PROBLEMS AND METHODS
OF LITERARY HISTORY

WITH SPECIAL REFERENCE TO
MODERN FRENCH LITERATURE

A GUIDE FOR GRADUATE STUDENTS

BY

ANDRÉ MORIZE

ASSISTANT PROFESSOR OF FRENCH LITERATURE IN
HARVARD UNIVERSITY

GINN AND COMPANY
BOSTON · NEW YORK · CHICAGO · LONDON
ATLANTA · DALLAS · COLUMBUS · SAN FRANCISCO

The Athenæum Press

GINN AND COMPANY · PRO-
PRIETORS · BOSTON · U.S.A.

INTRODUCTION

A memory and a wish are responsible for this book.

The memory is of years, already distant, when the author was privileged to study at the Université de Paris and the École normale supérieure under excellent masters. From these years he has brought away a feeling of special gratitude for the devotion with which these masters strove not only to communicate to their pupils a part of their own learning but also to initiate them into the actual methods of scientific work. He cannot forget the conferences on Saturday afternoons when, grouped about Professor G. Lanson, a few young men were made acquainted with the tools and the practical side of a study still new to them; or those hours when Lanson generously placed at their disposal the material destined to form the *Manuel bibliographique*; or, above all, the moments of personal contact when, with his wealth of erudition, his keen penetration, his strict but kindly criticism, he guided his students, started them on the right road and kept them in it, pointed out the stumblingblocks, and explained the best way to avoid them and to proceed with safety and success. Those were unforgetable lessons, and their memory, to which the author hopes not to prove faithless, will be found in every chapter of this book. The name of G. Lanson will appear several times, but the echo of his thought and of his very words will be heard on every page.

Other teachers gave no less invaluable help to their pupils, guiding them personally through the library stacks, showing them the principal bibliographical implements and illustrat-

iii

ing their use, thus supplying to the students in a few hours information that, left to their own devices, they could not have picked up in as many years. At other times a student would be asked to report to the professor and his comrades the results of his own researches, and together they would discuss the method, its merits and demerits. Every such occasion offered a fresh incentive to all the members of the class: they learned something more important than pedantic details or ingenious critical opinions—they learned how to work.

It is this memory, combined with the experience of several years of teaching in the United States, that roused in the author the wish to do the same good turn, as far as in him lay, to American students.

Indeed, there is always a troublesome transition between the end of undergraduate work and the beginning of graduate work. This difficulty is particularly noticeable when students reach the point of choosing the subject for a thesis and of attempting their own researches. Their zeal is, to be sure, unbounded, their diligence and conscientiousness are irreproachable; but it is impossible to deny that obstacles abound. In a word, and quite frankly, our young men do not know definitely enough how to work. They try to patch out this ignorance, for which they are not to blame, by an empiricism that may sometimes succeed, but that guarantees them insufficiently against deception and error. Too often they are seen wandering through the libraries "hunting for information", like a blind man hunting for a house in a strange city. They are satisfied with what they obtain in this way, without knowing that more—the really important—information exists elsewhere. They come up for even advanced examinations with a bibliographical ignorance that is at times disconcerting. Once the material is accumulated they do not always know how to arrange it with dexterity and skill: they feel like masons set to do an architect's task. Therefore, after months of research and exertion, they run the risk of producing a work, no matter how conscientious, that just misses being the definitive, or at any rate important, contribution intended. Loss of time, uncertainty, waste of energy and effort, at the expense of the final results,—such is, if not the usual, it must be confessed the sadly frequent, sight. This book will have realized its purpose if it is able to some extent to remedy this evil and to fill this gap.

The subject matter has been given, under the same title, as a course at Harvard University. This course, limited to a small number of pupils, has always been very informal, with conversation and free discussions constantly interrupting an exposition that sought to be clear and vivid rather than literary and eloquent. In arranging the lectures in book form the author has tried to keep the intimate, direct tone, the naturalness and ease, of unconstrained and unpretentious talks.

The aim is, first, to give to the novice in literary history a clear idea of the field he is entering—to define its characteristics and limits, its relations with the two neighboring provinces of literary criticism and history; next, to familiarize him with the indispensable implements and tools; lastly, to introduce him to the principal problems that may arise and to help him to find the solutions.

These problems, after all, are not endlessly varied: they fall under a certain number of headings, corresponding to different stages in the creation of a literary work and to its varying fortunes with the public; for instance, questions of linguistic or grammatical commentary and interpretation, questions of sources or of influence, questions of chronology or of authenticity, of biography or of bibliography, of lan-

guage, style, or versification. The student is never the first
person who has had to deal with them: others before him
have made the attempt; others have solved them. Their researches, considered particularly from the point of view of
method, form a treasure of accumulated experience on which
the present volume invites the newcomer to draw as often as
he can. Not, be it clearly understood, that he should become
the servile imitator of such and such a professor or scholar
or indulge in cunning plagiarism of successful methods. No,
the question is simply to follow the daily practice of technical or mechanical workshops: the apprentice stands beside the good workman whose hand and eye have acquired
skill and accuracy through years of training. He watches
him and asks questions; he strives to stamp on his memory
each phase of the process that transforms crude matter into
a finely finished work; he observes the deft fingers, the care,
the delicate, precise movements, that distinguish the experi-
enced craftsman from the unpracticed hand. He tries to
remember all this when he himself is seated at the bench
and working on his own account. This, and nothing else,
is expected from the student—to watch, observe, understand, and learn.

"To be useful to students has been my constant thought",
writes Lanson in his introduction to the *Manuel bibliographique*. The author wishes to repeat the formula here, restricting it still more: To be useful to graduate students,
working on French literature in American and English universities, has been his constant thought.

He has had especially in mind two types of young workers:
first, those that are just beginning their personal researches;
next, those that, after taking their A.M. or Ph.D. degree,
are continuing their careers in schools or colleges far re-

moved from the centres of scientific activity and historical investigation. He hopes to give them encouragement not to abandon personal work, and assistance in its accomplishment.

As occasion offered he has not hesitated to enlarge upon facts that are almost self-evident, upon elementary methods and precautions, even upon entirely practical advice; nor, in other places, has he avoided discussing more complicated problems, accessible only to students already far advanced. He has simply borne in mind the extremely diverse and unequal degrees of preparation found in the members of graduate courses; and experience has shown him, moreover, that sometimes it does no harm, even to the best students, to recall, if not to reveal, certain of these elementary, obvious, but very important points. Why should they not be as wise as M. Jourdain, who, when his master of philosophy asked him, "You know Latin, of course?" answered, "Yes, but go ahead just as if I didn't"? Perhaps the author will be reproached for going ahead too much as if his readers didn't!

Furthermore, certain demonstrations or discussions have been either developed fully or analyzed minutely, not at all because they were particularly original or interesting in themselves, but because as a rule they were newer to the students. The length of the various chapters corresponds less to the relative importance of the subject matter than to reasons or necessities that might be termed pedagogical.

Students must not suppose that they are herewith offered some variety of "Practical Receipt-Book," with the methods of literary history tabulated in rules and formulas, ready to be applied to fresh cases. Such an attempt could not be realized, and in any event would be absurd. They need not expect to be shown in these pages any short cuts for avoiding difficulties and obstacles. What they will find is a sort of atlas of literary history, a collection of maps of the country they plan to explore; on these are marked its intricacies and resources, and the safe highways from which the pioneers must start their explorations.

Lastly, this work will fulfill its author's earnest desire if it helps to develop in our young students, together with a taste for literary research, the attitude of mind that insures success, and that is nothing, after all, but scientific curiosity combined with scientific conscientiousness. A love of precision joined to aspirations toward general ideas; respect for historical facts, and warm appreciation of beautiful writings; minuteness in research, and breadth of view; finesse in analysis; strictness in criticism; penetration in æsthetic judgments; lastly, exacting loyalty toward oneself, toward facts, toward the ideas and the men studied,—these are a few of the valuable qualities that, thoroughly understood and thoroughly carried out, literary studies tend to develop. For the training of students there is no better school. May this book prove an acceptable introduction.

It is my pleasant task to extend hearty thanks to those who have been interested in the preparation of these pages: first, to Professor J. D. M. Ford, Chairman of the Department of Romance Languages at Harvard University, who welcomed and encouraged the idea of the course on which the book is based; to several of my colleagues and friends who have helped me with their invaluable advice, experience, and suggestions—in particular, to Professors Carleton Brown, Ronald S. Crane, and Percy W. Long; and, finally, to Miss Phyllis Robbins, who, with devotion and patience, has accomplished the work of transforming into a book for American readers these lectures of a French professor.

ANDRÉ MORIZE

CAMBRIDGE, MASSACHUSETTS

· CONTENTS

PAGE

INTRODUCTION iii

CHAPTER I. OBJECTS AND METHODS OF LITERARY HISTORY i

CHAPTER II. IMPLEMENTS AND TOOLS: BIBLIOGRAPHY . 13

Some works of general bibliography, 13. Bibliography of modern French literature, 16. Academic dissertations, 25. Large catalogues of libraries, 26. Bibliography of subjects involving the literary relations of France with other countries, 28. History of the French language, 29. Periodical literature, 30. Encyclopædias and large dictionaries, 33. Some practical advice, 34.

CHAPTER III. THE PREPARATION OF AN EDITION 37

Requirements of a good edition, 38. Different stages in the preparation of an edition, 38. Critical work for establishing and cleaning up the text, 39. Choice of a text as foundation of a critical edition, 47. Establishment and arrangement of the critical apparatus, 56. Reproduction of the text: questions of orthography and punctuation, 58. Linguistic and grammatical commentary, 62. Literary commentary, 63. Practical details of printing, 65. Examples of editions to study, 66.

CHAPTER IV. ESTABLISHING A CRITICAL BIBLIOGRAPHY . 70

Definition and object, 70. Critical bibliography of an author, 71. Examples to study, 76. Critical bibliography of a question of literary history, 80.

CHAPTER V. INVESTIGATION AND INTERPRETATION OF SOURCES 82

Definition of a source, 82. Importance of the study of sources, 84. Temptations and possible errors, 87. Various types of sources, 96. Direct sources, 96. Documentary sources, 101. Sources of detail, 104. Composite sources, 107. Oral and indefinite sources, 113. Sources of inspiration, 118. Graphic and plastic sources, 124. Principal fields for the investigation of sources, 127.

CHAPTER VI. CHRONOLOGY IN LITERARY HISTORY . . . 132

Importance of chronology, 132. Problems of chronology in literary history, 135. To fix the date of a work, 136. To fix the dates of the various parts of a work, 143.

PAGE

CHAPTER VII. PROBLEMS OF AUTHENTICITY AND ATTRI-
BUTION 157

The authenticity of the *Paradoxe sur le comédien*, 158. Problems of
attribution solved through bibliographical evidence, 170. *Opuscules*
and *Factums* of Pascal, 172. Problem of the attribution of the *Discours de la servitude volontaire*, 176. Methods in questions of authenticity and attribution, 189.

CHAPTER VIII. QUESTIONS OF VERSIFICATION 194

Bibliography of French versification, 196. Plan and methods of the
study of versification, 198. Lines considered separately, 200. Syllabic
structure, 200. Rhythmical structure, 200. Harmonic structure, 204.
Groups of lines, 206. Æsthetic commentary, 209.

CHAPTER IX. TREATMENT OF BIOGRAPHICAL MATERIAL
IN THE HISTORY OF LITERATURE 210

Importance of biographical precision in literary history, 210. Collection of the documents, 215. Treatment of documents; essential
points of literary biography, 217.

CHAPTER X. QUESTIONS OF SUCCESS AND OF INFLUENCE 225

Distinction between success and influence, 226. Definition of influence, 228. How may an influence present itself? 230. Active influences, 233. Retarded or arrested influences, 237. Mechanism and
mode of action of literary influences, 243. Simplification, elimination,
choice, 244. The image that each epoch or each milieu forms of a
work, 247. Tracing and measuring literary influences, 250. Possible
errors and necessary precautions, 259.

CHAPTER XI. THE HISTORY OF LITERATURE IN CONNEC-
TION WITH THE HISTORY OF IDEAS AND OF MANNERS 263

Questions in which literature and history cannot be considered isolated from each other, 264. Difficulties and precautions, 268. Relations between the literary work and its environment, 272. Influence
of the work on the milieu, 278. Methods of handling the facts, 282.
Importance of individual elements, 285. Remarks on method, 287.

CHAPTER XII. PREPARATION AND REDACTION OF A THESIS 289

Choice of a subject, 289. Approach and preparation, 291. Work of
organization: determination of problems, 294. Form and expression, 297.

CONCLUSION 300

INDEX 305

PROBLEMS AND METHODS OF LITERARY HISTORY

CHAPTER I

OBJECTS AND METHODS OF LITERARY HISTORY

To justify the existence and the methods of literary history is entirely superfluous nowadays, and it is no less superfluous to dwell upon the differences and likenesses between it and literary criticism. Our common sense tells us, if we do away with prejudices and futile scholarly discussions, that literary history, working in its own field, is trying neither to replace nor to oppose literary criticism. Literary history thinks that it can help literary criticism; can clear a path for it; can lighten its task of understanding, judging, and classifying literary works and the great movements of human thought. It offers its services as a devoted auxiliary, modest and self-effacing. It has no imperialistic designs: it covers enough territory already to have no need to encroach on that of a neighbor. It prepares the material for the critic but puts no restrictions on the way he should use it. If he has faith in impressionistic criticism, if he believes that the literary critic should surrender himself to the emotion produced by the book he is studying and then should express this emotion with precision and delicacy, he is free to do so. Literary history asks him only to base his personal reaction on facts that have been historically verified, to define his position clearly, and, when communicating a purely personal reaction to the public, not to believe or to make others believe that he is giving any added information about the work or its writer. "Impressionism", says Lanson, "is the only method that puts us in touch with beauty. Let us, then, use it for this purpose, frankly, but let us limit it to this, rigorously. To distinguish *knowing* from *feeling*, what we *may know* from what we *should feel*; to avoid *feeling* when we can *know*, and thinking that we *know* when we *feel*: to this, it seems to me, the scientific method of literary history can be reduced."[1]

If, on the contrary, the critic believes that he should explain and judge a work in the name of some preëxistent system, whether æsthetic, philosophic, or scientific; if he holds, with Boileau and the other dogmatic or authoritarian critics, that the criterion of excellence is conformity to some ideal or tradition; if he prefers, like Taine or Brunetière, to appropriate from science methods of classifying, explaining, or analyzing, to transfer to the field of literary criticism either the determinism of the physical sciences or the theory of biological evolution,—here again literary history denies neither the legitimacy of such points of view nor the interest of the results obtained. Let me repeat that it leaves each one free to use as he sees fit the facts that it puts at his disposal, but that it insists upon the necessity of his asking for the material, which it is ready to supply with every obtainable guarantee of historical accuracy. Now, laying aside all pedantic phraseology, the facts are these: those who have faith in literary history ask merely that the critic, before constructing systems, before praising or blaming, worshiping or scoffing, be sure that he *knows* exactly what he is talking about. They ask that before criticizing he be sure to criticize established facts, indisputable chronology, correct texts, ex-

[1] *Revue de l'Université de Bruxelles,* December, 1909.

act biographies; in short, as a watchword they would gladly adopt the old Latin proverb, modified for their use: "Primum scire, deinde philosophari."[1]

This craving for knowledge is, truly speaking, the only scientific part of their efforts. There is no scientific method in literary history in the sense that there is no method, however well adapted to a given science, that literary history can transplant and apply to its own researches. The illusion that this is possible is responsible for much poor and childish work: statistics and charts, evolution of species, and quantitative analysis are processes, methods, and hypotheses excellent in their place, but their place is not in literary history. For its purposes the scientific method is reduced to scientific conscientiousness and spirit—to the determination to leave nothing to guesswork, and, without stifling subjective impressions, to keep them entirely apart from substantiated facts.

Practically, what does this programme consist in? Its aim is to surround literary works with all the information needed to make them thoroughly understood. In detail the process is as follows:

1. To seize as completely and accurately as possible the meaning of the work—words and ideas, historical, philosophical, and artistic value.

2. To distinguish in each work between the part that originates with the writer and that in which imitations, reminiscences, traditions, can be detected.

[1] See Lanson, *De la méthode dans les sciences*, Vol. II, p. 223 : "We wish that, before judging Bossuet or Voltaire in the name of a doctrine or of a religion, there would be an effort to make his acquaintance, with no thought except to collect the greatest possible mass of authentic information, and to establish the greatest possible number of verified references. Our ideal is to construct a Bossuet and a Voltaire that neither Catholics nor Anticlericals can refute, with personalities that both will acknowledge to be true, and that both will then decorate with any sentimental characteristics they please."

3. To discover and analyze continually the interaction between literature and the multiple elements—intellectual or economic, political or moral, artistic or social—that form its environment.

In a word, the work of literary history is what has been aptly defined as "an attempt to comprehend historically and critically".[1]

This attempt to comprehend presupposes a large number of questions to study and problems to solve. The researches of literary history, like the laboratory experiments of psychology or of biology, have their own technique—practical methods of study and solution that prevent our going astray and wasting time and energy. No one should try to guess or to improvise these methods: it is far wiser to learn from those who have built them up and applied them with success.

These questions or problems may be classed under the following headings:

1. *Questions of bibliography*. What are the implements and tools of the good worker? How can the student find his way among the thousands of books, printed documents, and manuscripts that are available? Where will he turn for the heterogeneous information he requires? What will prevent his delving for months into a subject, only to learn too late that it has been excellently handled in some article that he did not know how to find? How can he avoid hunting for two or three hours for a fact that he could have verified in five minutes had he known where to go? Only those who have been thrown on their own resources before the thousands of cards in a catalogue, or in the labyrinth

---

[1] G. Cohen, "Une Chaire nouvelle de langue et de littérature françaises à l'Université d'Amsterdam," *Revue internationale de l'enseignement*, October 15, 1912. The article deserves to be read in full.

of a large library, will fully understand the need of some practical apprenticeship.

Besides, it is not entirely a question of being able to extricate oneself: other people have to be extricated also. To compile clear, complete, handy bibliographies of the important writers and subjects is one of the most urgent tasks for literary history. How, then, should this work be organized and carried out?

2. *Questions of criticism of the text.* In taking up the study of some book the first step is to examine the text. Is it correct and trustworthy? Or has it been transmitted to us with faults, omissions, interpolations, inadvertences of all sorts? In the latter case it must undergo a 'cleaning up', like that to which the ancient Greek or Latin authors are subjected. This is the preliminary work in preparing an accurate edition. How is it to be accomplished?

3. *Questions of interpretation and of explanation.* A text may be authentic and correct and yet be quite obscure, or decipherable only with difficulty. Read attentively and conscientiously any page of some famous writer; no matter how intelligent and cultivated you may be, there will be many things that at first sight leave a vague or incorrect impression, or none at all. "To understand that you do not understand" is the beginning of wisdom. Open Rabelais, Molière, Voltaire, Dante or Goethe, Milton or Cervantes; if you really know how to 'read', you will find many problems and stumblingblocks on every page. Words may be obscure, either because they belong to a special or technical vocabulary or because their meanings have changed since the book was written. Perhaps grammar and syntax puzzle you; they may differ from current use or from the general use at that time. Then there are many allusions—references to contemporary life, to the life of the author, to his reading,

to some fact of historical or local significance. All these allusions must be traced, analyzed, explained. In short, a commentary must be written, a grammatical, linguistic, explanatory, literary commentary of the text—a piece of work that, both in preparing and executing, needs great learning, perspicacity, and tact. This, after the establishment of a correct and critical text, is the second phase of editing.

4. *Questions of versification.* Whether in writing the commentary for a new edition, whether in literary criticism, whether as the object of a special, separate study, versification raises many difficulties. These difficulties, grave as they are for a Frenchman, are particularly formidable for a foreigner. To analyze and appreciate the rhythm, the harmony, and the artistic worth of a poem presupposes a mass of precise technical information and a long training of the ear. What, then, are the points to study? How is the commentary to be arranged? Where are the indispensable technical facts to be found? What definitions should be adopted? Finally, how shall the delicate skill be acquired that enables us to speak of French verse not as dry statisticians but as responsive, discriminating judges?

5. *Preparation of a critical edition.* Another urgent task for literary history is to furnish scholars as well as the general public with good editions of modern writers. This work also is exacting and complicated: the choice of the edition whose text shall be reprinted; the use to be made of manuscripts; the reproduction of the spelling and punctuation of the original editions; the establishment and arrangement of the critical apparatus and the various commentaries; the material details of the book—these are only a few of the problems that an editor must face. How can he succeed in such an enterprise?

6. *Questions of date and of chronology.* In literary criticism of whatever school there is no more frequent source of error than ignorance or uncertainty of chronology. The date printed on the title-page of a book is often not the exact date of publication; still oftener the date of publication is not the date of composition. Moreover, in many cases, in order to decide a question of influence or of imitation, not only the year of publication must be determined but the month, the week, the day. A precise knowledge of these chronological data is needed in order to give the work its true place in the author's life and in the literary development of his time.

On the other hand, many masterpieces, such as Montaigne's *Essais*, Voltaire's *Dictionnaire philosophique*, the *Confessions* of Rousseau, *Les Contemplations* of Hugo, have grown progressively, have been completed and enriched at intervals. To criticize them without first of all making sure of the date of composition of each of the parts would be to invite serious mistakes. With these fragmentary or autobiographical works fresh problems arise, calling for special methods.

7. *Questions of authenticity and of attribution.* If it is indispensable to establish a correct text, it is equally indispensable, in certain instances, to assure ourselves that the work is genuine, that it really belongs to the author to whom it is universally attributed. Doubtless, for most of the great modern works the question need never be raised. There are, however, many exceptions in the case of posthumous works, of correspondence, of libels published more or less clandestinely, or of collections into which pieces of suspected origin have insinuated themselves—in which the tares have been mixed with the wheat. By what methods should questions of this type be studied and answered?

8. *Questions of sources and of origins.* "Almost everything is imitation", writes Voltaire. "With books it is the same as with the fire on our hearths; we go to beg a light from our neighbors, we build a fire in our houses, and it belongs to all alike." Even if not "everything" is imitation, there is no doubt that every book stands partly for the creative thought of the writer, partly for his reading and documentary work. Sometimes he unconsciously fills it with vague reminiscences, half-forgotten reading, obscure suggestions; sometimes he intentionally borrows and imitates, even openly steals and plagiarizes, adding to his own structure stones that he may perhaps have freshly chipped but that he has not cut from the block. A search for all these elements is essential in determining the originality of a writer, his working methods, his literary inheritance and parentage. How should we carry out this investigation of sources and interpret the results?

9. *Questions of the formation and the transformation of a work.* As a general rule a book does not at the outset assume a definite and unchangeable form: it is the visible end of a long series of preparations and efforts and the beginning of another series of transformations. Between the moment when the first inspiration, the first projects, shape themselves in the author's mind and the day when, in his old age, he publishes the last edition of his book, there is a succession of intermediary stages, which reflect faithfully the changes in his taste, thought, and feelings. We must, then, find and study the outlines, rough drafts, fragments, and copies; we must follow the text through its various impressions, from the princeps to the definitive edition, collating, comparing, classifying the readings, corrections, additions, and suppressions, in order to trace the evolution of the author's ideas

and art. The results of this work will find a place in some critical edition, or in a general study of the formation of a writer or the genesis of a work; they will be worth exactly what the method used to obtain them is worth.

10. *Questions of biography.* Nearly every question that has been mentioned exemplifies the close connection between a writer's life and his work. This connection will, of course, be studied with greater exactness and profit the more completely the life of the author is known. How, then, is it possible to write what Sainte-Beuve calls "a well-composed biography"? Where are the documents to be found? How should they be turned to account? What special points should be brought out? In the life of every famous writer are there not certain questions and certain incidents that bear more directly than others on his work: geographic or ethnic origins; education and formation; first literary influences; periods of crisis and their causes; stages of evolution; relations with various contemporary social groups? Lastly, are there any models of literary biography, both historically unassailable and arranged with intelligence, clearness, and skill?

11. *Questions of success and of influence.* The life of a literary work really begins only on the day when, like Vigny's "bouteille à la mer", it is thrown into the great tide of human thought. Literary history should follow its destinies, its success, its influence. A work, though received in triumph, may disappear, leaving no trace; another, hardly noticed on its publication, may, as the years and centuries go by, exert an ever-widening power. What are the reasons for these vicissitudes? If it is true that, as the Latin poet says, "habent sua fata libelli", how should the *fata* and their caprices be studied? The history of the influence of literary

works is a splendid field for study, still nearly unexplored, in which several pioneers have already built monuments as landmarks and guides.

12. *Relations of the history of literature with the history of ideas and of civilization.* Finally, literary history looks farther than to the establishing of explanatory commentary, the naming of sources, and the tracing of influences. Often its horizon is enlarged to include the connection between the literary work and the general history of ideas and of civilization. In what degree is literature the 'expression of society'? In what degree is society shaped and modified by literature? What part does a book play in preparing great political crises or slow social evolution? Here are innumerable problems of vital interest, toward which in the last twenty-five years the work of many scholars has been directed—young scholars interested not only in philological study and psychological analysis but in the moral and social problems of history.

Such are the principal fields in which the student of literary history may exercise his powers. Before starting out, is it not a wise precaution to make inquiries as to the necessary equipment and the best route to his destination? The following pages are written in the hope of answering these inquiries.

First, the student must become familiar with the implements of his trade—the bibliographical material of French literature.

Next, he must take up, one after the other, each type of problem that has been mentioned. He should learn to state it, to define its terms, and to reach solutions. For him nothing will be so valuable as to study the works of those who have skillfully and successfully accomplished researches of this kind; perhaps, for the benefit of the inexperienced student, these works may be coaxed into giving up the secret of their methods.

Certainly no one can acquire true learning or genius through mere observation; but observation will help the conscientious young apprentice, who some day in the great workshop of his choice may become a skilled worker.[1]

[1] The few references given in the following list do not claim to offer a bibliography of literary criticism in general, or even of the "methods of literary history". They are intended merely to familiarize the student with the discussions mentioned in this chapter, and with the idea of literary history held today by its universally recognized representatives.

1. The essential reading is as follows:

LANSON, G. *De la méthode dans les sciences* (second series, 1911), pp. 221-264 ("La Méthode de l'histoire littéraire"). First published in *Revue du mois*, October, 1910, pp. 385-413; followed by an interesting discussion, April, 1911, pp. 486-497.

This reading is to be supplemented with several articles by the same author:

"Ouverture des conférences à la Faculté des lettres de l'Université de Paris," *Revue internationale de l'enseignement*, November 15, 1901, p. 385. See also same volume, p. 240.

"Histoire littéraire: résultats récents et problèmes actuels," *Revue de synthèse historique*, Vol. I (1900), pp. 52-83.

"Programme d'études sur l'histoire provinciale et la vie littéraire en France," *Revue d'histoire moderne et contemporaine*, April 15, 1903.

"L'Histoire littéraire et la sociologie," *Revue de métaphysique et de morale*, July, 1904.

"L'Esprit scientifique et la méthode de l'histoire littéraire," *Revue de l'Université de Bruxelles*, December, 1909.

Hommes et livres, Préface. 1895.

2. The following reading is recommended, as a means of gaining some knowledge of the various types, methods, or systems of literary criticism that have been mentioned in this chapter:

SAINTE-BEUVE. *Causeries du lundi*, Vol. XIII; *Nouveaux lundis*, Vol. VIII (two important articles on Taine); *Portraits littéraires*, Vol. III; *Correspondance*, Vol. I, p. 315, and Vol. II, p. 40.

TAINE. Introduction to the *Histoire de la littérature anglaise* (Babbitt edition); *Essais de critique et d'histoire*, particularly Préfaces of 1858 and 1866.

GIRAUD, V. *Essai sur Taine* (4th ed., 1909).

BRUNETIÈRE. Introduction to the *Évolution des genres*. 1890.

On Brunetière:
GIRAUD, in *Maitres d'autrefois et d'aujourd'hui*, 1913, and *Revue des Deux Mondes*, March, 1908, pp. 52–82.

FRANCE, A. *La Vie littéraire*, Préfaces in Vols. I and II.

BABBITT, I. *The Masters of Modern French Criticism* (1912). See the review of this book by D. Mornet, in *Revue d'histoire littéraire*, 1915, pp. 301–303.

HENNEQUIN, E. *La Critique scientifique* (2d ed., 1894).

RENARD, G. *La Méthode scientifique de l'histoire littéraire.* 1900.

PAUTHIER, H. and J. *L'Histoire littéraire.* 1911.

LANSON, G. "Les Études sur la littérature française moderne," *La Science française*, 1915.

MORNET, D. "Les Méthodes de l'histoire littéraire, étudiées à propos de l'histoire d'une œuvre: *La Nouvelle Héloïse*," *Revue des cours et conférences*, Vols. XXII¹ and XXII² (1913–1914).

MORNET, D. "Les Méthodes dans les récents travaux d'histoire littéraire," *Revue du mois*, June 10, 1914.

ESTÈVE, E. *Critique littéraire* (1915). Reprinted from *Mémoires de l'Académie Stanislas*, 1913–1914.

SERRURIER, C. *Introduction à l'histoire de la littérature française moderne.* Leyden, 1914.

URBAIN, C. "Histoire littéraire et érudition," *Revue du clergé français*, March 15, 1914.

GAYLEY, C. M., and KURTZ, B. P. *Methods and Materials of Literary Criticism.* Boston, 1920.

CHAPTER II

IMPLEMENTS AND TOOLS: BIBLIOGRAPHY

Before undertaking any kind of work the workman should learn to know his tools; without this indispensable familiarity he is doomed to an immense loss of time, to uncertain gropings, and to many mistakes. Doubtless each subject calls for a special bibliography, but to acquire this bibliography—and to acquire it by the shortest and safest route—it is necessary to consult a certain number of works of general reference, through which all special references are discovered, and in this way to be practically sure that nothing essential has escaped or been overlooked.

It is to this general bibliography of French literature, above all, that the student should introduce himself. A good idea, before starting to explore this limited province, is to take a look at the map of a vaster region, spread out in works of bibliographical reference of larger scope.

I. SOME WORKS OF GENERAL BIBLIOGRAPHY[1]

1. The first guide whose acquaintance it is well to make is C. V. Langlois, *Manuel de bibliographie historique* (Part I, 1901 (2d ed.); Part II, 1904). This book, intended pri-

---

[1] Is it necessary to say that the works mentioned under this heading are books of very general reference, which should be known and which are a help to the student in finding his way among the complicated paths of bibliography, but which need not be consulted every time that the bibliography on a particular question is being compiled? This remark would be unnecessary if experience did not prove that the error is sometimes committed by students whose critical sense does not equal their zeal and good intentions.

marily for students of history, makes a useful general introduction to any work in literary bibliography. The following paragraphs will be found especially profitable:

Sections 3–38, Bibliographies universelles.
Sections 63–68, Bibliographies nationales: France (very important).
Sections 95–98, Bibliographies générales.
Sections 129–131, Dictionnaires de biographie.
Sections 147–148, Presse quotidienne.[1]

2. For general bibliography prior to 1866 see the *Bibliotheca bibliographica* of J. Petzholdt,[2] particularly the following sections:

Pages 1–65, Einleitender Theil: works of general bibliography.
Pages 66–279, Allgemeiner Theil: general references; rare books; censured and forbidden works; and, especially, individual biographies in alphabetical order (pp. 156–279).
Pages 323–325, France.

[1] Langlois's *Manuel* will be the natural starting-point when the student of literature wishes to extend his bibliography in the direction of history proper, whether he is trying to acquire the indispensable historical background or whether he is clearing up some allusion or difficulty in interpretation. He should know, besides the *Histoire de France depuis les origines jusqu'à la Révolution*, published under the direction of E. Lavisse (1900–1911), and its continuation for the contemporary period (the chapters on the history of society and of fine arts and letters are excellent); P. Caron, *Bibliographie des travaux publiés de 1866 à 1897 sur l'histoire de la France depuis 1789* (Paris, 1912); and the *Répertoire méthodique de l'histoire moderne et contemporaine de la France* (from the Italian wars in the sixteenth century), begun in 1898, and published thereafter in supplements by the *Revue d'histoire moderne et contemporaine*. It is helpful also to know the other leading French historical periodicals: *Revue historique, Revue des études historiques, Revue des questions historiques*, and especially the *Revue de synthèse historique*, because of its bibliographies and "revues générales", or general surveys of the various fields of historical research.

[2] *Bibliotheca bibliographica. Kritisches Verzeichniss der das Gesammtgebiet der Bibliographie betreffenden Litteratur des In- und Auslandes, in systematischer Ordnung bearbeitet.* Mit alphabetischem Namen- und Sachregister (8vo). Leipzig, 1866.

Pages 325–339, French literature.

Pages 705–726, Literature, under the words *Frankreich, Poesie, Romane,* etc.

The reference to each work, which is usually exact, is followed by a critical note, short but valuable.

3. The classic but rather antiquated work of Petzholdt may be supplemented by the *Manuel de bibliographie générale* of H. Stein (Paris, 1898).[1] The classification of subjects is explained in pages x–xiv of the Introduction. The parts that particularly concern the history of literature are the following:

Pages 1–8, Bibliographies universelles.

Pages 21–24, France.

Pages 237–323, Philologie et belles-lettres, especially pp. 237–238, Généralités et répertoires nominaux; 268–271, Littérature française; 277, Traditions populaires (France) ; 281, Théâtre; 284, Romans; 288, Catalogues de thèses; 289, Littérature variée; 300, Bio-bibliographie littéraire; 309, Livres condamnés; 311, Anonymes et pseudonymes; 313–323, Presse périodique.

Pages 407–412, Histoire moderne et contemporaine.

Pages 421–424, Histoire de France.

Pages 433–434, Archives.

Pages 438–461, Histoire de l'imprimerie.

Pages 482–483, Livres à gravures.

Pages 497–554, Biographie.

The work is completed by two valuable Appendixes:

a. Répertoire des tables générales de périodiques de toutes langues (pp. 637–710), which shows, for each periodical, the nature, number, and date of the published indexes.

---

[1] The *Bibliographie des bibliographies* of L. Vallée (Paris, 1883; *Supplément,* 1884) is not to be recommended. It is obsolete, incomplete, and otherwise imperfect. If, however, Stein's book is not available, it may be useful to turn to the following chapters in Vallée's: p. 618, Bibliographie générale ; p. 621, Bibliographie spéciale; p. 623, Biographie; p. 664, France; p. 681, Histoire littéraire. See also the second part of the book, Table méthodique, under the names of French writers or of French provinces.

b. Répertoire des catalogues d'imprimés des principales bibliothèques du monde entier.[1]

4. Useful information may often be gained from the two following works: *British Museum Library, List of Bibliographical Works in the Reading Room* (2d ed., London, 1889), and W. P. Courtney, *A Register of National Bibliography*, which contains a good number of references to books or articles published in other countries than Great Britain (3 vols.) (London, 1905–1912). Lastly, the inexperienced student will avoid long and fruitless research by reading A. B. Kroeger, *Guide to the Study and Use of Reference Books* (3d ed.) (I. C. Mudge, Chicago, 1917).

II. BIBLIOGRAPHY OF MODERN FRENCH LITERATURE

THE *MANUEL BIBLIOGRAPHIQUE* OF G. LANSON

The book that should be a constant companion to the student is the *Manuel bibliographique de la littérature française moderne* (1500–1900), by G. Lanson, published in four parts (1909–1912), followed by a *Supplément* and an *Index général* (1914), and republished with corrections and additions in one volume in 1921.[2] Like all good tools the *Manuel* should be used intelligently; before expecting too much of it, it is wise to understand fully what it is meant to be.

---

[1] It is well to know of these catalogues when studying an author whose life or literary activity is connected with a particular locality : for instance, the catalogues of the libraries of Bordeaux for Montaigne and Montesquieu; of Geneva, Lausanne, or Neuchâtel for J.-J. Rousseau; of Lyons for Louise Labé, etc.

[2] Read good reviews of the book by F. Baldensperger, in *Revue de philologie française et de littérature*, Vol. XXIV (1910), p. 72, and Vol. XXVII (1913), p. 129; by D. Mornet, in *Revue du mois*, June 10, 1911, p. 732; by A. Monglond, in *Revue de synthèse historique*, Vol. XXVI (1913), p. 123; and by K. R. Gallas, in *Neophilologus*, Vol. I (1916), p. 308. The latter gives several interesting additions and corrections.

Here is a bibliography *à la française,* simple, clear, and methodical. There is no wish to impress the reader by accumulating titles and references; throughout there is an effort to simplify, to blaze trails through the immense bibliographical forest, and to lay out paths easy to follow and always leading somewhere. "The two principles that have guided me", writes Lanson, "have been (1) to show the way to what I have omitted; (2) to compose a handbook that corresponds to the culture and the practical needs of the average student of French literature. . . . To be useful to students has been my constant thought."[1] Therefore it must be borne in mind that the *Manuel* is not intended to give *all* the references that it is possible to gather, but aims only at directing the student where and how to find what he needs.

The book is composed of six parts: Introduction, Bibliographie générale; Seizième siècle; Dix-septième siècle; Dix-huitième siècle; Révolution et Empire; Dix-neuvième siècle. This division might cause inconvenience by cutting in halves writers who belong in two centuries, and by giving an inexact idea of the continuity of literary movements, did not the author prevent this in two ways: (1) a system of cross references makes it easy to piece together everything that relates to an author who lived in two centuries or who was interested in several branches of literature; (2) special chapters bring out clearly every period of transition and all transformations of literary ideals or theories.[2]

Taking the *Manuel bibliographique* as a whole, it is decidedly superior in two respects to all previous reference books of French literature.

[1] Préface, p. vii.
[2] See Vol. II, chap. xxvii, "Le Passage du dix-septième au dix-huitième siècle"; Vol. IV, chap. xi, "Du Romantisme au Parnasse," and chap. xii, § 3, "Du Parnasse au Symbolisme."

On the one hand, it constantly mentions the reviews and bulletins of learned societies. "A large part of the useful work is done by them, and it is these that students have the greatest difficulty in unearthing."[1] Often essential elements in a detailed study are buried in an article the importance of which could not be suspected from its title or origin.[2] Left to himself a student would hardly ever discover it.

On the other hand, the *Manuel* is much more, and much better, under its apparent dryness, than a list of titles and names. It is, indeed, a mine of valuable suggestions for studies to be undertaken and for the interpretation of great literary events. The author has "chosen a system that sketches a *design* for the methodical study of modern French literature", and "by the very arrangement of the subject-matter, has *suggested the work* that should be done".[3] In this way many features that do not usually find room in a bibliography are given their place, and their importance is made clear: for instance, works and discussions relative to the authenticity, the history, and the transformations of the texts; abundant lists of translations from ancient or foreign writers and of reprints of previous works of note (this makes a valuable contribution to the knowledge of the intellectual surroundings among which the great writers have developed); works on the sources that have been discovered for every important literary production; and, for each of the writers who have in their day been decisive elements in the general evolution of thought or of an artistic ideal, all the criticisms or apologies, discussions or controversies, that show the reaction of the reading-public. In the same way, several chapters are devoted to the evolution of doctrines,

---

[1] Préface, p. viii.
[2] For instance, many unpublished letters, biographical documents, etc.
[3] Préface, p. vii.

theories, literary or artistic ideals, and to the history of the social environment, condition of men of letters, pedagogical doctrines, *salons* and coteries. Every one of these chapters is full of interesting suggestions and opens new horizons to the student who tries to read them in the right spirit.

If a very matter-of-fact piece of advice is not out of place here, it may be said that a good practice is to have the *Manuel* bound interleaved with blank pages, on which each day, as the student progresses in his work, he will add such names, titles, and other information as will make the book far more than a tool—the friend of every working-hour.[1]

[1] The titles of the principal handbooks of the history of French literature are found in the *Manuel*. Here is a list of those that offer abridged bibliographical information of some value:

Histoire de la langue et de la littérature française des origines à 1900, published under the direction of L. Petit de Julleville (8 vols.) (1896–1899). Convenient bibliographies at the end of every chapter.

LANSON, G. *Histoire de la littérature française* (12th ed., 1914).

BRUNETIÈRE, F. *Manuel de l'histoire de la littérature française* (1897). Systematic and interesting; the bibliographical paragraphs may at times be misleading, in the sense that they contain almost exclusively the works used by Brunetière in evolving his highly systematic views.

WRIGHT, C. H. C. *A History of French Literature*. 1912.

HERRIOT, E. *Précis de l'histoire des lettres françaises* (1905). A good, clear, simple, fairly complete manual, with satisfactory bibliographical notes.

BRAUNSCHVIG, M. *Notre Littérature étudiée dans les textes* (2 vols.) (1920). By far the most convenient handbook now in existence, with bibliographies brought up to date, accurate information, and suggestive discussions. It is to be recommended highly to graduate students.

Although the two following books include much more than French literature, they supply most useful bibliographical material:

GAYLEY and SCOTT. *An Introduction to the Methods and Materials of Literary Criticism*. 1899.

GAYLEY and KURTZ. *Methods and Materials of Literary Criticism (Lyric, Epic, and Allied Forms of Poetry)* (1920). See especially the bibliographical appendix, pp. 787–846.

BOOKS OF LITERARY BIBLIOGRAPHICAL REFERENCE AND OF NATIONAL BIBLIOGRAPHY

Since Lanson's *Manuel* is, by its very definition, a selective list of authors and works, and since it is carried only to the year 1920, the student must supplement it by other sources of bibliographical information, so as to be able both to explore, if need be, the entire printed output of a given epoch and to follow, from day to day, the publication of all important new works that bear on literary history.

These two sources of information are (1) works that may come under the heading of bibliographical reference books, and registers of national bibliographies; (2) notices given periodically in the reviews and newspapers.

A. *Reference Books and National Bibliographies*

A convenient and reliable guide is R. A. Peddie, *National Bibliographies: A Descriptive Catalogue of the Works which Register the Books Published in Each Country* (London, 1912). "The official, semi-official, and trade bibliographies of a country", the author says, "are the bases of all bibliographical work. From them we learn (imperfectly in most cases) what books are published, and their subject indexes give us the first instalment of titles for our special bibliographies. It is necessary for all who make researches in any way touching the bibliographical field to become acquainted with these most valuable tools." The following are the essential bibliographies:

1. *France before 1840.*[1] For the sixteenth century, La Croix du Maine and Du Verdier, *Bibliothèque française*, the

[1] For more detailed information see Lanson, *Manuel*, Nos. 52–61.

revised and enlarged edition published by Rigoley de Juvigny (6 vols., 4to). Paris, 1772–1773.[1]

For the seventeenth and the early eighteenth century the most complete compilation of bibliographical data is found in T. Georgi, *Allgemeine Europäische Bücher-Lexici. Fünfter Theil in welchem die Frantzösischen Auctores und Bücher . . . geschrieben und gedrucket worden sind . . .* (fol.). Leipzig, 1742.[2]

For the eighteenth and the early nineteenth century, J. M. Quérard, *La France littéraire* (12 vols., 8vo). Paris, 1827–1864.[3]

2. *France after 1840.* Lorenz-Jordell, *Catalogue général de la librairie française,* begun in 1840, is made up both of volumes arranged alphabetically under the authors' names and of extremely valuable volumes of *Tables méthodiques.* It is subdivided in the following manner:

Vols. I–VI, 1840–1875; Vols. VII–VIII, *Tables.*
Vols. IX–X, 1876–1885; Vol. XI, *Tables.*
Vol. XII, 1886–1890; Vol. XIII, *Tables.*
Vols. XIV–XV, 1891–1899; Vols. XVI–XVII, *Tables.*
Vols. XVIII–XIX, 1900–1905; Vol. XX, *Tables.*
Vols. XXI–XXII, 1906–1909; Vol. XXIII, *Tables.*
Vol. XXIV, 1910–1912; Vol. XXV, *Tables.*
Vol. XXVI, 1913–1915; Vol. XXVII, *Tables.*

[1] For the fifteenth and sixteenth centuries the incomparable collection of bibliographical cards (250,000) of E. Picot has just (1920) been donated by his widow to the Bibliothèque nationale for the use of scholars and students. See also H. Omont, *Anciens Inventaires et catalogues de la Bibliothèque nationale,* Vol. I (*La Librairie royale à Blois, Fontainebleau et Paris au XVIe siècle* (1908)), and Beaulieux, "Supplément au Catalogue des livres du XVIe siècle (1501–1550) de l'Université de Paris," in *Revue des bibliothèques,* 1918.

[2] See also H. Omont, *Anciens Inventaires et catalogues de la Bibliothèque nationale,* Vol. IV (*La Bibliothèque royale à Paris au XVIIe siècle* (1914)).

[3] Completed by R. A. Peddie and Q. Waddington in *Table alphabétique des matières de la France littéraire de Quérard et de ses Suppléments.*

H. Le Soudier, *Bibliographie française* (second series), Vol. I, 1900–1904 (Paris, 1908), and Vol. II, 1905–1909 (Paris, 1911), supplemented by the weekly *Mémorial de la librairie française*, the monthly and yearly indexes of which are valuable.

Bibliographie de la France. Journal général de l'imprimerie et de la librairie, weekly, issued since 1811. This publication is the record of everything printed in France and delivered to the Ministry of the Interior in compliance with the law on the "dépôt légal", which requires a publisher to deposit a certain number of copies of every book or pamphlet he prints. Of course, books that for some reason have not been delivered are not mentioned, but as a rule this inconvenience is not of real importance. At the end of each year the *Bibliographie* is bound into one volume, completed by an index of authors, a list of new periodical publications, and a catalogue of subjects, the most important sections being: "Littérature française," "Sociétés savantes," "Sciences historiques," "Bibliographie," "Les Lettres."[1]

3. *France in the nineteenth century.* G. Vicaire, *Manuel de l'amateur de livres du XIXe siècle* (7 vols.) (1894–1910) and the *Table des ouvrages cités* (1920).

H. P. Thieme, *Guide bibliographique de la littérature française de 1800 à 1906* (8vo) (Paris, 1907) is indispensable to students of modern and contemporary French literature. It contains for each author (1) a chronological list of his works, with the name of the publisher; (2) a chronological list of the books in which the author is discussed; (3) a valuable list of articles from periodicals in all languages, relative to the author. The second part of the volume is devoted to works on the history of the language, literature, and

---

[1] A student of French literature should make a point of going at regular intervals to the library of the university to look through the latest numbers.

civilization of France. Although naturally rather summary, this sort of topic index is of great value.[1]

4. *Countries other than France*. For Germany the *Vollständiges Bücher-Lexicon*, by C. G. Kayser, covers German bibliography from 1750 up to the present time; it is supplemented by several subject indexes. The current bibliography is recorded (1) in *Hinrichs' Halbjahrs-Katalog der im Deutschen Buchhandel erschienenen Bücher, Zeitschriften, Landkarten, etc. Mit Registern nach Stichworten und Wissenschaften*, whose title, since 1916, has been changed to *Halbjahrs-Verzeichnis* etc. (for every year there are two indexes—one by authors, one by subjects); (2) in the *Wöchentliches Verzeichnis der erschienenen und der vorbereiteten Neuigkeiten des Deutschen Buchhandels*, which, since 1893, has continued the *Allgemeine Bibliographie*. This periodical corresponds to the *Bibliographie de la France*; it is arranged according to subjects.

For Great Britain the *English Catalogue of Books*, by S. Low, records all the English bibliography since 1835. Up to the volume 1881–1889 (London, 1893) the author index and the subject index are published in two separate parts; after that date they are printed together in one volume. The current register is the *Publisher's Circular*, a fortnightly publication.

For Italy we have (1) the *Catalogo generale della libreria italiana* (1874–1900), by A. Pagliaini (3 vols.) (Milan, 1901–1905), completed by an *Indice per materie* (Milan, 1910, A–F; 1915, F–P); (2) the *Bollettino delle publicazioni italiane ricevute per diritto di stampa*, issued by the

---

[1] As was inevitable, the *Guide bibliographique*, among its forty thousand odd references, includes many errors of detail. Some of these have been corrected in the *Revue critique*, Vol. II (1907), pp. 234–237, and in other reviews of the book.

National Library at Florence; (3) for current bibliography, the monthly *Bibliografia italiana,* founded in 1867 (very clearly arranged).

For the United States the most convenient reference books are the following: (1) the *American Catalog* (3 vols.), covering 1900–1910; (2) the *United States Catalog* (3 vols.: Vol. I, Books in print January 1, 1912; Vol. II, 1912–1917; Vol. III, 1918–1921), continued currently as the *Cumulative Book Index*; (3) for current bibliography, the *Publisher's Weekly.*[1]

5. *Anonymous and pseudonymous books.* Investigations, especially for the periods of absolute power, when clandestine literature was a necessity, will often lead the student to consult books, pamphlets, and controversial documents published without the author's name or under an assumed name. The real name will be found in the following works:

BARBIER, A. *Dictionnaire des ouvrages anonymes* (4 vols., 8vo) (3d ed., 1879).

QUÉRARD, J.-M. *Les Supercheries littéraires* (3 vols., 8vo) (2d ed., 1879).

BRUNET, G. *Supplément à la dernière édition des deux ouvrages précédents* (8vo). 1889.[2]

B. *Current Bibliography in Literary Periodicals*

There are several reviews that regularly supply ample lists of the books and articles on literary history published

---

[1] The new works of bibliographical reference, literary or otherwise, are recorded in *Bibliographie des Bibliotheks- und Buchwesens,* published as supplements (*Beihefte*) to the *Zentralblatt für Bibliothekswesen* (Leipzig), begun in 1905, and in the *American Library Annual* (New York), begun in 1912. For the national bibliographies of other countries see R. A. Peddie, *National Bibliographies* (London, 1912).

[2] Completed by H. Célani in "Additions et corrections au Dictionnaire des anonymes de Barbier," *Revue des bibliothèques,* October–December, 1901.

during a given period. Among them the most useful and the most complete are the following:

Revue d'histoire littéraire de la France. Reviews several important French daily papers, but, unfortunately, no foreign periodicals.

Kritischer Jahresbericht über die Fortschritte der romanischen Philologie, published by K. Vollmöller. Excellent; gives brief notices on the contents of the works or articles mentioned. The last volume that I have been able to see is No. XIII, for the years 1911–1912.

Modern Language Notes. Gives very valuable lists of new publications.

Zeitschrift für französische Sprache und Literatur.

Literaturblatt der germanischen und romanischen Philologie. Specially useful for its reviews of many German periodicals.

A *Yearbook of Modern Languages,* by G. Waterhouse, was published in 1920 (8vo) (Cambridge). The bibliographical notices are admittedly only a choice among many, and this choice seems rather arbitrary. In fact, the work does not fulfill the promise of its title, and in no way takes the place of the *Jahresbericht* of Vollmöller.

III. Academic Dissertations

The considerable number of theses, dissertations, and academic essays of all sorts devoted to some point in French literary history may be approached, for the various countries, through the following lists:

United States: *Library of Congress, List of American Doctoral Dissertations,* begun in 1912; annual; author and subject indexes.

Gerig, J. L. "Advanced Degrees and Doctoral Dissertations in the Romance Languages at the Johns Hopkins University. A

Survey and Bibliography," in the *Romanic Review*, Vol. VIII (1917), p. 328. Same survey for Harvard University, Vol. X (1919), p. 67, and for Yale University, Vol. XI (1920), p. 70.

FRANCE: MAIRE, A. *Répertoire alphabétique des thèses de doctorat-ès-lettres des universités françaises* (1810–1900), with subject index. Paris, 1903.

Catalogue des thèses et écrits académiques, annual official publication of the Ministry of Public Instruction. Begun in 1885.

GERMANY: KLUSSMANN, R. *Systematisches Verzeichnis der Abhandlungen welche in den Schulschriften sämtlicher an dem Programmtausche teilnehmenden Lehranstalten erschienen sind*, bibliography covering the period 1876–1910 (5 vols.). Leipzig, 1889–1916.

FOCK, G. *Bibliographischer Monatsbericht über neu-erschienene Schul- und Universitätsschriften*. Leipzig, 1890–1899.

Jahresverzeichnis der an den deutschen Universitäten erschienenen Schriften. Berlin, 1887 up to the present day.

For other countries useful information may be gathered from the following publication of the Bibliothèque nationale in Paris: *Catalogue des dissertations et des écrits académiques provenant des échanges avec les universités étrangères, et reçus par la Bibliothèque nationale*. Issued annually since 1884.

IV. LARGE CATALOGUES OF LIBRARIES

1. *British Museum*. An admirable document, of which students too often know but little, is the *General Catalogue of the British Museum Library*, justly called "the richest bibliographical collection in the world". It is published in six hundred parts (4to), usually bound in one hundred volumes. A *Supplement* completed in 1905 records the books added to the British Museum in the years 1882–1899.

The great value of the *General Catalogue* is that it gives not only each author with his works in his alphabetical place, but also (1) a very large number of subject entries, which constitute excellent bibliographical notices; (2) for each writer, after the list of his works, every book, pamphlet, or document that deals with him.

The catalogue is completed by the *Subject Index of the Modern Works added to the Library of the British Museum in the Years 1881–1900*, by G. K. Fortescue (3 vols.) (London, 1902–1903), with five *Supplements*, which bring the subject index up to 1915.

2. *Bibliothèque nationale*. The Bibliothèque nationale in Paris, although more complete in French literature than the British Museum, unfortunately does not provide the student with so accessible a fund of bibliographical information. The following material, however, is of great importance:

a. The *Catalogue général des livres imprimés de la Bibliothèque nationale*, begun in 1897, is printed now (1922) as far as the end of the letter *H*. It contains no subject entries—only a list of authors and of their works. Nevertheless, for every writer whose name is so fortunate as to begin with a letter that precedes *I* in the alphabet, the *Catalogue général* is the most complete bibliographical source.

b. The *Bulletin mensuel des nouvelles acquisitions françaises* is a precious record of current bibliography, especially under the headings "Biographie" and "Histoire littéraire".

c. The *Catalogue méthodique de l'histoire de France* consists of twelve volumes (4to) (Paris, 1855–1895) and contains material of great importance to literary history in Vols. IV (*Journaux et périodiques*) and IX–X (*Biographies individuelles*). The six volumes of *Suppléments* in autography are not on sale.[1]

---

[1] An excellent *Répertoire* by authors and subjects may be consulted in the reading-room of the Bibliothèque nationale and will quickly become familiar to those who work in Paris; it is a collection of index cards on which has been recorded every printed publication added to the Bibliothèque since 1882.

d. Library of Congress and other American collections.
Finally, an American student should know how to obtain
and how to use the index cards of the Library of Congress
and should be familiar with the most important of those
catalogues in which some information may be found for the
study of French literature.

By applying to the Chief, Card Division, Library of Congress, Washington, D. C., all the index cards relating to a
special topic can be purchased at a very low cost (one to
three or four cents each). This is often a convenient way of
collecting the elements of a correct and useful bibliography.

The most interesting catalogues for our purpose are the
following: *A Catalogue of the Bibliographies of Special Subjects in the Boston Public Library*, by J. L. Whitney, 1890
(see "France" and authors' names); *A Selection of Cata-
loguers' Reference Books in New York State Library* (Al-
bany, N.Y., 1903); *Catalogue of the Astor Library* (6 vols.);
*A Catalogue of the Allen A. Brown Collection of Books Re-
lating to the Stage in the Public Library of the City of
Boston* (1919); *Catalogue of the Molière Collection in Harvard College Library*, by Currier and Gay (*Bibliographical
Contributions*, Harvard College Library, Vol. IV, 1906);[1]
Peabody Institute Library Catalogue (13 vols.) (Baltimore,
1882–1895), which includes rare French books and valuable
extracts from periodicals, etc.

V. Bibliography of Subjects Involving the Literary
    Relations of France with Other Countries

Until F. Baldensperger and his collaborators publish their
much-needed *Bibliographie critique de la littérature com-*

---

[1] See also the catalogues of several special collections in the J. P. Morgan
Library: Corneille, Racine, Bossuet, Fénelon, Regnard, Le Sage.

parée, the essential source of information for all questions that deal with the literary relations between France and other countries is L. P. Betz, *La Littérature comparée, essai bibliographique* (2d ed. by F. Baldensperger, Strassburg, 1904). This clear, compact handbook first devotes several chapters to the literary relations of France with Germany, England, Italy, Spain, the Scandinavian and Slavic countries, the United States, and finally with Greek and Roman literatures. Then comes a stimulating chapter on what the Germans call *Stoffgeschichte*; that is to say, the history of the principal motifs, themes, and literary types of legendary, religious, or traditional origin.

Betz's book may be supplemented by articles and bibliographical references found in A. L. Jellinek, *Bibliographie der vergleichenden Literaturgeschichte* (Berlin, 1903), unfortunately discontinued and covering only the period June, 1902–June, 1903; *Zeitschrift für vergleichende Literaturgeschichte*, begun in 1888, discontinued in 1910; and *Revue de littérature comparée*, edited by F. Baldensperger and P. Hazard, beginning January 1, 1921, and destined to play for comparative literature the part played by the *Revue d'histoire littéraire* for the history of French literature.[1]

VI. History of the French Language

Even if a student has no intention of studying Romance philology in the accepted sense of the term, he may often find in his purely literary work difficulties in the language that expose him to many errors and misinterpretations. Whether he is preparing the annotation of a text, elucidating and discussing an obscure passage, or attempting to describe with precision an author's style, it is not enough for him to

---

[1] The *Journal of Comparative Literature*, begun in New York in 1903, has not been continued.

know Littré's *Dictionnaire* or the *Dictionnaire général de la langue française* by Hatzfeld, Darmesteter, and Thomas. The few works named below will be of use to him.

First, he will find the fundamental bibliography in the *Histoire de la langue française des origines à 1900*, by F. Brunot, which now covers the subject until the latter part of the seventeenth century and which for more recent periods may be supplemented by the chapters written by the same author for the *Histoire de la langue et de la littérature française* of Petit de Julleville. Lanson's *Manuel* will also supply interesting material.

The *Bibliographie de la syntaxe du français*, by Horluc and Marinet (*Annales de l'Université de Lyon*, 1908), is furnished with a copious index of words, expressions, and phrases, for which bibliographical references are given.

In E. Huguet, *Petit glossaire des classiques français* (Paris, 1907) many examples, picked for the most part from editions of the collection of the *Grands Écrivains de la France* (Hachette, Paris), are gathered, classified, and compared with definitions borrowed from the three large dictionaries of the seventeenth century: Richelet, Furetière, Académie française.

Abundant examples are also to be found in A. Haase, *La Syntaxe française au XVIIe siècle*, translated from German into French by Obert in 1898 (new edition, Paris, Delagrave, 1916).

VII. Periodical Literature

The reviews and magazines, whether of general interest or devoted to special branches, offer to the student—in ever-increasing numbers—essays, articles, or short notes indispensable to his studies but often difficult to discover. It almost seems as if nothing stamps a student's lack of experience and training so unmistakably as his embarrassment before the bulky collections of the various reviews. Unfortunately the practical knowledge of how to handle this essential material cannot be acquired by theoretical advice. The best method is to spend a few hours among the stacks in the library where the periodicals are stored, so as to see them at close range, to note which of them have tables of contents, and to learn which tables are reliable, which are incomplete or untrustworthy. It is also well, every month or every fortnight, to look over the new numbers of these periodicals and to jot down on cards the name of any article or note that might prove helpful.

There is, of course, no general index to the periodical literature of the world; yet several large indexes are of great assistance in digging out whatever material is to be found here. Some of the following works are not only of national range but include periodicals in many languages:

FRANCE. The *Répertoire bibliographique des principales revues françaises* of D. Jordell, discontinued in 1902, covers only 1897–1899. For more recent publications it is necessary to turn either to foreign indexes, not always reliable for French reviews, or to the collections and tables of the reviews themselves.

ENGLAND AND THE UNITED STATES. *Poole's Index to Periodical Literature* (2 vols. and 5 supplements) (Boston, 1891) covers the period 1802–1907. The *Review of Reviews, Index to the Periodicals of 1890–1902* (13 vols.) (London, 1891–1903) gives references to several periodicals not indexed in Poole. The *Reader's Guide to Periodical Literature* (New York, The H. W. Wilson Company), begun in 1900 and much improved during the last decade, is an excellent tool; some of the most important literary references are to be found in the volumes of *Supplement*, which index periodicals of more limited scope. Monthly lists enable the student to keep his bibliographical records up to date. The *Readers' Guide*, with its regular indexes, monthly lists, and supplements of various kinds, is complicated and at first sight disconcerting, but it is worth while to spend a few moments in making its acquaintance. The *Athenæum Subject Index to Periodicals* (London, 1916–   ), begun in 1915, publishes separate parts devoted to special subjects, such as *Language and Literature* (1916). The *Annual Magazine Subject Index*, edited by F. W. Faxon, Boston, begun in 1909, gives references to "a selected list of American and English periodicals" and may occasionally supplement Poole or the *Readers' Guide*.

GERMANY. Germany supplies three first-class indexes: The *Bibliographie der deutschen Zeitschriftenliteratur*, edited by F. Dietrich, begun in 1897 and issued currently, gives the contents of about a thousand periodicals in the German language. The *Bibliographie der fremdsprachigen Zeitschriftenliteratur*, edited by the same author, begun in 1911 and issued currently, is the most valuable index to periodicals in other languages than German; it too is undoubtedly in the first rank. The *Bibliographie der Rezensionen*, edited by A. L. Jellinek, begun in 1901, gives references to the reviews on German and foreign books appearing in about five thousand periodicals in all languages.

ITALY. *Catalogo metodico degli scritti contenuti nelle pubblicazioni periodiche italiane e straniere*; subject and author indexes; last volume published in 1914, covering 1907–1912.

BELGIUM. *Bibliographie de Belgique. Sommaire des périodiques*, begun in 1875, discontinued in 1914 (17 vols.). Brussels.

Besides the above indexes the student should be familiar with certain reviews especially interesting for our field, in which he will find notices and criticisms of the new books and follow the general orientation of researches in literary history :[1]

---

[1] To enumerate here all periodicals useful for literary history is impossible; the Index des abréviations at the beginning of Lanson's *Manuel* gives some idea of them.

Revue d'histoire littéraire de la France, since 1899. *Tables,* 1894–1899, published in 1900.

Revue de philologie française et de littérature, since 1887. *Index* of Vols. I–X, published in 1896.

Revue critique d'histoire et de littérature, since 1866. *Tables,* 1866–1890, published in 1895.

Literaturblatt für germanische und romanische Philologie, since 1880.

Archiv für das Studium der neueren Sprachen und Literaturen, since 1846. Edited by L. Herrig; often referred to as *Herrig's Archiv.*

Zeitschrift für französische Sprache und Literatur, since 1879.

Berliner Beiträge zur germanischen und romanischen Philologie, since 1893.

Die neueren Sprachen, since 1894.

Neophilologus (Groningen), since 1916.

Publications of the Modern Language Association of America, since 1884.

Modern Language Notes (Baltimore), since 1885.

Modern Language Review (Cambridge, England), since 1905.

Romanic Review (New York), since 1910.

Modern Philology (Chicago), since 1903.

Revue de littérature comparée (Paris), since 1921.

VIII. ENCYCLOPÆDIAS AND LARGE DICTIONARIES

There is no need to call the attention of American students to the *Encyclopædia Britannica* (11th ed., 1910–1911, 29 vols.), for they constantly use it in every imaginable way. They must, however, be reminded of two other important works: (1) the French *Grande Encyclopédie* (31 vols.) (Paris, 1886–1902), which, as far at least as the letter *M* or *N*, is excellent and contains certain articles that are

valuable contributions to literary history;[1] (2) *Brockhaus'
Konversations-Lexikon* (17 vols.) (Leipzig, 1892–1898).

France possesses no dictionary of national biography comparable to the English *Dictionary of National Biography*.
The old *Biographie universelle* of Michaud (2d ed., 1842–
1865) or the *Nouvelle Biographie générale*[2] of Didot (1857–
1866) should be mentioned, even if not recommended.

The *Dictionnaire critique de biographie et d'histoire* of
Jal (2d ed., 1871) brings new or unpublished documents,
or interesting corrections, to bear upon many obscure or
disputed points in the biography of important writers.

IX. SOME PRACTICAL ADVICE

When the student is collecting the bibliography of a subject, it is best to use index cards 3″ × 5″,—the size used practically everywhere for cataloguing. He should learn from
special treatises or from a careful inspection of the catalogue
of a good library how these cards ought to be made out.[3]

Scrupulous attention must be paid to the spelling of
proper names; it is a common experience to see students
hunting for a book, failing to find it, and giving up reading
it, only because the author's name is misspelled in their own
notes. Not less essential are such facts as the special edition
that has been used, its date, and its size.

In many cases it is advisable to copy bibliographical cards
several times, so as to have two indexes, one by authors, one
by subjects. For instance, here is a bibliographical card
correctly made out:

[1] For instance, articles "Académie," "Bossuet," "Corneille," "Diderot,"
"Molière," etc.

[2] Mediocre after the letter *L*.

[3] See G. E. Brown, *Indexing, A Handbook of Instruction* (London and New
York, 1921), or any other recent book on indexing.

LEBLOND (M. A.)

Leconte de Lisle d'après des documents nouveaux

Paris, Merc. de Fr., 1906, 16vo.

This card should be duplicated, in an abbreviated form, as often as is needed to enable the student to turn back to the book for every point on which the latter may give information. For example:

Sand (Influence de George)

LEBLOND (M.A.)

Leconte de Lisle, pp. 122–123

When the number of cards to be handled is large, it may be a good plan to use cards of various colors for different classes of reference: authors and subjects; books, periodicals, newspapers, etc; original texts, books of general information, old and modern works, etc.

Finally, if the library to which the student has access does not own some important book, he must remember that often it is possible to borrow from another university or from the Library of Congress.

Above all, he must not be alarmed or dismayed by the number of titles and references that have been piled into this chapter. He will find that a few afternoons—perhaps three or four—given up at the beginning of the year to a voyage of exploration through the mysteries of the library and its catalogue will save him whole weeks and often months. This is indeed the essential piece of advice: a good student must know these indispensable books of reference, handle them, look them over, make friends with them, and remember that, in libraries as well as in life, the only form of real and fruitful friendship is the one that does not confine itself to formal relations, but is built up on personal contact and frequent meetings.

CHAPTER III

THE PREPARATION OF AN EDITION

Although we can read the great Greek or Latin writers in editions as correct as the number and preservation of the manuscripts permit, editions that offer us the authentic and accurate text of many modern French writers are still lacking. An effort has been made in this direction in the last ten years, resulting in editions like those of the *Lettres philosophiques* of Voltaire or the *Méditations* of Lamartine (Lanson), the *Œuvres* of Vigny (Baldensperger), the *Profession de foi du vicaire savoyard* (P. M. Masson), Montaigne's *Essais* (F. Strowski), Hugo's *La Légende des siècles* (P. Berret), and certain others, which along their different lines may be considered as models. The task that remains is, however, enormous. We have no satisfactory edition of Rousseau's complete works; Bossuet, except the *Œuvres oratoires* and *Correspondance*, almost all of Marot and Fénelon, a large part of Voltaire, nearly the whole of Victor Hugo, and, I may say, most of the famous writers of the nineteenth century lack serious and critical editions.[1] Here is an immense and fruitful field. The preparation of an edition, with the study and research that it entails, offers admirable training for the student. And no task could be more useful; a good edition of a small work of importance is worth far more than five hundred verbose pages of pseudo-philosophy or pseudo-criticism.

---

[1] The so-called definitive edition of Baudelaire (1917) is as poor and inaccurate as an edition may well be (see *Revue d'histoire littéraire*, 1917, pp. 518–521).

I. Requirements of a Good Edition

A good edition of a modern literary text should answer at least the following requirements:

1. It should offer a correct text, that is to say, a text that reproduces as exactly as possible what the author wrote, free from all errors, inaccuracies, and alterations, whether owing to blunders of copyists or compositors, to the carelessness of the author, to ignorance, or to the prejudices of successive editors.

2. It should show the evolution of the text from the rough drafts, through the various editings and reprintings, to the final form adopted by the author.

3. It should clear up all difficulties and obscurities of the text: vocabulary, syntax, allusions.

4. It should supply a literary and historical commentary such that the work, with its sources and its historical, philosophical, controversial, or artistic value, may be entirely comprehensible to the reader.

5. It should be easy to handle and convenient, arranged and printed in such a way as to afford instruction and pleasure, with notes that elucidate and do not submerge the text.

II. Different Stages in the Preparation of an Edition

Let us suppose, then, that you have decided to undertake the task of editing one of the modern French works that it is so desirable to read from a correct and fully annotated text. As you proceed you will encounter all sorts of problems and difficulties, up to the moment when you return the last press proof to the printer. The problems or difficulties, corresponding to the successive stages in your work, can be grouped under the following heads:

1. Critical work for establishing and cleaning up the text.

2. Choice of a text to reproduce as the foundation of a critical edition.

3. Establishment and arrangement of the critical apparatus.

4. Reproduction of the text: questions of orthography, punctuation, etc.

5. Linguistic and grammatical commentary.

6. Literary commentary.

7. Practical details of printing.

CRITICAL WORK FOR ESTABLISHING AND CLEANING UP THE TEXT

You can readily see that the editor of a modern text is quite differently situated from the editor of a Greek or a Latin text. The latter has to contend with a certain number of manuscripts—the work of copyists, with which the author has had nothing to do; his task is to study, classify, and correct these manuscripts, so as, by means of them, to find as nearly as possible the original form of some work, otherwise unobtainable. The editor of a modern text, on the contrary, has to deal with at least five categories of documents:

1. Manuscripts[1] in autograph; often several successive autograph variants of the same work.

---

[1] The reading of the manuscripts of modern authors (from the sixteenth to the nineteenth century) requires methodical preparation and training. The student will find a good starting-point and many useful references in the last edition (which has been much improved) of M. Prou, *Manuel de paléographie*. He should next practice reading the various handwritings of different epochs in the excellent facsimiles of the manuscript of Pascal's *Pensées*,

2. Manuscript copies, not in autograph, which may have been either read and corrected by the author or derived from authentic manuscripts no longer extant.

3. Editions issued during the author's lifetime, whether published or supervised by him or printed independently.

4. Editions published after the author's death, but by persons, chosen by him or qualified for the task, who were in possession of papers that today are scattered or lost.

5. Printings by publishers which reproduce more or less exactly some authentic edition and often form the texts read by the mass of the public.

It is from among these that you must discover the true, pure text of the work you are editing. You will see later for what reasons an editor chooses one special text as the foundation of his edition. In certain cases internal criticism, conducted according to the strict methods of classical philology, is an indispensable auxiliary to the establishment and cleaning up of the text.

1. *Establishment of the text.* There are cases where the application of genuine philological methods of comparison and classification of the various readings[1]—the grouping of texts by families and the establishing of their derivation,

---

of the 'exemplaire de Bordeaux' of Montaigne's *Essais* (both published by Hachette), or in the many examples in A. de Bourmont, *Lecture et transcription des vieilles écritures* (*XVIe, XVIIe, XVIIIe siècles*) (1881), in J. Kaulek and E. Plantet, *Recueil de fac-simile pour servir à l'étude de la paléographie moderne* (*XVIIe et XVIIIe siècles*) (1889), in the *Musée des Archives Départementales* (1878), or in the collection of the *Autographic Mirror*.

[1] Is it necessary to mention that the collating of the various readings should be accomplished with the maximum of patience and care? There is no more tedious undertaking, nor one more calculated to exhaust the power of concentration. Yet, though not all variations of the text need have a place in the commentary of an edition, they should always be completely collated. It is wise to do this work piecemeal, and to have other people check it up. A convenient method is to make a faithful copy of the original edition (or of some other that in particular cases may seem more authentic) ; to leave wide

without any historical or literary considerations—makes it possible to distinguish the true text, which should be the authority in every critical edition. A typical example of philological methods is the work of J. Bédier[1] on the text of the *Entretien de Pascal avec M. de Saci*; his use of internal criticism may be summarized as follows:

Statement of the problem. Of what value is the text of the *Entretien* that is reproduced in every edition of Pascal? Is it a compound of several texts? an arbitrary choice of various readings? A critical text must be established.

Elements of the problem. Seven texts of the *Entretien* are in existence (five manuscript copies and two early editions) no one of which has been directly copied from any of the other six. The connection and derivation of these seven texts—known as *G, M, J, F, B, D, T*—must be established.

Method employed. Collation and critical comparison of the different readings.

Successive results obtained:[2] *a.* All the seven texts are derived from the same original *O*, which is already faulty.

b. D, G constitute one family = *V*.

c. F, J, T, B, M constitute a second family, which is divided into subfamilies:

(1) *F, J, T* constitute a small group = *Z*.

(2) Group *Z* is related to *B*. Therefore *B* forms with *Z* (= *F, J, T*) a family = *Y*.

margins and plenty of space at the top and the bottom of the pages, and to note therein the readings of the different editions. By a "faithful copy" must be understood the minute reproduction of words, spelling, typographical peculiarities, punctuation, paging, etc. Some small detail, seeming at first sight insignificant, will perhaps enable you to classify an edition definitively. Another piece of advice: do not expect hypotheses and conclusions to become clearly distinguishable until you have finished your collation.

[1] *Études critiques*, pp. 3–18, 19–80. Paris, 1903.

[2] Every reading that has influenced these results is, of course, found in Bédier's pages.

(3) *Y* is related to *M* through a copyist *X*.

d. T has occasionally made use of *D*.

Final classification. Expressed by this figure:

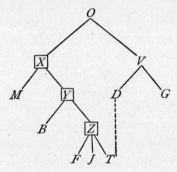

Conclusions. Restoration of the original text (archetype) *O*, except in a very few instances where passages occur in *X* that are not in *V*, and vice versa; and even in these it is possible, in ten cases out of twenty, for obvious reasons to make a choice. "We need only apply obediently the rules that our classification of manuscripts imposes on us, to see the original text establish itself of its own accord; the mere weighing and comparing of the various groups of manuscripts should always restore the genuine readings, and cause the false to eliminate themselves like dross."[1] After this process we are in possession of the best possible text of the *Entretien avec M. de Saci.*

This, then, is a valuable result obtained by purely internal methods of criticism. Such methods may be applied also to what I call cleaning up the text.

2. *Cleaning up the text.* If you are working on a manuscript or an edition, you will inevitably find yourselves confronted at times with a word, an expression, or a sentence that either has no sense at all or only an inadmissible one.

---

[1] *Études critiques*, p. 48.

There are absurdities in the current texts of our best writers,[1] sometimes even in the original texts. These must be cleaned up, and for this purpose philological methods must again be used. To arouse your curiosity, incite ingenious hypotheses, and lead you to reason correctly, I know no better guide than the *Manuel de critique verbale appliquée aux textes latins*, by L. Havet.[2] To be sure, the work is intended for students of Latin philology; but as, after all, the psychology of transcribers and the mechanism of scholia, interpolations, or omissions are in the main invariable, we may well seek Havet's advice as to method.

It is possible to cite innumerable instances of emendations of details[3] both ingenious and amusing. I must content myself with a few, each exemplifying a different manner of treatment.

a. In 1774 Meusnier de Querlon, publishing the *Journal de voyage* of Montaigne, prints the following sentence: "M. de Montaigne disoit s'agréer fort en ce détroit . . . et n'y trouvions incommodité que de la plus espesse et insupportable poussière . . . Dix heures après, *M. de Montaigne disoit que c'estoit la lune de ses tretes*: il est vrai que sa

---

[1] In all the derivative editions of Hugo may be found the following lines:

> La rose épanouie et toute grande ouverte,
> Sortant du frais bouton comme d'une urne *ouverte*,
> Charge la petitesse exquise de sa main . . .

A recent history of French versification, written in English by Kastner, mentions (p. 55) without wincing this "negligence" in one of Hugo's most perfect poems. If Kastner did not care to tamper with a text of Hugo, he might at least have consulted the original edition of 1859: the word there is *verte* (see P. Martinon, "Sur deux textes de Hugo et de Vigny," *Revue d'histoire littéraire*, 1908, pp. 129–130).

[2] 4to. Paris, 1911. See especially §§ 62–127.

[3] You should emend in this way only with extreme caution and when the emendation is imperatively demanded. Beware of those "reckless infelicities of correction" that are the hall marks of those who are always ready to correct when the text is merely obscure or too difficult for them.

coustume est . . . de faire manger l'avoine à ses chevaus avant partir au matin du logis. Nous arrivames . . . de grand nuict à Sterzinguen." In 1889 the Italian editor D'Ancona reproduces[1] this incomprehensible text, adding in explanation De Querlon's childish note: "Parce que cette poussière obscurcissant le jour, ne lui laissait, ainsi que la lune, que ce qu'il fallait de clarté pour se conduire." L. Lautrey, publishing a new edition of the *Voyage* in 1906,[2] makes the following correction: "Dix heures après (*M. de Montaigne disoit que c'estoit là l'une de ses tretes*, etc.) nous arrivames . : ." Because a parenthesis is properly placed and an apostrophe restored, the sentence recovers its meaning.

b. The edition of André Chénier by H. de Latouche (1819), and even the first impression of Becq de Fouquières's admirable edition, print in the *Iambes* the absurd line

Pauvres chiens et moutons, toute la bergerie . . .,

which the Hellenist J. Thurot, inferring a corrupt reading of the manuscript, emends in this convincing way:

Pâtres, chiens et moutons, . . .

c. In *L'Esprit pur*, of Alfred de Vigny, every edition, including the definitive edition by Ratisbonne, gives these lines:

L'écrit universel, parfois impérissable,
Que tu graves au marbre, ou *traînes* sur le sable.

A nonsensical text, yet one that Brunetière quotes in *L'Évolution de la poésie lyrique*,[3] and L. Dorison in *Alfred de Vigny poète philosophe*.[4] The last line should be changed to

Que tu graves au marbre, ou *traces* sur le sable.[5]

---

[1] P. 96. [2] Hachette, Paris. [3] Vol. II, p. 27. [4] P. 204.
[5] G. Dalmeyda, "Note sur un vers de Vigny," *Revue d'histoire littéraire*, 1910, p. 619. Dalmeyda justly remarks that "when it is a question of texts

d. In the *Journal d'un poète,* again by Vigny,[1] we read: "Le Capitaine fit connaissance avec un passager. Homme d'esprit, il lui dit . . ." This ridiculous punctuation should be corrected thus: "Le Capitaine fit connaissance avec un passager homme d'esprit. Il lui dit . . ."[2]

e. At other times the correction is found by turning to the original text, which has been corrupted by successive editors. In the eighteenth *Lettre philosophique* of Voltaire, after a somewhat free translation in verse of Hamlet's soliloquy, the Kehl editors and their successors insert a transitional sentence followed by a literal translation in prose; they then return to the text of 1734: "Ne croyez pas que j'aie rendu ici l'Anglais mot pour mot; malheur aux faiseurs de traductions littérales!" This interpolation is utter nonsense. Lanson reëstablishes the sequence of ideas by suppressing the editors' addition.[3]

f. The scrutiny of handwritings will often suggest an hypothesis that may lead to some useful emendation. In the first edition and in all subsequent editions of *La Prière* by Lamartine is found this text,[4] which Lamartine himself failed to notice:

> Ma pensée, embrassant tes attributs divers,
> Partout autour de *toi* te découvre et t'adore,
> Se contemple soi-même, et t'y découvre encore.

A. Hauvette, another Hellenist, observing that "in Lamartine's manuscripts initial *s* is elongated and nearly straight" and that although "Lamartine usually crosses his *t* with a

---

that have been read and reread, habit and memory exert a strangely conservative force." Good advice about method. See also P. Martino, "Note sur trois corrections au texte de *L'Esprit pur,*" *Revue d'histoire littéraire,* 1919, p. 119. He tries to give an explanation of the traditional text, and insists quite rightly upon the necessity for extreme prudence in corrections of this kind.

[1] P. 28.   [2] E. Estève, in *Revue d'histoire littéraire,* 1914, p. 451, note.
[3] Edition of the *Lettres philosophiques,* Vol. II, p. 82.   [4] Line 53.

horizontal stroke, he almost as invariably omits this horizontal stroke when *t* recurs in the same word or hemistich", corrects the passage thus:

Partout autour de *soi* te découvre et t'adore,

which correction is verified[1] in the *Correspondance*.[2]

What conclusions as to method can be reached from these examples?

1. Never allow an incomprehensible, ridiculous, or inconsistent reading to remain in the text without correction or comment.

2. Look for the possible origin of a corrupt reading in the chirographical peculiarities of the manuscript; in an error by the compositor of the first edition; in the editor's negligence or ignorance; in an inadvertence on the part of the author.

3. Make a conjecture as to the emendation. Strive to verify your conjecture by consulting the manuscripts, by

[1] Vol. II, p. 89.

[2] *Bulletin de la société des humanistes français*, 1901, pp. 52–53. Another example is found in Bossuet's *Sermon sur l'honneur du monde*: "Cet homme s'est enrichi par des concussions épouvantables, et il vit dans une avarice sordide; tout le monde le méprise; mais il tient *bonne table à ses mines* à la ville et à la campagne,"—an unintelligible text. Lebarq suggests "*à ses ruines*" ("*in a way that will ruin him*"), but the correction is poor French and inconsistent with the context. Another guesses "*tient bonne table, a ses mines*" ("*puts on airs*"), which is a pointless, unnatural expression. Rébelliau suspects an inversion of words by Bossuet's hasty pen and reads "*tient bonne mine à ses tables*". Here the plural is hardly admissible. Finally, A. Croiset, the learned Greek scholar, noticing that in words beginning with *con* Bossuet sometimes expresses the prefix by the abbreviation $\tilde{c}$, and noticing besides that in his handwriting *u*, *n*, *v* are indistinguishable, believes that the six downstrokes and *es* that compose the word *mines* should be read $\tilde{c}vives$, or *convives*: "*tient bonne table à ses convives* à la ville et à la campagne".

See other examples of ingenious emendations in *Annales romantiques*, July, 1906, pp. 248 and 377; in *Revue d'histoire littéraire*, 1912, pp. 409–410; in the edition of Vigny published by F. Baldensperger, *Wanda*, viii; and in the entire collection of the *Bulletin de la société des humanistes français*.

studying the different readings, or by considering the rest of the work.

4. Comment upon these corrupt or doubtful passages in your notes, even if you do not succeed in correcting them satisfactorily.

CHOICE OF A TEXT AS FOUNDATION OF A CRITICAL EDITION[1]

We have seen that Bédier chose from among seven texts of the *Entretien avec M. de Saci*—five manuscript and two printed. When Lanson undertook the editing of the *Lettres philosophiques*, he was confronted by more than twenty-five texts printed before Voltaire's death. I myself found over forty in editing *Candide*.[2] For the *Profession de foi du vicaire savoyard* Masson was obliged to study at least seven different manuscripts and more than twenty-five printed editions.

This, then, is the essential question: What text should be selected as a foundation for the new edition? There are two aspects of the matter to consider: (1) Should the preference be given to manuscripts or to editions? (2) From among the editions which should be selected?

1. *Should preference be given to manuscripts or to printed editions?*

Above all, resist the temptation to ascribe, as Bédier says, "a kind of mystical superiority to every manuscript over every printed text"[3] Unquestionably, nothing is more invaluable than a manuscript written or revised by the author; nothing is more natural than the tendency to give this abso-

---

[1] See Langlois and Seignobos. *Introduction aux études historiques*, pp. 51–56.
[2] Voltaire, *Candide*, with Introduction and Commentary. Published by A. Morize (Société des textes français modernes), Paris, 1913.
[3] *Études critiques*, p. 6.

lutely 'authentic' text preference over all others. To do so, however, is in certain cases an error.

An excellent instance of a rigorous critical treatment is Bédier's study on *Le Texte des "Tragiques" d'Agrippa d'Aubigné*, in which he proves that at times an edition must be preferred to the best manuscript.[1]

Elements of the problem. a. There are four texts of *Les Tragiques* contemporaneous with the author:

A, edition of 1616, not acknowledged by D'Aubigné, though published by him.

B, enlarged edition without name of place or date; acknowledged by D'Aubigné.

T, Tronchin manuscript, prepared under D'Aubigné's direction and corrected by his hand.

L, London manuscript, corrected by D'Aubigné and forming part of his widow's inheritance.

b. These four texts, all authentic, present serious divergencies.

c. Of the three modern editions that we possess,[2] one reproduces *A* with some corrections or additions taken arbitrarily from *B*; the other two reproduce *T* without giving any reasons for this choice.

Problem. a. To classify these four texts chronologically.

b. To discover the definitive form, to be used as the basis of a modern edition.

First phase: elimination. a. Facts observed: The text of *A* is an incomplete and imperfect rough draft. On the other hand, *L* copies all *T*'s faults without exception and adds some of its own. Therefore *L* is simply a derivative of *T*.

b. Conclusion: Elimination of *A* and *L*; *T* and *B* remain.

---

[1] *Études critiques*, pp. 3–18.

[2] Lalanne edition (1857); Read edition (1872); Réaume and De Caussade edition (1877).

Second phase: classification. What is the relation between *T* and *B*? There seem to be only two possibilities: *T* is a revision previous to *B*; *T* is a revision subsequent to *B*. A detailed study of the variants shows, however, that *T* is not the source of *B*, for often *B*, in agreement with *A*, gives a better reading; *B* is not the source of *T*, for often *T*, in agreement with *A*, gives a better reading.

Third phase: critical work. See line 190:

A, Vainqueur, *mais hélas! c'est vaincre à la Cadméenne.*
T, Vainqueur, *comme l'on peut vaincre à la Cadméenne.*
B, Vainqueur, *comme l'on peut c'est vaincre à la Cadméenne.*

The correction of *A* in *T* is intelligible; but where did the ridiculous line in *B* come from?

A fact to be observed: *B* borrows the first hemistich from *T*; the second, from *A*.

Fourth phase: hypothesis. After 1616 (*A*) D'Aubigné revised his poem only once (*T*). At the time his revision was printed he did not send his manuscript copy (*T*) to the printer; he sent a copy of *A*, corrected by hand above the text, in the margin, or on interleaving-paper. In line 190, when transferring the correction "comme l'on peut" from *T* to the margin of *A*, he inadvertently crossed out in *A* only "mais hélas!" without including the words "c'est", which *B* scrupulously reproduces.

Corroboration of the hypothesis. a. D'Aubigny made similar mistakes in lines 361 and 1216.

b. The manuscript bears the autograph memorandum "donné à l'imprimeur le 5 aoust". Yet the condition of the manuscript shows that it never went to a printer. Thus D'Aubigné, after writing his corrections on a copy of *A*, merely made a note of the date on which he gave his new text to the printer.

Fifth phase: verification of the hypothesis. *a.* The slight divergencies between T and B can be logically explained.

b. Any serious fault in A, corrected in T, fails to appear in B.

c. A bad error in French, contained in T, not in A, disappears from B at the time the proofs are corrected.

Conclusion. *a.* B is the definitive form of the text decided upon by the author.

b. We have no correct edition of D'Aubigné.[1]

From this study, and from others like it,[2] we can frame the following suggestion as to method:

When the choice lies between an impression published by the author himself and manuscripts, even if in autograph, that precede the impression, the impression is generally of greater value than the manuscripts.

The question of selecting between the manuscript and printed editions may take many other forms:

a. An edition has perhaps been made after the author's death, with the help of manuscripts no longer extant. The manuscripts that we possess may be merely preparatory or imperfect forms (this is the case with certain of Diderot's works). Here again the edition is more trustworthy than the manuscript.

b. Suppose that, as the author has left only rough drafts, the editions have been prepared without even his posthumous participation. If so, we must turn to the manuscript. A typical case is the *Pensées* of Pascal.[3]

c. We may have an edition issued without the author's supervision, as well as his manuscripts in a more or less final

---

[1] Except of the first book, published under the direction of Bédier, Paris, 1896.

[2] For instance, the study of the *Provinciales* of Pascal. See Molinier edition (*Pensées*, Préface), and Brunschvicg edition, Vol. IV, p. 101.

[3] Some valuable information may be gained by seeing how the first editors did their work.

form. Then we naturally choose the manuscripts. This is the situation with André Chénier (d. 1794), whose works were first published by Henri de Latouche in 1819. Chénier's manuscripts, accessible today, have been used as the foundation for the editions of J. M. de Heredia and of P. Dimoff.

d. Lastly, the real text is found in the manuscripts if the author, during an era of absolute power or of persecution, has been forced to alter or soften down his work for the printer,[1] or if he has adapted it to the exigencies of the stage.[2]

From these instances, then, we can derive a second suggestion as to method:

When dealing with manuscripts and printed editions we should choose the text that brings us closest to the author's definitive and complete thought.

2. *How to choose from the printed editions*[3]

The choice of a printed edition may range between two extremes: (1) the princeps, or original edition; (2) the last edition issued during the author's lifetime.

As with the manuscripts, absolute and inflexible methods would be dangerous here. In fact,

a. The original edition may be only an imperfect and unfinished sketch; for instance, D'Aubigné's *Les Tragiques*.

---

[1] For example, many philosophical writings of the eighteenth century.

[2] See P. and V. Glachant, *Essai critique sur le théâtre de Victor Hugo*, pp. 223–259. 1902.

[3] Work of the kind treated here is impossible without a fairly minute knowledge of the technical processes of bookmaking during the epochs in question. See some very useful suggestions in the article by R. B. McKerrow, "Notes on Bibliographical Evidence for Literary Students and Editors, etc.," *Transactions of the Bibliographical Society*, Vol. XII, pp. 213–318 (London, 1914). For instance, the author shows (p. 220) in what ways "bibliographical evidence will often help us to settle such questions as that of the order and relative value of different editions of a book; whether certain sections of a

b. The last edition is not necessarily superior to those that precede.

c. An intermediate edition may represent more exactly than either of these the author's intention.

Let us consider some examples:

(1) Voltaire, *Candide*. Between the text of *Candide* of 1761, altered in certain details and amplified, and the original text of 1759, I chose that of 1759, because it was the precise form in which Voltaire hurled this bomb into the philosophical arena of his century.

(2) Rabelais, *Pantagruel*. Abel Lefranc chose the last edition of *Pantagruel*, as representing the work perfected and enlarged as Rabelais desired.[1]

(3) Calvin, *Institution chrétienne*. In the case of the *Institution chrétienne*, Abel Lefranc preferred the first French text, of 1541, both because that date is of capital importance in the history of the French language and of French thought and because the last text (1560) published during Calvin's lifetime, translated from the Latin edition of 1559, abounds in errors and corrupt readings.[2]

book were originally intended to form part of it or were added afterwards; whether a later edition was printed from an earlier one, and from which; whether it was printed from a copy that had been corrected in manuscript, or whether such corrections as it contains were made in the proof; and a number of other problems of a similar kind, which may often have a highly important literary bearing".

[1] Rabelais, *Œuvres complètes*. Published by A. Lefranc (Vol. I, 1912; Vol. II, 1913).

[2] Calvin, *Institution de la religion chrétienne* (text of 1541). Published, in 2 vols., by Lefranc, Chatelain, and Pannier, 1911.

It is the text of 1560 that is reissued by Baum, Cunitz, and Reuss in Vol. XXXI of the *Corpus Reformatorum*. If the additions in the Latin edition of 1559 are indeed Calvin's own, its translation, the French text of 1560, is much altered after Book I, chap. vii. See Lanson, in *Revue historique*, 1894, pp. 60–76, and J. Demeure, in *Revue d'histoire littéraire*, 1915, pp. 402–407. The text of 1541 is the genuine French text, and the only Calvin text published by Calvin.

(4) Lamartine, *Méditations*. The text of the *Méditations* commonly on sale includes, besides the 1820 collection, eleven poems subsequent to 1830; the discourse *Des destinées de la poésie*, which dates from 1834; and the *Commentaires* in prose, a sort of inexact and belated confessions. Now, the *Méditations* has special literary significance as the expression of the souls of 1820 who hailed in Lamartine their eagerly awaited poet. Literary history needed a good edition, which should reproduce not the composite publication of 1849 but the important little book of 1820; this was supplied by Lanson.[1]

(5) Ronsard, *Poésies*. Until 1914 we had only two modern editions of Ronsard: that of Blanchemain,[2] whose text is a spurious mixture of readings picked up here and there and of the editor's inventions; and that of Marty-Laveaux,[3] which reproduces the text of 1584 as it was arranged by an older and less spirited Ronsard, often very different from the Ronsard of the early days of the Pléiade. Laumonier[4] has undertaken to reissue the first edition of each collection, adding in footnotes the later emendations and changes. This makes it possible for us to read the poems in all their freshness, to follow Ronsard's development, and to get to the heart of an epoch when "the art of expressing a thought was in the making, and was steadily advancing".

These few examples show:

(1) That it is impossible to give a rule, or even a general suggestion, as to the choice of a text as the foundation for an edition.

(2) That in a great number of cases it is well to choose the first form of an important work.

---

[1] In 2 vols (8vo) (*Collection des grands écrivains*, 2e Série). Hachette, 1915.
[2] 1857–1867.   [3] 1887–1893.
[4] Société des textes français modernes. Hachette, 1914 et seq.

(3) That, after all, the editor's endeavor should be to select and reproduce the text that has the greatest historical significance.

Selection, however, is not always easy, even after deciding to rely on the first edition. Several editions differing considerably from one another may bear the same date. Among these the original must be found. This is the case with Rousseau's *Discours sur l'inégalité* and *Émile*; Voltaire's *Lettres philosophiques* and *Candide*; several of Pascal's *Provinciales*; and many other works.

Once more, it is naturally impracticable to lay down rules for discovering this true original text. Each editor must find the specific method that will accomplish his purpose. Here are two examples that illustrate different processes:

(1) Voltaire, *Lettres philosophiques*. Lanson decided to publish the text of the *Lettres philosophiques* of 1734. But he found two editions of 1734, and, curiously enough, both are authentic.

(a) The Basle edition (London, 1734), brought out through the efforts of Thieriot, a friend of Voltaire.

(b) The Amsterdam edition (Rouen, 1734), brought out by the publisher Jore.

Both texts in the first place came from Voltaire, who sent a copy to Thieriot and a copy to Jore; corrections to Thieriot and corrections to Jore. How is it possible to choose? Lanson decides by means of external criticism, both historical and psychological.

(a) Voltaire himself corrected Jore's proofs; he did not see Thieriot's and repeatedly complained of Thieriot's negligence (evidence furnished by the *Correspondance*).

(b) Coincident with Thieriot's edition an English translation was being made in London from the copy sent by Voltaire. Now the English translation agrees often with the edition of Jore, not with the edition of Thieriot, whose "friendly emendations" are thus ruled out.

(*c*) Finally, "the *Lettres philosophiques* is interesting through its rôle in the history of ideas. . . . The work is a polemic. Therefore, the edition must be selected that gave offense to the authorities, and was censored and condemned." This is Jore's edition.[1]

(2) Voltaire, *Candide*. In the case of *Candide* the text of 1759 seemed to me the most interesting historically. But I had before me thirteen editions dated 1759; which was the correct one? This time I was guided by bibliographical and critical considerations. Through an examination of typographical ornaments and of other details I recognized the edition that came from Cramer's press (the press usually employed by Voltaire at that period); through a minute study of a curious copy[2] I discovered in several places a text that antedates the original edition.[3]

---

[1] *Lettres philosophiques* (ed. Lanson), Vol. I, Introduction, pp. viii–xii. This piece of criticism demonstrates (1) the importance of the testimony furnished by correspondence; (2) the importance of translations (compare the case of the *Institution chrétienne*); (3) the importance of judiciary proceedings, censorship, etc. for every book that influences the history of ideas.

[2] Introduction critique, pp. lxxxi–lxxxvi.

[3] A study of the various recent editions mentioned as examples draws attention to two conditions of frequent recurrence:

1. It may happen that although an author has revised and improved his text, we are not justified in supposing that the minor changes are by him. They may have been made by the printer and overlooked by the author.

2. It may happen that an author, wishing to reprint some work, is satisfied to take a worthless copy of a former unauthorized edition, to make his additions or changes in this, and to pass over unnoticed the many little mistakes or peculiarities of the text he is using. Thus the new edition introduces fresh faults into the very text that the author desires to perfect.

ESTABLISHMENT AND ARRANGEMENT OF THE CRITICAL APPARATUS

You have now collated all the texts, manuscript or printed, of the work that you intend to edit. You have chosen a text as the foundation for your work, and you have a perfect copy of it. What are you going to do with this material?

The next step is to establish the critical apparatus of your edition; that is to say, to arrange alongside your fundamental text all the readings that will help the reader to follow the history and the development of the text.

1. Observe that I say "all the readings that will help the reader"—not simply "all the readings". Even though you are obliged in your preparatory work to study and to collate every divergent form of the text, it would be a childish display to crowd into your "adnotatio critica" all the readings that you have accumulated in your notes. For the really interesting modifications would disappear, submerged by this deluge of useless detail. Therefore in your introduction rid yourself of the editions that have no bearing on the history of the text. Refer to them, describe them—and leave them.[1]

2. You should follow some plan that will make your critical apparatus clear and readable. Do not force the reader to turn back to the introduction or to the list of symbols to find out what it is all about. In designating the different editions, avoid letters, such as the Greek alphabet, that have no significance. Use either the last two figures in the date of the edition, or a letter that recalls its essential character. Your reader will remember without difficulty that 59 stands for the edition of 1759; *K*, the Kehl edition; *L* and *T*, the London and Tronchin manuscripts respectively; 75[8],

---

[1] See how Lanson deals with them in *Lettres philosophiques*, Introduction, pp. xiii–xiv.

Volume VIII of the 1775 edition. Symbols of this kind explain themselves.

3. When the same reading is found in successive editions derived one from another, do not encumber your notes by enumerating each one. Do not write out 1552, 1553, 1567, 1572, but simply 52–72.

4. Where should you put your critical apparatus? This depends chiefly upon its size and upon the importance that you wish to attach to it. I am opposed to arranging the various readings at the end of the volume, or even at the end of the chapter, book, or canto. By this system the reader is given an irksome task, and the readings, massed together far from the text they are supposed to elucidate, lose in life and interest. In most cases it will be quite convenient to put the critical apparatus on each page, between the text and the historical or exegetical notes. The general effect will be much clearer if you use different type for these three sections.

In certain extreme cases it will be necessary to resort to special processes. Masson, when editing the *Profession de foi du vicaire savoyard*, wished (1) to give us the text of the original edition and (2) at the same time to enable us to trace, through the very important manuscripts, the development of the work, thought, and art of Rousseau. Therefore he decided to arrange his text and his readings on two pages:

The left-hand page, mainly critical, gives the versions of the four manuscripts, and shows the progress of Rousseau's work, from such beginnings as we can reach, up to its completion (the text of each manuscript is distinguished by a different type); the right-hand page, mainly historical, reproduces the original edition (with the readings of subsequent editions), and points out the sources of Rousseau.[1]

[1] Introduction, p. xcviii.

This method, although admirable in this instance and doubtless applicable to certain other works, such as *Les Martyrs*
of Chateaubriand or *La Tentation de Saint Antoine* of Flaubert, would, however, have no advantage for most of the
works that we wish to see well edited.

REPRODUCTION OF THE TEXT: QUESTIONS OF ORTHOGRAPHY AND PUNCTUATION[1]

To reproduce a text is more easily said than done. It is a
delicate task with even a printed text, and often impossible
with manuscripts or copies. In the sixteenth century "spelling" can hardly be said to have existed. In the seventeenth
century, though an effort was made to regulate it, few con-
formed to the regulations.[2] In the eighteenth century all
was chaotic; many writers took no interest in the question;
Voltaire left his printers free to "régner sur ce petit peuple-
là". Besides, a number of important texts were printed in
foreign countries by foreign typographers. With manuscripts
the uncertainty is even greater: at some periods no distinction was made between writing *i* and *j*, or between *u* and *v*,
etc.; famous authors, such as Montesquieu, have strange
orthographical frailties;[3] Mme de Tencin's letters would be

---

[1] See L. Clédat, "Sur l'établissement du texte de Boileau," *Revue de philologie française*, Vol. I (1917), pp. 1 ff. (in particular, pp. 9–10, on the reproduction of orthography).

[2] See F. Brunot, *Histoire de la langue française*, Vol. IV, pp. 83–167.

[3] Here is a specimen of Mme de la Fayette's spelling and punctuation: "Il
ny a un jour que lon ne parle icy de vous escrire toutes les soirees se finissent
en disant mon dieu escriuont donc a ce pauure mr de Pomponne mandons luy
combien nous nous ennuyons de ne lauoir plus et lenuie que nous auons quil
reuienne cela ce dit touts les soirs . . ."

Here is a quotation from Bossuet:

"Pardonnez nous si nous entandonssi mal vôtsre grandeurs etayezagreable-
ces iddees grossieres que nous nousformons denotre felicite durant lexiletla
captiuite de cesteuie . . ." (quoted by Brunot, *Histoire de la langue française*,
Vol. IV, pp. 159 and 166).

a disgrace to a little girl eight years old; Hugo himself and Lamartine[1] overlooked many inadvertencies.

What are you going to do in reproducing your text? On the plea of scientific precision, shall you thrust upon your reader a text that is nearly indecipherable? Or, on the ground of its illegibility, shall you treat it as you please— correcting, unifying, modernizing? Here again you must discriminate and give proof of judgment and fine critical sense.

1. It is useless to preserve anything that is obviously some stupid mistake of the printer or an oversight on the part of the author. Nevertheless, point out the slip in your critical apparatus, for it may serve to identify the edition.

2. If you are the first to reëdit a very rare text, reproduce the original with scrupulous fidelity (with the above reservation). However, the addition of a few capitals, periods, or colons, while not affecting the exactness of the reproduction, will help greatly in the reading of it. Do not fail to specify in your introduction what decisions you have made.

3. Certain authors have idiosyncrasies of spelling that they cling to. In this case do not interfere with them; on the contrary, make them very plain. Rousseau chose to write *dégré* for *degré*; *réligion* for *religion*, etc. Masson[2] gives a brief list of these orthographical preferences.[3] Likewise, Voltaire decided after 1734 to print *français, anglais*, instead of *françois, anglois*, etc. This interesting fact in the history of the language should be carefully noted.

---

[1] See Des Cognets, "Étude sur les manuscrits de Lamartine," in *Mélanges d'histoire littéraire* (Bibliothèque de l'Université de Paris), Vol. XXI, pp. 109–197; P. V. Glachant, *Essai critique sur le théâtre de Victor Hugo* (1902), p. 55, note 1.

[2] *Profession de foi*, p. 583.

[3] See, for some valuable suggestions as to method, pages cvii–cviii of the introduction.

4. You will find texts, especially in manuscript, that use abbreviations without any coherent system. In the greater number of cases there is no objection to adopting throughout either *M*. or *Monsieur*, *&* or *et*, etc., even when the original vacillates between the two forms.

5. In editions that are intended not for savants but for the general public or for schools and colleges, to modernize the spelling, whether wholly or in part, is quite admissible; but these are not cases that involve critical methods.

6. Punctuation is a difficult question to handle. Only by a thorough knowledge of its history, and especially of the habits of your author, will you reach a legitimate solution. Frequently the punctuation of the original texts is incoherent, representing only the whim of the printer; it is for you, in such instances, to make the text readable, while departing as little as possible from the original. When the author himself has determined the punctuation, leave it alone. Again, if faulty punctuation alters the idea or confuses the sense, arrange it to fit the meaning.[1] Lastly, remember that even at a comparatively recent date punctuation marks did not have the same value that they have today.[2]

The question is of particular importance in editing poetry, as here it is closely related to rhythm. The punctuation of

---

[1] Here is an emendation by J. M. de Heredia in his edition of the *Bucoliques* of Chénier (p. 80). Instead of

   Les fleurs ne sont plus tout; le verger vient d'éclore,

he reads,

   Les fleurs ne sont plus; tout le verger vient d'éclore.

[2] See D. Mornet, *L'Alexandrin français dans la deuxième moitié du XVIIIe siècle*, pp. 38–42. He points out that printers and authors commonly used the semicolon (;) as we use the comma (,). Thus Rousseau punctuates: "Soyez-en sûre, aimable Claire; je ne m'intéresse pas moins que vous au sort de ce couple infortuné; non par un sentiment de commisération qui peut n'être qu'une faiblesse; mais par la considération de la justice . . ." (*Nouvelle Héloïse*, Vol. II, p. 2; text of the two principal editions).

writers such as Chénier, Hugo, Vigny, or Leconte de Lisle is all-important, although their editors have too often failed to recognize this fact. Compare these two texts taken from Chénier's *Le Jeune Malade*. The first is that of Latouche[1] and of Becq de Fouquières[2]; the second is reproduced by Dimoff from the autograph manuscript. Is it not evident how different the comment on the rhythm and expression would be for each version?[3]

<table>
<tr><td style="text-align:center">1</td><td style="text-align:center">2</td></tr>
</table>

1	2
Ma mère, adieu; je meurs, et tu n'as plus de fils.	Ma mère, adieu. Je meurs; et tu n'as plus de fils.
Non, tu n'as plus de fils, ma mère bien-aimée.	Non, tu n'as plus de fils. Ma mère bien-aimée,
Je te perds. Une plaie ardente, envenimée,	Je te perds. Une plaie ardente, envenimée,
Me ronge; avec effort je respire, et je crois	Me ronge. Avec effort je respire; et je crois
Chaque fois respirer pour la dernière fois.	Chaque fois respirer pour la dernière fois.
Je ne parlerai pas. Adieu; ce lit me blesse,	Je ne parlerai pas. Adieu. Ce lit me blesse.
Ce tapis qui me couvre accable ma faiblesse;	Ce tapis qui me couvre accable ma faiblesse.
Tout me pèse et me lasse. Aide-moi, je me meurs.	Tout me pèse; et me lasse. Aide-moi. Je me meurs.
Tourne-moi sur le flanc. Ah! j'expire! O douleurs!	Tourne-moi sur le flanc. Ah j'expire. O douleurs!

The subjects of orthography and punctuation, in short, are infinitely complicated. They require art, tact, taste, on your part. Here again the best method is, after studying

---

[1] 1819.   [2] 1862.

[3] This example is interesting in showing that even the most impressionistic and subjective criticism implies an initial study of literary history and of its precise methods; that is, unless you are disposed to be as enthusiastic over Latouche's punctuation as over Chénier's rhythms.

thoroughly the individual case, to decide what liberties you may allow yourself so as to present the text in the form desired by its author, without obliging your reader to decipher hieroglyphics or to wrestle with absurdities.

LINGUISTIC AND GRAMMATICAL COMMENTARY

The linguistic and grammatical commentary aims at explaining every difficulty that your text may present in vocabulary, grammar, syntax, and versification. Obviously, the earlier the text the more necessary it becomes. What most of the work of the fifteenth and sixteenth centuries and many passages previous to 1650 really need is translation.

As soon as you have acquired material for the commentary, the questions again arise : How must you choose? How shall you arrange it?

1. In choosing, the following is a safe principle: Keep in your notes only such data as to vocabulary or language as are indispensable for understanding the text. The rest is padding and ostentation. If you chance upon a curious or interesting word, do not take the occasion to write its complete history; examples filched from dictionaries and crowded into the same page as the text make your work tedious and obscure. Avoid anything that sounds like a philological dissertation. Discuss only the special points that need clarifying. Reject all but the necessary remarks.

2. The arrangement will depend entirely on the scope and purpose of the commentary; that is to say, on the kind of work you are editing. There are difficulties in arranging the commentary either as footnotes or at the end of the volume. If as footnotes, the notes will be overloaded, and, in trying to lighten them, serviceable and sometimes necessary material will be discarded; if at the end of the volume, or of

separate parts of the volume, your comments will be of far less benefit to the reader. Here are a few suggestions:

a. When your commentary is not bulky, insert it below the text with the other notes.

b. When it is bulky, a good plan may be to divide it into two parts: one part, for observations on grammar or syntax, to be arranged as footnotes; the other, for remarks on vocabulary, in a glossary at the end of the volume. Asterisks in the text would then refer the reader to the glossary.

c. In the case of very important grammatical and syntactic commentary, you might index every remark of the kind made in the notes, supplying in this way the elements and the plan of a study on the language of your author.[1]

At all events, bear in mind that you are not writing a philological contribution to the history of the language, but are elucidating a difficult text. Everything that does not directly further your aim must be sacrificed without compunction.

LITERARY COMMENTARY

The literary commentary should include all remarks and notes, whether historical, biographical, philosophical, or æsthetic, all discussions on sources or influences, all bibliographic or iconographic information, necessary for understanding the text.

During the preparatory work you will accumulate an enormous and somewhat confused mass of documents of every kind and origin. Resist the temptation to insert them all in your notes. They have helped you, but they are not all indispensable to your reader. Therefore, here again, to know how to choose is the beginning of wisdom.

---

[1] The editions of Molière or of Racine in the *Collection des grands écrivains de la France* furnish admirable examples.

But how should you choose? The principle of choice has, I think, been formulated perfectly by Lanson: "To know how to retain from your exhaustive researches the material that is called for by the nature of the text."

Lanson means that you should begin by deciding (this will prove your perspicacity and tact as an editor) what constitutes the special interest of your text—what gives it importance in the author's life, or in the history of ideas or of some particular literary theory or *genre*. Pick out from your notes those that are related to this aspect of the work and that help to explain it. Leave the others, or take only the most important. For instance,

1. Saint-Simon's *Mémoires* requires, above all, historical commentary: information about the people and events mentioned; explanation of obscure allusions; correction of errors; completion of fragmentary anecdotes. This has been supplied in Boislisle's large edition.[1]

2. Works that are more or less autobiographical should on every point be criticized, verified, and explained, in notes that weigh them against accurate critical biographies of their authors. We are still waiting for such an edition of Rousseau's *Confessions*.

3. Philosophical, theological, and polemical works should have their environment restored. Your notes should bring out the relation of a work to previous or contemporary systems and doctrines; the writer's standing; the current of ideas he followed or tried to stem. Under this heading come the *Pensées* of Pascal, the *Sermons* of Bossuet, the *Émile* of Rousseau, the *Génie du christianisme* of Chateaubriand. For many of these the commentary should be especially on the sources.[2]

---

[1] *Collection des grands écrivains.* Hachette.
[2] The study of sources will be treated in a special chapter.

4. Other works, on the contrary, have chiefly an æsthetic interest. The notes should, therefore, in each case lay stress upon the artist's effort to reach or to approach perfection; upon the means he employs; upon the degree of his success or failure. It happens frequently that such literary commentary is inseparable from the study of the various readings and successive transformations of the text. The novels of Flaubert, and the poems of Chénier or of Leconte de Lisle and many of Lamartine's or Hugo's, are well suited to criticism of this kind.

Is it necessary to say that there are no 'air-tight partitions' between these compartments? The question is, primarily, to use intelligence in deciding what direction your commentary should pursue; what aspect you should emphasize; how much space you should devote to each category of notes.

Lastly, by an attentive study of several good editions you will best serve your apprenticeship.

PRACTICAL DETAILS OF PRINTING

I sum up here these suggestions of an entirely practical nature, intended not to exhaust the subject but to indicate how such details as are involved in the final work on an edition may judiciously be handled.

1. Whenever possible put all the annotation, critical or historical, on the same page as the text. This is its proper place, where it is most effective.

2. Distinguish with special type the different sections of the page: text, various readings, notes.

3. Use simple, intelligible symbols.

4. When you have selected a system of symbols, adhere consistently to it from the beginning of the book to the end.

5. Do not fail to equip your edition with the necessary indexes and tables of contents: "Livre sans index, livre à peu près perdu" has been justly said.

6. Do your utmost to insure the typographical correctness of your text, of the various readings, and of the notes.

EXAMPLES OF EDITIONS TO STUDY

In order to become acquainted with applications of the various methods, you will find nothing of greater value than to spend some hours in familiarizing yourself with certain recent editions. I subjoin a list, which may be altered or enlarged at your pleasure.

1. In the *Collection des grands écrivains de la France,* published by Hachette, study preferably *Molière* (Despois, Mesnard, and Desfeuilles); *La Bruyère* (Servois); *Racine* (Mesnard); *Pascal* (Brunschvicg); *Saint-Simon* (Boislisle).

2. The Société des textes français modernes has published, beginning in 1905, a series of critical and annotated editions, among which the most instructive as regards method seem to me to be the following:

VOLTAIRE. *Lettres philosophiques* (Lanson). 1909.
DU BELLAY. *Œuvres poétiques* (Chamard). Since 1908.
SENANCOUR. *Obermann* (Michaut). 1912 and 1913.
VOLTAIRE. *Candide* (Morize). 1913.
RONSARD. *Œuvres complètes* (Laumonier). Since 1914.
HEROET. *Œuvres poétiques* (Gohin). 1909.

3. The publication of the *Pensées* of Pascal forms one of the most complicated and interesting problems in editing. All the documents on that question are readily accessible. See especially the introductions to the Michaut edition[1] and

[1] 1897. See A. Gazier, "G. Michaut, Les *Pensées* de Pascal," *Revue d'histoire littéraire,* 1897, pp. 624–626.

to the Brunschvicg edition[1]; the *Manuel bibliographique* of Lanson, Nos. 4632–4651; and the complete photographic reproduction of the manuscript published by Hachette.

4. Not less instructive is the history of the edition of Montaigne's *Essais*. Nos. 2552–2569 of the *Manuel* refer you to some useful sources for this study. See in particular the Bordeaux edition, published by Strowski, beginning in 1904, and the photographic facsimile of the precious copy in the Bordeaux Library.

5. It has been said that the edition of Rousseau's *Profession de foi du vicaire savoyard* by Masson[2] "sets a standard for publications of this kind, and is the model edition that (while modifying the plan and the method to suit particular cases) we should always try to approximate".[3] You have seen above in what an ingenious way Masson arranges his commentary and critical apparatus. An introduction, which is an example of masterly terseness, explains (*a*) the history of the composition and the publication of the *Profession*; (*b*) the development of the text traced through the manuscripts and the editions; (*c*) the method of the present edition.

The historical commentary, the result of formidable research, is concentrated upon the following points: (*a*) works that Rousseau alludes to, and that he refutes; (*b*) origins of his art and erudition; (*c*) biographical events that are reflected in his work; (*d*) texts, possibly but not necessarily known to Rousseau, that form "the intellectual and moral atmosphere for his maturing mind".

It must indeed be a fine edition that deserves the commendation that "every detail in the critical apparatus or in the commentary serves some purpose".

---

[1] 1904.   [2] 1914.
[3] Lanson, in *Revue d'histoire littéraire*, 1917, p. 322.

Since these editions will be useful as material for critical observation rather than as models for beginners to imitate, I add the names of some excellent works on a more restricted plan, which will give you a correct idea of the edition of an important, though more limited, text.

1. Rabelais, *Lettres d'Italie*, published by Bourrilly (8vo) (1910). The book has a successful typographical arrangement, full, judicious notes, and a convenient index.

2. Rabelais, *Le Quart Livre de Pantagruel* ("édition partielle", Lyon, 1548), critical text published by Champion with introduction by Plattard (8vo) (1909). Its good points are a clear text, well-arranged readings, a wisely planned introduction, and lucid and complete notes.

3. D'Aubigné, *Les Tragiques*, Livre I, *Misères*, published under the direction of Bédier (16mo) (1896).

4. Claude Binet, *La Vie de P. de Ronsard*, published by Laumonier (8vo) (1910). The work shows immense erudition, which, in my opinion, slightly overbalances the text. There is a good critical commentary. I should prefer to have the historical commentary arranged at the bottom of the page of text rather than at the end of the volume.

5. Voltaire, *Correspondance* (1726–1729), published by Foulet (1913). This edition is a model of the critical method applied to the establishment of a text. The notes and appendix clear up many faults or inaccuracies of previous editions.

6. In the last few years four editions have been published that are well worth examining: Lamartine's *Méditations*, edited by Lanson (2 vols.) (1915); *La Légende des siècles*, edited by Berret (2 vols.) (1920); *Télémaque*, edited by A. Cahen (2 vols.) (1920); *Adolphe*, edited by G. Rudler (1919). In breadth of learning that never submerges the text, in discriminating commentary, and in perfect arrange-

ment they stand for an ideal that is, perhaps, a little discouraging but that certainly may act as an inspiration.[1]

[1] Those who wish to undertake the proper editing of any of the important texts of the nineteenth century would do well to know that under the French law a writer's works belong either to his editors or to his heirs for a period of fifty years, to the day, after his death. Therefore, no one can publish, in part or in full, any work thus protected without a preliminary understanding with its legal owners. Also, by a very recent law, the duration of the war (1914–1918) is not to be included in the legal fifty-year period: the period is to be lengthened by five years. Thus the authors who should have become 'public property' during 1920 do not become so until 1925; among them are Mérimée, Montalembert, Alexandre Dumas père, Jules de Goncourt, Prévost-Paradol. Other writers whose works will become public property within the next few years are the following: during 1926, Émile Deschamps; during 1927, Théophile Gautier; during 1928, Ernest Feydeau, Glatigny; during 1929, Michelet, Guizot, Jules Janin, Charles Asselineau; during 1930, Quinet, Tristan Corbière; during 1931, George Sand, Mme Louise Colet, Fromentin, Henri Monnier; during 1932, Thiers; during 1933, Claude Bernard, etc.

CHAPTER IV

ESTABLISHING A CRITICAL BIBLIOGRAPHY

The establishment of the critical bibliography of a writer, of an important work, or of a question of literary history is one of the most useful services that a young scholar can render to science. Let it be clearly understood that he should not think of undertaking any work comparable to those huge bibliographical monuments that usually represent more than a quarter of a century of patient, skillful research; for example, *Voltaire, Bibliographie de ses œuvres*,[1] by G. Bengesco, or the *Bibliographie des recueils collectifs de poésie publiés de 1577 à 1700*,[2] by F. Lachèvre. On the contrary, it is a question of a work with a definite aim that is sufficiently modest not to mean the sacrifice of a lifetime; it is a question of choosing a very limited subject, of placing at the disposal of anyone it concerns all the serviceable references, correctly presented, verified, and criticized.

Today, for no matter what subject, the list of printed references is long, at times formidable. If an investigator were always obliged to consult an exhaustive list of these references, he would inevitably be overwhelmed. Suppose that a historian were to venture upon the study of Jeanne d'Arc: in the catalogue devoted to her by H. Stein, which does not contain the manuscript documents, he would find more than twelve thousand entries. He would need at least thirty years for the mere perusing of these twelve thousand printed documents. And, to quote the saying of a French humorist, by that time he would be either dead or crazy, or would be be-

---

[1] In 4 vols., 8vo. 1882–1891. [2] In 4 vols., 4to. 1901–1905.

ginning all over again on the amount of new material printed during those thirty years.

This is the reason for the existence of critical bibliographies—works not of accumulation but of choice, not of piling up but of clearing up. For their given subjects they should tell the reader: At the present day, here is a list of what you must read or examine. Here are the writer's works, with the indispensable bibliographical data. Here are the publications that contain information worth consulting. The rest is mediocre or bad, verbiage or rubbish.

By this means, in from fifty to one hundred pages, it is possible to offer a very helpful bibliographical introduction.[1] It often happens that the bibliography of a thesis may or should be presented in this form.

How can such a work be prepared, compiled, and arranged?

It is understood that you are in possession of the requisite materials, that you have established and verified all index cards relating to your subject, as has been explained in Chapter II ("Implements and Tools: Bibliography"), and that these have been classified, studied, and appraised. There remains to make of them a convenient and accurate little book.

Let us take two different cases: the critical bibliography of an author; the critical bibliography of a subject.

CRITICAL BIBLIOGRAPHY OF AN AUTHOR

A study of the best critical bibliographies published recently, together with sound common sense, will indicate that the most logical and satisfactory divisions are the following:

1. *A short biographical notice.* Give in detail the chronology of the writer's life.

---

[1] See F. Funck-Brentano, *Introduction aux bibliographies critiques* (8vo, 7 pp.). Paris, 1899.

2. *Manuscripts.* Compile as complete a list as possible of the manuscripts, telling where they are to be found (location of the library, call number, etc.) and what they are (autographs or copies, well or poorly preserved). Analyze the contents, specifying what use has been made of these manuscripts in the printed works and bringing to light those that may be still inedited. For correspondence, if the case arises, mention where the letters are stored and the whereabouts, if known, of all scattered letters, such as those described in the catalogues of autographs, etc.[1] Mention in addition which of the manuscripts are accessible to the public and how they may be consulted.

3. *Works (or articles) published during the author's lifetime.* Describe in its chronological position each work that was published during the author's lifetime. This description necessitates a technical knowledge of at least the elementary facts about book production, and especially about the mechanical side of it. Perhaps this is as good a chance as any to insist upon the dangers of the average student's ignorance on this subject: the art of printing is linked in too intimate a way with literary history to be safely neglected. Whether in establishing a critical bibliography or in preparing an edition or the critical apparatus of an important text, it is often possible to solve questions more rapidly and surely by simple bibliographical evidence than by purely literary methods. No book exists for French literature that in this respect compares with Ronald B. McKerrow's excellent treatise *Notes on Bibliographical Evidence for Literary Students and Editors of English Works of the XVIth and XVIIth Centuries,* published in the *Transactions of the Bibliographical So-*

---

[1] Especially the catalogues of private or public collections or of public sales. See, for example, the catalogues of Charavay, in France, or that of the Dreer Collection or of the Anderson Collection, in America.

ciety.[1] The examples are, of course, taken from English writers, but many of the principles and suggestions can without difficulty be applied to works printed in France. Besides concise and clear details about the making of a printed book and the various stages in the process,[2] the student will find some useful technical information on the importance of signatures,[3] imprints, and initials; on the part played by watermarks in determining the size of a book; on the exact meaning of the terms 'edition' and 'issue' (p. 260), with an explanation of the particular cases that may arise; on the way to distinguish a first impression from those that follow (pp. 264 ff.); on how to tell whether two copies belong to the same edition (pp. 270–272); on the importance of 'cancels' (French *cartons*) and the means of detecting them. This preliminary study will be of the greatest service for the descriptions that must be included in your critical bibliography.[4] The following recommendations should also be carefully observed:

Reproduce with minute exactness the full title-page, including the arrangement of the lines (separate them by short, vertical strokes). Do not neglect any details or imperfections in the imprint, ornaments etc.

[1] Vol. XII, pp. 213–321. London, 1914.

[2] "Elementary instruction in the mechanical details of book production need occupy but a few hours of a university course of literature, and it would, I believe, if the course were intended to turn out scholars capable of serious work, be time well spent" (p. 220). *The Practice of Typography*, by T. L. De Vinne (4 vols.), is an excellent introduction.

[3] A 'signature' is a distinguishing mark (letter or number) placed at the bottom of each sheet of a book, to indicate its place to the folder and binder. —For any difficulty about the meaning of foreign technical terms see *Vocabulaire technique de l'éditeur, en sept langues* (Berne, 1913) and H. Ramin, *Vocabulaire anglais-français et français-anglais des industries du livre* (Paris, 1920).

[4] You will find some good technical advice in F. Madan, "On Method in Bibliography," *Transactions of the Bibliographical Society*, Vol. I, pp. 91–102; and G. W. Cole, "Compiling a Bibliography" (New York, 1902) (reprinted from the *Library Journal*, 1902).

Note the date of publication with the greatest possible accuracy. For modern or recent books, thanks to the *Journal de la librairie* and to publishers' announcements, the month or the week of their appearance may often be determined.

Next, mention all subsequent editions, recording each interesting alteration, whether in the title or in the contents of the volume. Make plain, whenever you can, the motives for these alterations.

Reproduce any fragments, prefaces, forewords, suppressed passages, etc. that have disappeared from the current editions and that may be of interest in tracing the history of the author's thought.[1]

When it is a question of collections of poetry, essays, or treatises, give in detail the contents of the volume, which may vary from one edition to another.

Group together any information that gives an idea of the circulation of the work (numbers of copies printed at each impression, reviews in journals and periodicals, etc.).

For each volume state the number of pages and, for certain old editions, the irregularities of paging, signature, interesting illustrations, or typographical ornaments, woodcuts, headpieces and tailpieces, etc.

When there are several volumes, or a complete or incomplete collection of an author's works, establish and record the date of publication of each volume.

Many modern writers, particularly since the beginning of the nineteenth century, have first published their works as articles in reviews or journals (Chateaubriand, Lamartine, Hugo, Vigny, Musset, Sainte-Beuve, Renan, Taine, Bourget,

---

[1] See, for instance, Taine's remarkable pages, exhumed by V. Giraud in his *Bibliographie critique de Taine*, particularly (p. 13) an admirable portrait of Sainte-Beuve suppressed from the Préface of the *Essais de critique et d'histoire*.

Anatole France, among others). Your critical bibliography should contain the answers to the following questions relating to such articles: Where and when did they appear? Were they included in some later work or were they put to no further use? If they were used, did they conform to the original text?

4. *Posthumous works.* In addition to the details already suggested, you will note the conditions under which posthumous works have been published: Who was responsible for their publication? How much was the editor guided by directions left by the author? Is his work satisfactory, and may it be considered definitive? If errors, omissions, or corruptions exist, what are they?

5. *Correspondence.* Enumerate the published collections of correspondence; ferret out the letters not included by the editor of the correspondence, stating whether they were overlooked by him at that time and have been published later, or are still in manuscript.

6. *Works to be consulted.* It is on the question of works to be consulted that your bibliography should be truly critical. Your aim should be, in directing your reader to what is really useful, to save him the time and the trouble of hunting up and reading hundreds of pages, either empty of information or definitely superseded by more recent or more scientific works. Your entries should be followed by brief, precise criticisms. If a valuable review has been published, give the reference.

In particular, call attention to the information that lies hidden in the periodicals, the proceedings of learned societies, and other compilations. This is an essential part of your task.[1]

---

[1] Take care to state the number of pages in each article. This gives an idea of its importance if not of its thoroughness.

When a work has aroused a controversy, group the refutations, apologies, and parodies round it; make clear the stand taken by adversaries and defenders; in short, restore the work to its exact environment.

Finally, do not omit to "date your bibliography almost to the day, so that the reader may know definitely when your bibliographical investigation ended".[1]

To present all this material conveniently, several arrangements are possible. It is for you to choose that best suited to the specific question you are treating.[2] One of the most favorable methods, I think, consists in dividing your references into *General Studies* (in chronological or alphabetical order, or classified under *books* and *periodicals*—this last arrangement has little to commend it) and into *Particular Studies* (subdivided into studies relating to successive works, studies relating to ideas or doctrines, studies relating to biographical detail, etc.).

7. In any case, the work should be completed by one or more indexes, where, distinguished by different kinds of type, the names of persons and the titles of works should be enumerated.

EXAMPLES TO STUDY

Here are four examples of bibliographies constructed in this manner, demonstrating each from a different point of view how helpful it is to undertake and accomplish successfully a work of this kind.

1. C. Urbain, *Bibliographie critique de Bossuet* (8vo, 31 pp.) (Paris, 1900). In this little book, completed on

---

[1] Funck-Brentano, *Introduction aux bibliographies critiques.*

[2] Every bibliographer while making his investigation [I should add, "and arranging his material"] should act as if at some future time he intended to write a comprehensive work upon the subject of his labors, and was simply making a preliminary survey and record of the field, with this as his main purpose constantly in view.—G. W. Cole, *Compiling a Bibliography*, p. 4

September 15, 1899, the student will find the following points particularly worth his notice:

a. The compactness and precision of the biographical data (pp. 1–2).

b. The description of the various editions of Bossuet.

c. The bibliographer's criticism of each edition, summing up the work of the editor and explaining to what extent the text may be considered authentic (pp. 18–21 and passim).

d. The grouping of the "References from Contemporaries" (p. 21) and the "Refutations and Apologies" (p. 29).[1]

2. V. Giraud, *Taine, Bibliographie critique* (8vo, 81 pp.) (Paris, 1902), completed in March, 1902. This is a true model of its kind, condensed, clear, intelligent, interesting to read. The reader should pay particular heed to the following points:

a. The clearness of the paragraph devoted to Taine's manuscripts (p. 2).

b. The definiteness and completeness of the information on every article published by Taine, together with its 'history'; that is to say, the record of how Taine afterwards used it, as well as valuable extracts from the passages that are not reproduced in the later publications (pp. 3–43).

c. The full account of the various transformations of the *Essai sur les fables de La Fontaine* (p. 5), and the publication of the *Histoire de la littérature anglaise* (pp. 21–23).

d. The equal clearness and thoroughness of the data on the references and of his estimate of them; for instance, the work of G. Barzellotti (p. 54).

e. The publication, in the paragraph *Fragments de la correspondance*, of several letters scattered among the reviews

---

[1] Another bibliography on Bossuet, *Bibliographie raisonnée des œuvres de Bossuet* (16mo) (published by Verlaque, Paris, 1908), offers an occasion for instructive comparison. Verlaque's is perhaps more complete, though certainly less critical, than Urbain's, which it will neither supersede nor overshadow.

or catalogues, and a critical study (p. 47) resulting in the rectification of the date of one of these letters.[1]

3. G. Rudler, *Bibliographie critique des œuvres de Benjamin Constant* (8vo, 108 pp.) (Paris, 1908). Except in an appendix that makes no pretense of completeness, Rudler does not attempt to give a bibliography of works on Benjamin Constant. His chief aim is to make an inventory of Constant's manuscripts and works, corresponding to the period covered by his other book, *La Jeunesse de Benjamin Constant* (Paris, 1908). A student should study this *Bibliographie critique* in particular for the classification of papers, the discussions concerning the dates of certain letters, the description of the manuscripts, and the publication of a large number of inedited letters and documents.

4. G. A. Tournoux, *Bibliographie verlainienne; contribution critique à l'étude des littératures étrangères et comparées* (16mo, 172 pp.) (Leipzig, 1912). Tournoux has conceived his book along entirely different lines and with quite another purpose from the critical bibliographies of Urbain and Giraud.[2] He desires, by the establishment of a methodical bibliography, to trace the dissemination and the influence of Verlaine's work in the different countries throughout the world. Considering successively the French-speaking countries, and then Spain, Portugal, Italy, Rumania, Greece, Germany, England and English-speaking nations, Holland, and the Scandinavian, Slavic, and Czechic countries, he ex-

---

[1] See, for the same sort of work, Martino, "Bibliographie critique de Fromentin," *Revue africaine,* 1914 (reprinted separately); A. Maire, *L'Œuvre scientifique de Blaise Pascal: bibliographie critique* (8vo, Paris, 1912) (a remarkable work); H. Cordier, "Essai bibliographique sur les œuvres d'A. R. Le Sage," *Bulletin du bibliophile,* January, 1908–December, 1909; and G. Michaut, *Bibliographie des écrits de Sainte-Beuve,* at the end of his thesis entitled *Sainte-Beuve avant les "Lundis".*

[2] A true critical bibliography of Verlaine has still to be compiled and would be a useful, interesting subject for a Ph.D. thesis.

amines, in each one, the literary or critical studies, translations, anthologies, poems on Verlaine, and even the poems that have been set to music. The work has for us a double interest:

a. It illustrates, on the one hand, the fact that from these bibliographical studies, if they are well done, however dry and narrow they may seem, general ideas of wide, keen interest may be derived. This *Bibliographie verlainienne* throws into strong relief the influence and expansion of the poet's work; it is immediately evident that "whereas he has been popular in Germanic and Slavic countries, he has had only a cold reception among the Latin peoples, with the exception of the Spanish: let this fact be explained by those critics who are specially concerned with literary psychology and race affinity. However widespread the diffusion of his work, Verlaine has not been translated in his entirety. His translators have confined themselves to introducing a limited number of his poems into their languages. They must have followed some system in their choice. What has guided them? Why has a certain author in a certain country preferred a certain piece? There is material for many investigations, as regards not only Verlaine's genius but the character of those who have translated him, or for whose benefit he has been translated."[1]

b. On the other hand, a contribution of this type gives interesting suggestions; it opens to our students a vast and enticing field. Without choosing too extensive or too weighty subjects, but preferably some recent authors for whom American libraries can more readily furnish the necessary resources, many analogous works may be successfully undertaken. I have in mind studies of critical bibliography on Hugo, Dumas, Flaubert, Maupassant, or Zola, in America

[1] Introduction, p. ix.

or in England; on the dissemination and reputation in France of American or English authors, or, indeed, of great writers of other nationalities, such as Tolstoi or Ibsen. Subjects like these could be treated by a group of graduate students working in collaboration in a seminar under a professor's supervision.

CRITICAL BIBLIOGRAPHY OF A QUESTION OF LITERARY HISTORY

Having considered the critical bibliography of an author, we are naturally led to a second type of bibliography—that of a complete subject, or of a movement of ideas.

The principles and rules evidently remain unchanged; they are merely adapted to the different subject matter. Here again it is precision, judicious choice, critical appreciations enabling the reader to lay his hand on something that would be difficult or impossible to discover for himself, reliable and discriminating erudition, that we should struggle to attain.

Suggestions for a subject might be multiplied indefinitely: (1) A critical bibliography of a literary *genre*:[1] dramatic pastoral; classic tragedy (its origin); romantic drama; comedy of manners.[2] (2) A critical bibliography of a literary school or epoch: *préciosité*; revival of the taste for antiquity at the end of the eighteenth century; fantastic literature during the romanticist period; realistic or naturalistic

---

[1] See, for example, H. Vaganay, *Le Sonnet en Italie et en France au XVIe siècle. Essai de bibliographie comparée* (8vo) (Lyons, 1903).

[2] Here is a supplementary suggestion, found in the *Revue d'histoire littéraire* (1906), p. 501: "A bibliography that should include the keepsakes, the collections of extracts, and the literary periodicals of the Romantic school, would lead to the discovery of many pages by the best French authors of the nineteenth century not contained in their works, and would supply a powerful tool, and many suggestions, for literary historians and bibliophiles."

schools. (3) A critical bibliography of the relations of literature at a given time with the fine arts, with philosophy, or with music. (4) Above all, a critical bibliography of a great writer's influence in his own or in a foreign country— a question that involves both the bibliography of a writer and the bibliography of a subject.

An admirable example of the latter is the *Bibliographie critique de Goethe en France,* by Baldensperger (8vo) (Paris, 1907). I know few books in which bibliographical information is presented with more acumen and skill or in a manner more stimulating to the reader's mind. The dryness of the references is constantly relieved by brief and adequate commentaries, valuable quotations, and ingenious comparisons. This excellent model, which a student must not expect to equal in his first attempt, will, nevertheless, point out where and how to proceed.

CHAPTER V

INVESTIGATION AND INTERPRETATION OF SOURCES

It is not possible to reason in a discriminating manner about an author's thought or art or to make a sound estimate of his originality unless in advance we have discovered and explained whence his ideas have come; by what influences he has been affected; what writers have stimulated or nourished his thought; what books he has imitated, adapted, sometimes calmly copied,—in short, what are the sources of his work.

First, it is necessary to agree on the definition of a source. To discover the sources of a work does not mean only the malicious pleasure of pointing out in footnotes all passages reproduced with varying degrees of fidelity or servility from another author. It does not mean merely the childish satisfaction of catching, let us say, Chateaubriand or Hugo 'in the act'—the relish of showing beyond a shadow of doubt that some page of the *Voyage en Amérique* or some line in *La Légende des siècles* is nothing but a more or less clever appropriation from the text of an obscure traveler or of a forgotten journalist:

Not, indeed, that such criticism is unjustified or useless. I should say even that it is necessary, and this for several reasons. First, because it keeps our admiration from straying toward points that do not deserve it. Next, because it throws valuable light on the working-methods of the writer whom we are studying. Lastly, because in this way we become better acquainted with the character of the writer, with his scruples as to originality or even as to literary probity. Yet we must concede that plagiarism was formerly regarded in a very different light from what it is today. If Montaigne blandly transcribes entire fragments from other writers, no one in the France of his day thought of blaming him. Even in the seventeenth and eighteenth centuries public opinion was still indulgent in this regard; it was not until the last century that plagiarism was condemned as out-and-out dishonesty. Up to that time an author had a sort of recognized right to "take what he wanted where he could get it".

Discovering a source means something besides bringing to light and indicating literal imitations or conformity of one text to another. It means investigating, finding, analyzing, and discussing the material of all kinds that may have contributed to the formation and the expression of a great writer's thought: first, without doubt, passages directly borrowed (whether admittedly or not), conscious or unconscious imitations of some predecessor; but in addition other sources, less obvious, less easy to define, sometimes scarcely tangible —sources at least as important as the former. Such would be the perhaps remote effect of education; the impress left by something hastily read; the recollection of a conversation; the influence of literary, political, social, or religious environment—the stamp of some tradition, not always to be traced to a particular book, but reacting upon the writer through his friendships, his associations, and the salons, academies, and social sets of every sort that he has frequented. These form the atmosphere that an author is obliged to breathe, no matter how determined he may be to shut himself up in his 'tower of ivory'; they cannot fail to affect him in some degree, positively or negatively, whether he is swayed unconsciously or whether he resolutely takes the opposite stand.

When we speak of atmosphere, of environment, we must remember that the literary works studied and admired today represent only a small part of the total production of the period in which they appeared. For every masterpiece or work of real worth that has come down to us there are hundreds, if not thousands, that have sunk forever into the oblivion they deserve. There was a time, however, when the works that are now condemned were widely read; frequently they had a brilliant though brief success. They helped to form the 'ambient' in which our famous writers have been developed, and, therefore, the extent to which they have provided or confirmed these writers' ideas should be taken into account. If you examine *La France littéraire* of Quérard or glance through Voltaire's or Grimm's *Correspondance*, the files of the *Année littéraire* or of the *Journal des savants*, you will gain a superficial notion of what Voltaire, Rousseau, or Diderot very likely used to read, week after week, month after month—material that, thought out anew, transformed, worked over and over, may have reappeared in their writings. We are disposed to accept too readily the false theory that great writers read only great writers—that geniuses merely pass on the torch from one to the other. Nothing is more untrue. A certain celebrated page by Rousseau can be traced to his having recently read the *Journal encyclopédique*; a brilliant witticism of Voltaire was his reaction to a passage by an obscure and ignorant Jesuit Father. It is necessary, then, in order to clarify and understand the great and glorious works to spend much time with the mediocre and insignificant.

This labor of investigating and discovering sources of every kind is important, as we have seen, because it is the indispensable condition for determining the originality of an author.[1] A time-honored custom that dominates the methods of instruction in every country concentrates the study of the history of literature round its masterpieces. If it is a question of instruction only, nothing is more legitimate; it is always better to read in our classes, and to require our students to read, Corneille than Alexandre Hardy, Chateaubriand than W. Bartram, and Anatole France than the Abbé de Villars. However, the moment that we undertake a historical and critical study of the master writers the point of view changes. It then becomes a question of discovering exactly what kind of men they were, what new ideas they contributed, and how much they availed themselves of traditions, of preëxisting thought and learning. This knowledge is acquired only through as complete a study as possible of the sources from which they borrowed. It is all very well to say that Rousseau introduced into eighteenth-century literature the type of the "bon sauvage" and that he first expressed the "sentiment de la nature"; that Voltaire imported English Deism into France; that Du Bellay's *Deffence et illustration de la langue françoise* was little short of revolutionary. These assertions on the part of the lecturer or the critic who scorns 'facts' and limits himself to 'ideas' may, indeed, be the occasion of magnificent rhetoric, whose least defect will be its absolute erroneousness. Nevertheless, patient and thorough study of the sources—not infrequently leading to the discovery of forgotten documents —has proved that the "bon sauvage" existed long before Rousseau, who exploited rather than invented a notion al-

---

[1] As a good example of the study of an author's originality taken in connection with an examination of his sources, see J. Plattard, *L'Invention et la composition dans l'œuvre de Rabelais* (Paris, 1909); in particular, chap. i, "Les Rapports de l'œuvre de Rabelais avec la littérature romanesque de son temps," and chap. vi, "L'Humanisme."

ready on the way to general acceptance; that *La Nouvelle Héloïse* did not create the feeling for nature in the eighteenth century but gave expression to it; that Voltaire's Deism is of French rather than English extraction, and that when he left for London in 1726 his ideas were well established on that point; finally, that the first book of the *Deffence et illustration de la langue françoise* is hardly more than a translation, sometimes verbatim, of a similar work published for the vindication of the Italian language. If, unhappily, there were not still many critics and philosophers who refuse to admit the necessity of researches of this kind, it would be superfluous to lay stress upon them.

In the second place, the search for sources is important for establishing derivations and legacies from other writers and epochs. Again, it is only by a careful inventory of the sources, the direct imitations, or the less obvious influences that the degree of dependence between two authors or two periods may be fixed. Take André Chénier as an example: how much does French Romanticism owe to him? How can we answer this question otherwise than in empty words before we have listed all possible comparisons between him and Lamartine, Vigny, Hugo, and the rest? Even when the list has been made, it is evident that we have not answered the question (this is a point that we must not lose sight of), but we shall, at least, have material with which to answer, a basis for reasoning—we shall not be building in the air.

Finally, the search for sources is important because it attracts attention to certain works and certain writers, little known and oftentimes forgotten, who in their day were the vehicles for ideas, or the 'exciters' for producing the thought of more renowned writers. Between the radiance of the seventeenth century and the brilliant epoch of eighteenth-century philosophy there has long been for us a sort of black hole; the study of the sources of the famous writers of the eighteenth century is dragging out of this obscurity many writers who, during the transition period, were their precursors and their inspiration.

As 'source-hunters' we do not tread a safe path; before proceeding further we should be warned against certain temptations and certain possible errors.

1. First, we must avoid becoming 'source-maniacs'; that is to say, adopting as a postulate the theory that a specific source necessarily underlies each passage, each line, of the text in question. Alfred de Musset says, "It is imitating someone to plant cabbages" ("C'est imiter quelqu'un que de planter des choux"), and it is always "imitating someone" to write a book. We cannot speak or write without borrowing the words of others; as La Bruyère declared long ago, "everything has been said, and we are too late by the seven thousand years and more that men have existed, and thought." We must not, on the pretext of pointing out a source, multiply comparisons that are nothing but vague coincidences of words or of thought, or uninteresting repetitions of banal and everyday ideas. Amusing examples are found in E. Dreyfus-Brisac, *Un Faux Classique, Nicolas Boileau*,[1] or *Plagiats et réminiscences, ou Le Jardin de Racine*.[2] If Ronsard writes,

> Les matelots à la peur *indomptés*,

and you find in Boileau,

> Immolent trente mets à leur faim *indomptable*,

should you conclude from this, as does Dreyfus-Brisac, that Boileau has here copied Ronsard? It is also unwarrantable

---

[1] Paris, 1901.   [2] Paris, 1905.

to discover plagiarisms, or even sources or simple reminiscences, in resemblances of the following kind:

Accablé de malheurs, d'ennui et de tristesse . . .

ALEXANDRE HARDY

Et que simple témoin du malheur qui l'accable.—RACINE

Echauffant les glaçons de cette âme cruelle . . .—HARDY

Et, de sang tout couvert, échauffant le carnage.—RACINE

At this rate, when M. Jourdain says to his servant,
"Nicole, apportez-moi mes pantoufles", he certainly is guilty
of several barefaced plagiarisms. Therefore do not let us
hunt for sources or influences where none exist.

2. On the other hand, when we have found a source, we
should not think that it is the only one—the only possible
one. We must avoid what I call the 'hypnotism of the unique
source.' Take warning from those authors of monographs
who, having devoted themselves largely to the study of one
person, are as a result obsessed with a tendency to detect
his influence on every side. Lanson alludes to this when
he writes, "We study Lamennais's influence upon Hugo or
Lamartine, and we close our minds to all the channels by
which the same ideas, the same opinions, could have been
simultaneously supplied to them".[1] He is thinking of the
two books, by C. Maréchal, entitled *Lamennais et Victor
Hugo*[2] and *Lamennais et Lamartine*.[3] Maréchal is without
doubt the greatest authority on Lamennais in the world. For
years he has made him the centre of his studies, of his interests, and of his literary affections. What, then, is more
natural than the tendency to discover Lamennais in every
famous writer who could possibly have read him? Incon-

[1] *De la méthode dans les sciences*, Vol. II, p. 251.
[2] 1906.   [3] 1907.

testably his influence is real and deep and should be mentioned and studied; but it should be taken into account (which Maréchal apparently has not cared to do) that Hugo and Lamartine have felt other influences contradictory or corresponding to Lamennais's. It is obvious that in his poem *La Providence* Lamartine uses every Christian argument against despair. "He takes them from Lamennais", Maréchal would say. As a matter of fact, they are the commonplace, traditional arguments by which Christian theology seeks to aid all those whom life discourages and disillusions. Lamartine did not need Lamennais's help to discover and express them.

These remarks apply also to those who are hypnotized not merely by a man but by an idea or a theory. Take, for instance, the book entitled *Montesquieu et la tradition politique anglaise en France; les sources anglaises de "L'Esprit des lois,"* by J. Dedieu.[1] Throughout its pages we feel the author's unconscious desire that everything in the *Esprit des lois* should be English—his constant inclination to furnish, alongside Montesquieu's text, fragments of Sidney, Locke, Mandeville, Gordon, Arbuthnot, Warburton, or Bolingbroke. It seems to us that Dedieu, while working on the text, always had one question uppermost in his mind. This question was not, Is there a source for this passage, and if so what is it? It was rather, Can I not find some English quotation as a source for this passage? This ill-advised method, although it did not entirely interfere with the usefulness of his book, clearly led him to assert the English origin of some passages of Montesquieu that are merely reminiscent of classic Greek or Roman texts. Furthermore, he has not taken into account that "there has existed, at least since the Renaissance, a mass of notions and opinions, often contradictory, which forms a sort of intellectual atmosphere breathed by all Euro-

[1] Paris, 1909.

pean students and scholars. Some principle, whose origin is sought by certain critics in the works of Clarke or even of Bolingbroke, may be traced to the most venerable manuals of Roman law."[1]

Therefore it behooves us, as I have tried to show, not to hunt for a single source, or a single category of sources, where there are many and of various kinds. Nor should we look at a text through a stained glass that prevents our detecting the differences in shade or the odd medley of colors.

3. In the third place, we should avoid the danger of reasoning from a resemblance to a direct dependence. We touch now upon one of the most indispensable precautions in the investigation of sources—that which applies to 'intermediaries.' A writer expresses some idea; another expresses the same idea. We should not be in too great a hurry to say that the second took the idea from the first, even if nothing contradicts the theory. We should make sure that between the two there does not exist a third writer, and perhaps a fourth, who served to transmit the idea, sometimes, indeed, under a new aspect.

This question of intermediaries furnishes an occasion for various comments on the method of investigating sources.

a. Even the fact that a writer inserts a literal quotation does not prove that he has read the book from which it is copied. There may have been a middleman who supplied the quotation ready to hand. Montaigne quotes Calpurnius and Prudentius without having read either the one or the other. The three passages from each that are found in the *Essais* were taken from the writings of his friend the learned Justus-Lipsius.[2] Therefore, for the study of Montaigne's

---

[1] H. Barckhausen, in *Revue d'histoire littéraire*, 1910, p. 407.

[2] See P. Villey, "Amyot et Montaigne," *Revue d'histoire littéraire*, 1907, p. 714; and *Les Sources et l'évolution des "Essais" de Montaigne*, Vol. I, pp. 92 and 203.

sources it is the text of Justus-Lipsius that is interesting, not that of Calpurnius or of Prudentius. In the same way Montaigne quotes Florus, Frontinus, Polybius, Vegetius, although he has read none of them. Every fragment is copied from the *Politicorum Libri Sex* of this Justus-Lipsius, the middleman whom Montaigne consults.

We must pay careful attention, especially in the case of ancient writers, to the collections of axioms, maxims, adages, and extracts of all sorts, which, as inexhaustible and varied treasure-troves of facts, quotations, sayings, similes, and anecdotes, obviate the necessity of reading the original works. Villey shows that Montaigne owes much to these miscellanies. He cites[1] from the *Apologie de R. de Sebond*[2] a certain passage containing four quotations and two examples (from Terence, Sophocles, Athenæus, and *Ecclesiastes*). Do not suppose, however, an equal diversity in Montaigne's preparatory reading; for the four quotations and the two examples are already grouped by Erasmus on one page in his *Adagia* under the title "Fortunata Stultitia."

It may perhaps happen that the very writer for whose sources we are looking acts as intermediary between himself and a remote text. With some particular work in view, or simply to preserve some useful or interesting passage, he may keep a more or less systematic notebook. Later, when another work is in preparation, he consults this compilation of facts and quotations (in the same way as the volumes of maxims and anecdotes) long after he has forgotten the remainder of the texts from which he copied them.

Montaigne, for instance, gathers for his own use a number of exact quotations from Latin writers. He reads his Seneca, picks out the phrases that have impressed him, and,

[1] Villey, *Les Sources et l'évolution des "Essais,"* Vol. II, p. 15.
[2] Montaigne, II, 12.

without any particularly diligent study of the author, writes an *Essai* composed of his maxims.[1]

MONTAIGNE[2]	MAXIMS FROM SENECA
C'est ce qu'on dit, que le sage vit tant qu'il doit, non pas tant qu'il peut; et que le present que nature nous ait faict le plus favorable et qui nous oste tout moyen de nous pleindre de nostre condition, c'est de nous avoir laissé la clef des champs.	Sapiens vivit quantum debet, non quantum potest.—*Epistle* 70 Nil melius aeterna lex fecit.—*Epistle* 70 Hoc est unum cur de vita non possumus queri.—*Epistle* 70 In aperto nos natura custodit.—*Epistle* 70
Elle n'a ordonné qu'une entrée à la vie, et cent mille yssuës.	Unum introïtum nobis ad vitam dedit, exitus multos.—*Epistle* 70
Pourquoy te plains-tu de ce monde? Il ne te tient pas: si tu vis en peine, ta lascheté en est cause; à mourir, il ne reste que le vouloir:	Neminem tenet (vita) . . . ? Nemo nisi vitio suo miser est.—*Epistle* 70 Scias ad moriendum nihil aliud in mora esse, quam velle.—*Epistle* 70
Ubique mors est: optime hoc cavit Deus. Eripere vitam nemo non homini potest; At nemo mortem: mille ad hanc aditus patent.	Seneca, *Phœnissæ*, Act I, line 151.
Et ce n'est pas la recepte à une seule maladie, la mort est la recepte à tous maux. C'est un port tres-asseuré, qui n'est jamais à craindre, et souvent à rechercher.	Non tantum hujus morbi, sed totius vitae remedium est.—*Epistle* 78 Portus est, aliquando petendus, nunquam recusandus.—*Epistle* 70
Tout revient à un: que l'homme se donne sa fin, ou qu'il la souffre, qu'il coure au devant de son jour, ou qu'il l'attende;	Nihil existimat sua referre, faciat finem an accipiat, tardius fiat an citius.

---

[1] Villey, *Les Sources et l'évolution des "Essais,"* Vol. II, p. 17.
[2] II, 3; Vol. III, p. 26.

D'où qu'il vienne, c'est tous-jours le sien: en quelque lieu que le filet se rompe, il y est tout, c'est le bout de la fusée.

Nemo nisi suo die moritur.—*Epistle* 69

Ubicumque desines, si bene desinis, tota est (vita).—*Epistle* 77

La plus volontaire mort, c'est la plus belle.

Bella res est mori sua morte.—*Epistle* 69

La vie despend de la volonté d'autruy; la mort, de la nostre.

Vitam et aliis approbare quisque debet, mortem sibi.—*Epistle* 70

En aucune chose nous ne devons tant nous accommoder à nos humeurs qu'en celle-là.

In nulla re magis quam in morte, morem animo gerere debemus.—*Epistle* 70

La reputation ne touche pas une telle entreprise, c'est folie d'en avoir respect.

Ad id consilium fama non pertinet.—*Epistle* 70

Le vivre, c'est servir, si la liberté de mourir en est à dire.

Vita, si moriendi virtus abest, servitus est.—*Epistle* 70

In this instance Montaigne the collector of the Latin maxims is the intermediary between Seneca and Montaigne the writer of the *Essai*.

Voltaire furnishes us with similar examples. During the long years when he was preparing the *Essai sur les mœurs* he filled many books with notes and references, preserving here an entire passage, there a single sentence, here an amusing anecdote, there a date or a dry detail; sometimes merely copying; sometimes adding a reflection of his own, incisive, scoffing, caustic. The *Sottisier*[1] and part of the *Œuvres inédites*[2] are instances of miscellanies, or collections, of this type. From such collections arise in Voltaire's mind, at a later date, memories, reminiscences, and allusions which we should be amazed to find grouped together did we not know that they had already been combined on the occa-

[1] Vol. XXXII (ed. Moland).
[2] Vol. I. Published by F. Caussy, Paris, 1914.

sion of a previous work. The chapter in *Candide* about
'Le Pays d'Eldorado'[1] is for the most part constructed in
this way. Here again, it is the author himself who has been
the middleman between the original texts and their distant
echo found in his pages.

b. A special category of intermediaries, to which attention must be called, is composed of translations and editions.

Frequently when a writer borrows or receives his inspiration from some ancient or foreign text, it is not the original
version that has influenced him but a translation or an
adaptation. It is clear in this case that some turn of phrase,
some detail of expression,—some error perhaps,—may not
originate with the author but with the translator. What
Villey says of the translations used by Montaigne may be
widely applied:

We must find out, as regards each author, whether Montaigne
read the text or a translation, and, when he used a translation,
whose translation it was. Suppose that Montaigne chooses an
expression that happily conveys the meaning of the Latin phrase:
is the choice his own, or did some translator prompt him? Suppose that he mistranslates: shall we impute the mistake to him,
or lay the blame elsewhere? A translator is often a collaborator,
and also often a traitor. We must know how far Montaigne has
been aided and how far betrayed.[2]

This Villey has accomplished in a masterly fashion in his
works on the sources of the *Essais*.

[1] Chap. xviii.

[2] For instance, Amyot translated Plutarch in 1572, after which date editions
succeeded one another rapidly. Now on page 172 of the first edition he
writes, "Sylla ayant pris la ville de Péruse condamne tous les habitants à
mourir, excepté son hôte". But *Péruse* is an error for *Préneste*, corrected in
the second edition. Montaigne copies the passage, writes *Péruse*, and never
afterwards changes it. No more evidence is needed. See Villey, in *Revue
d'histoire littéraire*, 1907, p. 715.

Problems of the kind are frequent among writers who quote from the Bible. What translation do they use? Silvestre de Sacy's? a Catholic or a Protestant version? For a poet like Vigny the question is interesting.[1]

In "Les Trois Cents," one of the poems in *La Légende des siècles*, Hugo is inspired by Herodotus, but not by the Greek text: he has taken the translation of Du Ryer, as E. Fréminet has conclusively shown.[2]

Finally, along these same lines, it is useful and often possible to determine exactly what edition an author has followed. On the one hand, he may have found in a certain edition some unusual readings, which are retained in the borrowed fragment. On the other hand, he may have used the notes, commentaries, or introductions of some particular edition as additional material. For instance, Montaigne[3] quotes an anecdote about Saint Louis from a "tesmoing très digne de foy", whom he sincerely believes to be Joinville; whereas it is Anthoine de Rieux, who in 1547 published the first edition of Joinville, but in a disfigured, mutilated, highly colored form. The identification of the edition used exonerates Montaigne.[4] In like manner we find several lines transferred intact to the *Essais* from a note by Lambinus in his edition of Lucretius.[5]

4. Another tendency should be resisted, which, though resembling the mania for sources, differs essentially from it. I call it the obsession for the written source. Suppose that in the course of your studies you come upon a passage evidently not original with your author: you feel convinced that beneath it is a source of information that can be reached;

[1] See H. Alline, "Deux Sources inconnues des premiers poèmes bibliques de Vigny," *Revue d'histoire littéraire*, 1907, pp. 627–636.
[2] *Mélanges d'histoire littéraire*, Vol. XXI, pp. 4–6. 1906.   [3] I, 38.
[4] Villey, *Les Livres d'histoire moderne utilisés par Montaigne*, p. 38.
[5] Ibid. p. 16.

you find yourselves launched upon a tedious and endless chase after a clue to the document used in the mysterious passage. You will not find it, for the excellent reason that there is no such document. You have chanced upon one of those sources that we have already mentioned,—unwritten sources, information assimilated by the author in conversations, in his daily pursuits,—influences that you cannot hope to trace. In this case be resigned to your ignorance; or, if circumstances permit, apply to the problem the appropriate method, of which farther on we shall have examples.

It remains now for us to form an exact idea of the nature of a source, and of what aspects it may assume. This may be gathered from a series of examples, proceeding from the simplest to the most complex—from the fragment directly borrowed to the vague and almost intangible suggestion. It is needless to say that this classification is not absolute, that there are no perfectly distinct types of sources. They are of all kinds; their degree of relationship to the text inspired by them is infinitely variable, and those that follow are given merely as samples.

1. *Direct sources*. A passage may be almost literally transcribed.

MONTAIGNE[1]

Nous semblons proprement celui qui, ayant besoin de feu en iroit quérir chez son voisin, et y en ayant trouvé un beau et grand s'arreteroit là à se chauffer, sans plus se souvenir d'en raporter chez soi.—I, 25

AMYOT

. . . comme si quelqu'un ayant affaire de feu en alloit chercher chez ses voisins, et là y en trouvant un beau et grand, il s'y arrestoit pour toujours à se chauffer, sans plus se soucier d'en porter chez soi.—*Comment il faut ouïr*, fol. 30, V°

[1] Quoted by De Zangroniz, in *Montaigne, Amyot, Saliat*, p. 36.

MONTAIGNE[1]

J'ay vu (dit Arrius) autresfois un éléphant ayant à chacune cuisse un cymbale pendu et un autre attaché à sa trompe, au son desquels tous les autres dansoient en rond, s'eslevant et s'inclinant à certaines cadences selon que l'instrument les guidoit; et y avoit plaisir à ouyr cette harmonie.—II, 12

ARRIAN

J'ay veu autrefois un elephant ayant à chacune cuisse un cymbale pendu, et un autre attaché à sa trompe, au son desquels tous les autres elephants dansoient en rond, proprement et à certaines cadences, tantost s'elevant en l'air, ores s'inclinant, selon que le son et la cadence du premier le requeroient: et y avoit plaisir à ouyr l'harmonie de ces cymbales.—Translation by Witard, p. 327

CHATEAUBRIAND[2]

L'hibiscus, cette herbe énorme, qui croît dans les lieux bas et humides, monte à plus de dix ou douze pieds, et se termine en un cône extrêmement aigu : les feuilles lisses, légèrement sillonnées, sont ravivées par de belles fleurs cramoisies, que l'on aperçoit à une grande distance.—*Voyage en Amérique*, p. 84

BARTRAM

L'*hibiscus coccineus* croît à dix ou douze pieds de haut, en se divisant régulièrement de manière à former un cône aigu. Ses branches se subdivisent de même et sont ornées de grandes fleurs pourpres, qu'on aperçoit à une grande distance.—W. BARTRAM, *Travels*, etc. (Dublin, 1793), p. 102

VICTOR HUGO[3]

C'est dit ; va les chercher. Mais qu'as-tu ? Ça te fâche ?
D'ordinaire tu cours plus vite que cela !
—Tiens, dit-elle en ouvrant les rideaux, les voilà !

Les Pauvres Gens (1854)

---

[1] Quoted by Villey, in *Les Livres d'histoire moderne utilisés par Montaigne*, p. 169.

[2] Quoted by Bédier, "Chateaubriand en Amérique," *Études critiques*, p. 203.

[3] See P. Berret's article "*Les Pauvres Gens* et *Les Enfants de la morte*," *Revue universitaire*, April, 1916, pp. 265–272. He points out that, besides the poem by C. Lafont, Hugo had read in the *Presse* (to which he subscribed)

Charles Lafont

"Adoptons les enfants de cette malheureuse. . . .
Tu ne me réponds pas? Parle, tu m'embarrasses.
Blâmes-tu mon dessein? Non, puisque tu m'embrasses.
Va chercher les enfants."—"Tiens," dit-elle, "ils sont là!"

> Les Enfants de la morte (1851)

Victor Hugo[1]

—Ça, dit Roland, je suis neveu du roi de France,
Je dois me comporter en franc neveu de roi.
Quand j'ai mon ennemi désarmé devant moi,
Je m'arrête. Va donc chercher une autre épée,
Et tâche cette fois qu'elle soit bien trempée.
Tu feras apporter à boire en même temps,
Car j'ai soif.

> Le Mariage de Roland, ll. 52–58

Jubinal

Olivier, lui dit-il, je suis le neveu du roi de France, et je dois agir comme un franc neveu de roi; je ne puis frapper un ennemi désarmé; va donc chercher une autre épée qui soit de meilleure trempe, et fais-moi en même temps apporter à boire, car j'ai soif.—Article from the Journal du dimanche, November 1, 1846

The borrowed passage may be found in a modified or transposed form.

on December 10, 1852, a sort of plagiarism in prose of the poem, ending with these words, which resemble even more closely than Lafont's the text of La Légende des siècles: "Va les chercher!—Tiens, dit-elle en tirant les rideaux du lit, les voilà!" In Hugo's manuscript the first version is "Tiens, dit-elle en tirant les rideaux, les voilà!" See also Berret's edition of La Légende des siècles, pp. 740 ff.

[1] Quoted and annotated in P. Berret, Le Moyen Age dans La Légende des siècles et les sources de Victor Hugo, p. 34. See also Berret's edition of La Légende des siècles, p. 161.

MONTAIGNE[1]

Cleomenes disoit que, quelque mal qu'on peut faire aux ennemis en guerre, cela estoit par dessus la justice, et non subject à icelle, tant envers les dieux que envers les hommes,—et, ayant faict trève avec les Argiens pour sept jours, la troisième nuict après, il les alla charger tous endormis et les defict, alleguant qu'en sa trève il n'avoit pas esté parlé des nuicts. —I, 6

AMYOT

Il avoit faict trève pour sept jours avec les Argiens: la troisieme nuict après, . . . il les alla charger, . . . et comme on lui reprochoit qu'il avoit faulsé la foy jurée, il respondit qu'il n'avoit pas juré de garder les trèves la nuict: au demeurant que quelque mal que l'on peut faire à ses ennemis . . . cela estoit par dessus la justice et non subject à icelle, tant envers les dieux qu'envers les hommes.—*Les Dicts notables des Lacédémoniens*, fol. 217, V°

CHATEAUBRIAND[2]

Le P. Aubry se pouvait sauver, mais il ne voulut pas abandonner ses enfants, et il demeura pour les encourager à mourir par son exemple; jamais on ne put tirer de lui un cri qui tournât à la honte de son Dieu ou au déshonneur de sa patrie. Il ne cessa, durant le supplice, de prier pour ses bourreaux et de compatir au sort des victimes. Pour lui ar-

CHARLEVOIX

Le Père de Brébeuf se riait également des menaces et des tortures mêmes; mais la vue de ses chers néophytes cruellement traités à ses yeux répandait une grand amertume sur la joie qu'il ressentait de voir ses espérances accomplies. . . . Les Iroquois le firent monter seul sur un échafaud et s'acharnèrent sur lui. . . . Tout cela n'empêchait pas le ser-

---

[1] Quoted by De Zangroniz, in *Montaigne, Amyot, Saliat*, p. 29. Here the modifications and transpositions may be explained by the difference between Montaigne's purpose and Amyot's: in Montaigne's version the moral reflection precedes the exposition of the fact that illustrates it.

[2] Quoted by Bédier, in *Études critiques*, pp. 279–280. The additions or modifications are due to considerations of art and of style. The aim has been to increase the picturesqueness of the description and to fill out the rhythm.

See also G. Chinard, "Chateaubriand. *Les Natchez*, livres I et II. Contribution à l'étude des sources de Chateaubriand," *University of California Publications in Modern Philology*, Vol. VII (1919), pp. 201–264.

CHATEAUBRIAND (Continued)

racher une marque de faiblesse, les Chéroquois amenèrent à ses pieds un sauvage chrétien, qu'ils avaient horriblement mutilé. Mais ils furent bien surpris quand ils virent ce jeune homme se jeter à genoux, et baiser les plaies du vieil ermite, qui lui criait : *Mon enfant, nous avons été mis en spectacle aux anges et aux hommes.* Les Indiens, furieux, lui plongèrent un fer rouge dans la gorge pour l'empêcher de parler. Alors, ne pouvant plus consoler les hommes, il expira. On dit que les Chéroquois, tout accoutumés qu'ils étaient à voir des Sauvages souffrir avec constance, ne purent s'empêcher d'avouer qu'il y avait dans l'humble courage du père Aubry quelque chose qui leur était inconnu. . . . —*Atala*

CHARLEVOIX (Continued)

viteur de Dieu de parler d'une voix forte, tantôt aux Hurons, qui ne le voyaient plus, tantôt à ses bourreaux, qu'il exhortait à craindre la colère du ciel. . . . Un moment après on lui amena son compagnon (le P. Lallemant) qu'on avait enveloppé depuis les pieds jusqu'à la tête d'écorce de sapin, et on se préparait à y mettre le feu. Dès que le P. Lallemant aperçut le P. de Brébeuf dans l'affreux état où on l'avait mis, il frémit d'abord, ensuite lui dit ces paroles de l'Apôtre : *Nous avons été mis en spectacle au monde, aux anges et aux hommes.* . . . Il courut se jeter à ses pieds et baisa respectueusement ses plaies. . . . Les barbares enfoncèrent dans le gosier du P. de Brébeuf un fer rougi au feu. . . . Son courage étonna les barbares et ils en furent choqués, quoique accoutumés à essuyer les bravades de leurs prisonniers en semblables occasions.—*Histoire de la Nouvelle France*, Vol. I, pp. 292–293

At other times the borrowing is particularly interesting from the point of view of the author's style. The important fact is no longer that the writer has taken ideas from someone else and has woven them more or less adroitly or boldly into the texture of his book : it is a question of thoughts that have become like his own and have been engraved on his mind because they appealed to him, because they agreed with his own imagination and taste. The study of such sources throws much light upon the writer's artistic personality.

MONTAIGNE[1]

Il est advenu aux gens véritablement sçavans ce qui advient aux espis de bled: ils vont s'élevant et se haussant la tete droite et fière tant qu'ils sont vuides, mais quand ils sont pleins et grossis de grains en leur maturité, ils commencent à s'humilier et à baisser les cornes. Pareillement, les hommes ayant tout essayé et tout sondé, n'ayant trouvé en tout cet amas de science et provision de tant de choses diverses rien de massif et de ferme, et rien que vanité, ils ont renoncé à leur présomption et reconnu leur condition naturelle.—II, 12

AMYOT

Ainsi comme les laboureurs voient plus volontiers les espis qui penchent et se courbent contre la terre que ceux qui pour leur légèreté sont haults et droicts, d'autant qu'ils les estiment vuides de grain et qu'il n'y a presque rien dedans. Aussi entre les jeunes gens qui se donnent à la philosophie, ceux qui sont les plus vuides et qui ont moins de pois, ceux-là ont du commencement l'assurance, la contenance, . . . et puis quand ils se commencent à remplir et à amasser du fruict des discours de la raison, ils otent alors cette mine superbe. —*De la vertu morale*, fol. 37, E[2]

2. *Documentary sources.* More often than not the source is some reading undertaken by an author to gain information on a detail of his subject, and summed up in a note such as we all make when we are verifying a doubtful point. For a historical work the sources are the documents that the historian discovers, studies, criticizes according to scientific methods, and cites either in his footnotes, appendixes, or

[1] Quoted by Villey, in *Les Livres d'histoire moderne utilisés par Montaigne*, p. 198.

[2] To the examples quoted here may be added, in particular, P. Henriot's article in *Revue du temps présent*, August 2, 1912, where it is shown that Victor Hugo, in his *William Shakespeare*, calmly pilfered from Guizot's *Shakespeare et son temps*. See also the many articles that point out Stendhal's barefaced plagiarisms, especially C. Stryienski, "Les Dossiers de Stendhal," *Mercure de France*, October, 1903; P. Arbelet, *L'Histoire de la peinture en Italie et les plagiats de Stendhal* (1913); M. Barber, "Encore un plagiat de Stendhal," *Mercure de France*, February 1, 1920; F. Gohin, "Stendhal plagiaire de Mérimée," *Minerve française*, 1920.

bibliography. In the case of a literary work, a work of art, the scaffoldings, thanks to which we can follow and 'check up' the investigations of the historian, have been torn down. The documents, the sources, are cleverly absorbed into the texture of the work. It is, however, necessary to separate them, to see in what way they have been used, and how they have stirred the imagination, the thought, or the emotions of the writer. Examples might be given by the hundred; a few must suffice to illustrate what precedes.

Let us begin with a scientific document. When Voltaire discusses Newton in the *Lettres philosophiques*,[1] he takes his information for the most part from *A View of Sir Isaac Newton's Philosophy* by Dr. Pemberton.[2] While reading it he makes notes, of which the substance, and frequently the detail, reappears in his composition.[3]

VOLTAIRE	PEMBERTON
Monsieur Newton fait voir que la révolution du fluide dans lequel Jupiter est supposé entraîné n'est pas avec la révolution du fluide de la terre comme la révolution de Jupiter est avec celle de la terre. —*Lettres philosophiques* (Lanson edition), XV, Vol. II, p. 18	Sir Isaac Newton finds that the time of one entire circulation of the fluid wherein Jupiter would swim, would bear a greater proportion to the time of one entire circulation of the fluid where the earth is, than the period of Jupiter bears to the period of the earth.— *A View* etc., Vol. II, p. 138

J. Morel, "Recherches sur les sources du *Discours de l'inégalité*,"[4] gives many examples of documents that may be called 'philosophical.'

The category of documentary sources par excellence, however, is that of the historical sources. Here again it would

---

[1] XIV–XVI. [2] London, 1728.

[3] For particulars as to the material borrowed from Pemberton, see the commentary on these three letters in Lanson's edition of the *Lettres philosophiques*, Vol. II. [4] *Annales Jean-Jacques Rousseau*, Vol. V.

be possible to extend indefinitely the list of examples. None are more instructive than those offered by Berret in his splendid work entitled *Le Moyen Age dans La Légende des siècles, et les sources de Victor Hugo*.[1] We shall have occasion to return to him when treating the 'sources of inspiration'; even at this stage Berret enables us to follow Hugo's documentary processes with marvelous precision. He studies and completes the catalogue of Hugo's library at Guernsey; knows what books he had at his elbow on the shelf in his little room; what newspapers and magazines he read; what clippings he made, and how he filed them and attached them to the manuscripts where they were used. In short, he lets us sit beside Hugo at work and watch his daily methods.

If we study the chapters devoted to such poems as *L'Aigle du casque, Ratbert, Le Parricide*, we shall be spectators of Hugo accumulating his notes,—dipping into *Quentin Durward*, the *Dictionnaire universel* by Moreri, a little-known *Introduction à l'histoire du Danemark* by Mallet, and many other books. While preparing the poem *Ratbert* he goes in quest of proper names of an imposing sonority and of the right length to fit his line; we catch him busy with his list, first hunting in the article "Malespine," in Moreri's *Dictionnaire*, then simply running through the letter *V*, picking up here and there such names as strike his fancy.[2]

> La même flamme court sur les cinq Mérindades;
> Olite tend les bras à Tudela qui fuit
> Vers la pâle Estrella sur qui le brandon luit;
> Et Sanguesa frémit, et toutes quatre ensemble
> Appellent au secours Pampelune qui tremble.

Le Jour des rois, line 206

On divisait le royaume de Navarre en *cinq Mérindades* qui étaient: Mérindade de *Pampelune*, d'*Olite*, de *Sanguesa*, d'*Estella*, de **Tudela**.[3]— Moreri's *Dictionnaire* (Art. "Navarre")

---

[1] Paris, 1911.　　[2] P. Berret, loc. cit. pp. 201 ff.　　[3] Loc. cit. p. 162.

The inevitable conclusion reached by Berret[1] is that the investigation of documents gives an entirely new idea of Hugo's processes of composition, and of the origin and growth of his inspiration.[2]

3. *Sources of detail.* It is necessary only to open some good modern edition and look through the commentary, or glance at the tables of contents of any of the special reviews, —*Revue d'histoire littéraire, Modern Language Notes,* etc., —to find innumerable examples of sources of detail. Many of these sources are incontestable; many are doubtful; some are based on hardly acceptable analogies.

Comparisons that show merely from what work the author has taken a certain fact, allusion, or proper name have no great interest. They are, moreover, generally the easiest to make. Most of the editions of ancient writers, and many historical books or collections, have tables of contents or indexes that do away with much drudgery. The information of real value is that concerning the action of the author's mind—the way in which his memory and emotions are roused.

Voltaire, in the course of a chapter in *Candide* (1759), tells us that "Pangloss enseignait la *Métaphysico-théologo-cosmolo-nigologie*"—a magnificent word, which makes us think of Rabelais. How is it formed? From a distant

---

[1] Pp. 387–396.

[2] Other examples of historical documentation of the same kind are studied by E. Huguet in his articles "Quelques sources de *Notre-Dame de Paris*," *Revue d'histoire littéraire,* 1901, and "Notes sur les sources de *Notre-Dame de Paris*," loc. cit., 1903. See also, for documentary sources, J. Vianey, *Les Sources de Leconte de Lisle,* and A. Hamilton, *Sources of the Religious Element in Flaubert's Salammbô* (Johns Hopkins Press, Baltimore, 1918); and especially H. Chamard's and G. Rudler's remarkable work, "La Documentation sur le XVIe siècle chez un romancier du XVIIe : les sources historiques de *La Princesse de Clèves*," *Revue du seizième siècle,* 1914.

recollection, on the one hand; with ironical intent, on the other. A long while before, he had read in the *Mémoires de Trévoux*, February, 1737,[1] an article by the Jesuit Father Castel, which called Leibnitz's system "une *doctrine physico-géométrico-théologique*". The expression is underlined in the text read by Voltaire. We know in this way how the form of the pleasantry became lodged in his marvelous memory. On the other hand, the person whom Voltaire attacks most violently in *Candide* is the German metaphysician Christian Wolf, whose followers honor him for having coined and circulated the term "cosmology"; therefore Voltaire includes it in the extravagant, derisive vocable with which he baptizes the doctrine of Pangloss. As for *nigologie*, is any comment needed? The amusing, ridiculous word serves as a fitting completion of the jest. Here, then, the source of the detail throws light upon the actual workings of Voltaire's mind.

Other instances, by illustrating the capacity of Voltaire's memory, help us to understand how he could construct with such astonishing ease paragraphs containing allusions and reminiscences traceable to I know not how many volumes, published at different times, on every conceivable subject. "Je suis la fille du pape Urbain X et de la Princesse de Palestrine", says "la Vieille" in *Candide* in beginning her story. Why this connection between the names Urbain and Palestrine? Because twenty years previously they had appeared in one sentence in the *Annales de l'Empire*. Or again, when Candide and his little troop arrive at Buenos Aires, they present themselves to the governor "Don Fernando d'Ibaraa y Figueora y Mascarenes y Lampourdos y Souza". Voltaire's agile mind gathered this imposing name from

[1]P. 469.

material found in five scattered volumes, and from the list of accomplices in the attack against the king of Portugal, September, 1758; that is, at the very moment when Voltaire was writing his novel.[1]

VOLTAIRE	HISTOIRE DES SÉVARAMBES
Il donna l'ordre à ses ingénieurs de faire une machine pour guinder ces deux hommes extraordinaires hors du royaume. Trois mille bons physiciens y travaillèrent; elle fut prête au bout de quinze jours et ne coûta pas plus de vingt millions de livres sterling, monnaie du pays. On mit sur la machine Candide et Cacambo. . . . Ce fut un beau spectacle que leur départ, et la manière ingénieuse dont ils furent hissés . . . au haut des montagnes.—*Candide*, chap. xviii, p. 124	Il nous dit qu'il nous mènerait au haut de la montagne par une voie qui peut-être nous surprendrait. . . . Nous trouvâmes divers grands traîneaux attachés à de gros câbles qui descendaient du haut de la montagne où ils étaient attachés. . . . Quand nous y fûmes montés, on donna un coup de sifflet, et l'on tira une petite corde qui allait vers le haut; aussitôt, nous sentîmes monter notre traîneau fort doucement; . . . par ce moyen, nous montâmes ce rideau de montagnes sans aucune peine, et sans être tirés ni par hommes ni par chevaux.—2d ed., 1716, Vol. I, pp. 156–157

The form—the light and nimble narrative—is Voltaire's own; but to the obscure Denis Vairasse, author of the *Histoire des Sévarambes*, he owes the first idea of the marvelous machine.

In certain cases the study of these sources of detail permits us to form a lifelike picture of the writer's literary processes. A typical instance is the thirteenth of the *Lettres philosophiques*, again by Voltaire.[2] We find him with a page or two to write on the infinite variety of ways in which "the

---

[1] *Candide* (A. Morize edition), pp. 3 and 58.
[2] Lanson edition, Vol. I, p. 166, and *Commentaire*, p. 178.

great philosophers have positively settled the nature of the soul of man". Hastily opening a copy of Bayle's *Dictionnaire*, he turns to the precious table of contents at the back, hunts up some supplementary information in the body of the work, and composes his eight or ten paragraphs. Sometimes he is so hurried that he is satisfied with the synopses furnished him by the table; he goes too fast, skips a line in his reading, and attributes to one the theory of another.

VOLTAIRE	BAYLE
Le divin Anaxagoras . . . affirma que l'âme était un esprit aérien, mais cependant immortel. Diogène . . . assurait que l'âme était une portion de la substance même de Dieu. . . . Épicure la composait de parties comme le corps.	*AME*. . . . Elle est un être aérien selon Anaxagoras, 219, et selon Diogène le Physicien, II. 297ª, et une portion de la substance de Dieu selon Cesalpin, 118ᵇ. . . . Était composée de plusieurs parties selon la doctrine d'Épicure, III. 101ª.[1]

We see that through heedless reading the doctrine of Cesalpino is transferred to Diogenes. At Voltaire's door, as at many another's, instances of this kind of inadvertence may be laid.

4. *Composite sources.* It would be a great mistake, as we have already pointed out, to think that when a source exists there is but one source for each passage or each detail. A poem or a page of prose is often a sort of mosaic, inlaid more or less intentionally, sometimes in an almost inextricable manner, with reminiscences or fragments of varied nature and origin. Take, for instance, the following poem by André Chénier, a real piece of marquetry, where traces of ancient authors, especially Greek, are recognizable in every line. For the sake of brevity I restrict myself to giving the references.[2]

[1] The numbers and letters refer to the volumes, pages, and columns of the *Dictionnaire*.

[2] From the Becq de Fouquières edition, p. 56. Paris, 1872.

Chénier

Pleurez, doux alcyons! ô vous, oiseaux sacrés,
Oiseaux chers à Thétis, doux alcyons, pleurez!
Elle a vécu, Myrto, la jeune Tarentine!
Un vaisseau la portait aux bords de Camarine:
5 Là, l'hymen, les chansons, les flûtes, lentement
Devaient la reconduire au seuil de son amant.
Une clef vigilante a, pour cette journée,
Dans le cèdre enfermé sa robe d'hyménée,
Et l'or dont au festin ses bras seront parés,
10 Et pour ses blonds cheveux les parfums préparés.
Mais, seule sur la proue, invoquant les étoiles,
Le vent impétueux qui soufflait dans les voiles
L'enveloppe. Étonnée, et loin des matelots,
Elle crie, elle tombe, elle est au sein des flots.
15 Elle est au sein des flots, la jeune Tarentine!
Son beau corps a roulé sous la vague marine.
Thétis, les yeux en pleurs, dans le creux d'un rocher,
Aux monstres dévorants eut soin de le cacher.
Par ses ordres bientôt les belles Néréides
20 L'élèvent au-dessus des demeures humides,
Le portent au rivage, et dans ce monument
L'ont au cap du Zéphyr déposé mollement;
Puis de loin, à grands cris appelant leurs compagnes,
Et les Nymphes des bois, des sources, des montagnes,
25 Toutes frappant leur sein et traînant un long deuil,
Répétèrent, hélas! autour de son cercueil:
"Hélas! chez ton amant tu n'es point ramenée;
Tu n'as point revêtu ta robe d'hyménée:
L'or autour de tes bras n'a point serré de nœuds,
30 Les doux parfums n'ont point coulé sur tes cheveux."

La Jeune Tarentine

CLASSICAL REMINISCENCES

1. Catullus, *Carm.* III.
2. Virg. *Georg.* I. 399.
   Theocritus, *Idyl.* VII. 57.
   Euripides, *Iph. in Taur.* 1089.
4. *Schol. Pind. Olymp.* V. 1.
5. Several Greek Epithalamia.
6. Lucretius, I. 97.
   Xenocrates Rhod. *Anth.* VII. 291.

Antipater Thessal. *Anth.* IX.
   215; *Anth.* VII. 188.
8. Euripides, *Alc.* 160.
11. Virg. *Æneid.* VI. 338.
15. Bion, *Eleg.*
19. Propertius, III. vii. 67.
22. Strabo, VI. i. 7.
   Anth. VII. 1.

Composite sources are met with everywhere, either in the case of authors such as Chénier, Montaigne, and the poets of the Pléiade, whose minds are crammed with quotations, recollections, and details of Greek, Latin, or Italian literature; or in the case of those who, having read extensively with a definite work in view, exhibit in some later book traces of this reading which, though partly effaced, transformed, or distorted, are yet unmistakable. Voltaire's works bristle with reminiscences of this kind. Examine this short passage from *Candide*:

Tout étant fait pour une fin, tout est nécessairement pour la meilleure fin. Remarquez bien que les nez ont été faits pour porter des lunettes, aussi avons nous des lunettes. Les jambes sont visiblement instituées pour être chaussées, et nous avons des chausses. Les pierres ont été formées pour être taillées et pour en faire des châteaux; aussi Monseigneur a un très beau château . . . (p. 5).

These five or six lines, written in 1759, are the combination of almost as many memories, some of which date back more than twenty years. The passage "les nez ont été faits pour porter des lunettes" is taken from the Jesuit Hartsœcker, whose *Recueil de plusieurs pièces de physique*[1] Voltaire read at Cirey at the time when he was working on

[1] 12mo. Utrecht, 1730.

Newton with Mme du Châtelet.[1] He discovered in it the
following passage[2]: "Je crains fort que quelque railleur ne
s'avise de dire ici . . . que *Dieu a donné en partie le nez à
l'homme pour la commodité d'y mettre des lunettes.*" He justified the forebodings of the obscure Jesuit when, in his *Élé-
ments de la philosophie de Newton* (1738), he used the jest
for the first time: "Parce qu'au bout d'un nombre prodigieux
d'années les besicles ont été enfin inventées, doit-on dire que
Dieu a fait nos nez pour porter des lunettes?"[3] The idea had
lodged in a corner of his brain, to reappear twenty years later.

In reading the pious dissertations of Pluche in *Le Spectacle de la nature* (1732) Voltaire found[4] some absurd passages on the "perfections de la jambe". These had already
supplied him with the following remark: "Les hommes portent des chaussures; direz-vous que les jambes ont été faites
par un être suprême pour être chaussées?"[5] The way for
the joke in *Candide* has been paved.

When, in November, 1756, Voltaire's friend Thieriot sent
him the works of "l'illustre vicaire Derham", he read in the
Physico-theology[6]: "Le Créateur a fait naître des *matériaux*
par toute la terre, *convenables aux édifices.* . . . Quelle bonté
immense du Créateur, . . . cette variété immense de plantes
. . . et de *pierres*!" Here are noses, legs, and stones, gathered from voluminous and scattered reading.

An even clearer example of Voltaire's habit of using, in a
work of fiction, material collected for some more serious
work is Chapter XVI in *Candide*, on the Oreillons.[7] I give
a short extract from it, with corresponding references.

---

[1] See Moland edition, Vol. XXXIII, p. 347.   [2] P. 25.
[3] Vol. XXII, p. 565.   [4] Vol. V, pp. 45–51.
[5] *Dialogue entre Lucrèce et Posidonius*, Vol. XXIV, p. 62. 1756.
[6] Vol. I, p. 324. Translated into French in 1726.
[7] On pages 96 ff. of my edition may be found all the references. Here I am
obliged to choose and abridge.

Candide[a]	References
A leur réveil, ils sentirent qu'ils ne pouvaient remuer; la raison en était que pendant la nuit les	[a] The entire passage abounds in personal recollections; Voltaire had seen in Paris, in 1723, four cannibals from Louisiana. Many of his impressions of that time are contained in a letter of October, 1737, and also in the *Essai sur les mœurs* (ed. Moland, Vol. XII, p. 388).
Oreillons,[b] habitans du pays, les avaient garottés avec des cordes	[b] Garcilaso de la Vega, *Histoire des Incas* (1737), Vol. I, p. 91: "Ils se perçaient les oreilles . . . les Espagnols les nommèrent pour cela *Orejones*, ou *hommes à grandes oreilles*." See also La Condamine, *Relation abrégée du voyage* etc., p. 105.
d'écorce d'arbre.[c] Ils étaient entourés d'une cinquantaine d'Oreil-	[c] *Voyages de François Coréal* (1722), Vol. I, p. 195: "Ils *garrottent* le prisonnier avec des *cordes de coton*."
lons tout nus,[d] armés de flèches, de massues et de haches de cail-	[d] Numerous references from the books of travel consulted for the *Essai sur les mœurs*.
lou:[e] les uns faisaient bouillir une grande chaudière; les autres	[e] *Voyages de François Coréal*, Vol. I, p. 236: "Nous trouvâmes *une cinquantaine* de Guapaches *armés de flèches et de massues*"; and Vol. I, p. 228: "Ils *rôtissent* leurs prisonniers et les mangent . . . Ils ont pour arme une espèce de *massue*; ils se servent pour couteaux de *pierres* qu'ils aiguisent."
préparaient[f] des broches, et tous criaient: "C'est un Jésuite, c'est	[f] *Voyages de François Coréal*, Vol. I, p. 171: "*préparatifs* pour le massacre de quelque captif dont la chair doit les régaler."
un Jésuite; nous serons vengés,[g]	[g] *Voyages de François Coréal*, Vol. I, p. 232: "Les prêtres de ces sauvages *haïssent mortellement* les Jésuites. . . ."
et nous ferons bonne chère;[h] mangeons du Jésuite, mangeons du Jésuite."	[h] Moratori, *Relation des missions du Paraguay* (1754): "Ils se proposaient de *faire un excellent repas* de la chair du P. Ruiz, qu'ils *croyaient*

CANDIDE (Continued)

REFERENCES (Continued)

Candide s'écria: " . . . nous allons certainement être rôtis ou bouillis[j] . . ." Cacambo ne perdait jamais la tête: "Ne désespérez de rien", dit-il au désolé Candide: "j'entends un peu le jargon de ces peuples,[k] je vais leur parler."—"Ne manquez pas", dit Candide, "de leur représenter quelle est l'inhumanité affreuse de faire cuire des hommes, et combien cela est peu chrétien."[1]

devoir être fort délicate, parce que les Jésuites sont les seuls au Paraguay qui fassent usage du sel."

[j] Garcilaso de la Vega, Vol. I, p. 45: "Sans attendre que la chair soit ou *rôtie ou bouillie*, ils la mangent goulûment. . . ."

[k] *Voyages de François Coréal*, Vol. II, p. 30: "Mon interprète, qui savait une partie du *jargon de ces peuples*, me servit beaucoup dans cette occasion."

[1] Herrera, *Histoire générale des conquêtes des Castillans* (1671) (quoted in the *Essai*), 3d decade, p. 312: "Un prêtre lui fit entendre que, pour se sauver, il fallait *vivre selon la loi de Jésus-Christ en cessant de manger de la chair humaine.*" See also page 393: "Ils sacrifiaient des hommes, ils les *mangeaient*, ils faisaient d'autres choses abominables, du tout *contraires à notre sainte foi; ils mangeaient ceux qu'ils captivaient, dont Dieu était fort offensé.*"

Reminiscences occur throughout the chapter, and also in the pages that describe the travelers' stay in Eldorado. As a part of the researches and documentation for the *Essai sur les mœurs* (1756) every book cited had been read by Voltaire, and the curious or valuable passages entered in his notebooks. These passages he had, in his rôle of historian and critic, incorporated in the *Essai sur les mœurs*; he had, however, through his labors of documentation accumulated a reserve of concrete or picturesque details, a store of exact or evocative terms, which, when the time came, he was to introduce, in his rôle of novelist, into the pages of *Scarmentado* or *Candide*.

It is true that these details have suffered various distortions; the interest and fruit of this study of sources is precisely to show how the alterations take place. Some are involuntary, resulting from the inaccuracies of memory of the novelist who invents a tale with his head full of material that he attempts neither to dismiss nor to recall. Others are voluntary, a means of transforming some flat, colorless document into a paradoxical or controversial satire or caricature. In this respect the study of composite sources is a valuable auxiliary to literary analysis.

5. *Oral and indefinite sources*. Lastly, in the investigation of the sources of the details of a work, there is a class, as important as it is difficult to trace, which deals with the oral and indefinite sources,—in other words, with whatever inspiration a writer owes to his environment (literary, political, artistic, or religious), to the thousand and one contacts that stimulate his thought or his imagination and give birth to an idea, a word, or a clever expression. Is it necessary to say that, in most cases, these sources are bound to elude us, and that we must be resigned? It would be absurd to expect to grasp the intangible: we should risk obtaining for our pains only worthless and ridiculous results.

Before giving up, however, we must push on as far as we can. It is, in fact, possible in many cases, if not to clear up a definite point, at least to group together a certain amount of information, a number of facts, quotations, and details of all sorts, that will help us to study the genesis and growth of a writer's thought or style. We can try to reconstruct an environment of opinion, thought, literature, or art. We can revive the atmosphere of certain political or religious discussions: turn ourselves into Jansenists, the better to explain Pascal; into philosophers, to study Diderot; into Bretons, to follow the young Renan. We can examine newspapers, periodicals, the innumerable short articles called forth by special events, where are recorded the freaks of public opinion, the transformations of customs, the fluctuations of thought. With their aid we may get in touch with the facts, the ideas, that have reacted on our author.

There remain the conversations, the oral sources, forever beyond our reach. Here we must accept the inevitable. Yet, in some cases, by means of articles, letters, or contemporary references, we may hope to guess the possible or probable topics of these conversations—a delicate and most uncertain method, to which we shall have the prudence never to attach a demonstrative value.

A few examples follow of indefinite sources, or, to be more exact, of the reconstruction of an intellectual or literary environment.

a. Lanson, in his commentary on the *Lettres philosophiques*, attempts in several places to "*reconstruct the condition of English public opinion and thought* that gives rise to certain of Voltaire's assertions".[1] He accumulates quotations from authors whom Voltaire may have known; refers to facts that may have impressed him; gives information illustrating what the public round him was feeling and thinking. See his notes on the ninth letter, "Sur le gouvernement," and the remarks that preface it:

This letter is the result of everything that Voltaire has read or heard in discussions on politics and on the origins of the English Constitution . . . Many of my extracts will serve to show the *condition of public opinion opposed or reflected by him*, rather than writings from which he acquired definite information. It was a subject threshed out daily in the newspapers, as it undoubtedly was in conversation. It is, therefore, necessary to be very cautious in naming his sources.[2]

[1] Introduction, pp. l ff.   [2] Vol. I, p. 108.

Observations of the same sort on another subject are found in the commentary of the eighteenth letter, "Sur la tragédie":

Here it can never be a question of an investigation of sources, in the strict sense of the word, except for a small number of facts. Voltaire's æsthetic judgment is the result of a lifelong training and a preference for French art. Nevertheless, it depends also in great measure on conversations held with cultivated Englishmen, whose acquaintance he had made. I cite a certain number of texts, to be taken less as direct sources of Voltaire than as *evidence of the state of English public opinion about English writers*.[1]

These remarks are excellent and fitted for wide application.

b. Morel, in his "Recherches sur les sources du *Discours de l'inégalité*,"[2] deals with analogous cases, which, nevertheless, differ somewhat from the above. He tries to "replace Rousseau in the genuine intellectual surroundings where his thought was formed; to show that there were vital influences inducing him to read certain books already out of date". Turning, for instance, to the study of Rousseau's personal relations with Diderot, he points out the significance of these relations in the formation of Rousseau's ideas. He "reconstructs" the Diderot whom Rousseau knew, to whose "incandescent" conversation he listened. He pictures Diderot seized by the "pedagogical mania" that made him "harangue" unceasingly. Diderot is an insatiable giver of good advice; he is full of general information, of plans that others, who have the time, may carry out. He indicates the destination and the route: he himself has not patience for the pilgrimage. He must have lavished such advice on Rousseau. Morel tries to piece it together as far as possible, by analyz-

---

[1] Vol. II, p. 88. It is in this connection that Lanson gives the list of plays by Shakespeare and other authors produced in London during Voltaire's stay.

[2] *Annales Jean-Jacques Rousseau*, Vol. V (1909), pp. 119–198.

ing and studying the ideas expressed by Diderot before 1754 and by comparing them with the *Discours de l'inégalité,* mentioning also with great scrupulousness the necessary limitations of such a method and the impossibility of reviving everything supplied to Rousseau by Diderot's vigorous, enthusiastic utterances.[1]

c. To the same category belongs the problem arising whenever an author has been shaped by what has gone before him—whenever his work, whether in substance or in form, is the product of literary tradition, resembling not one but a hundred others and imitating all without imitating any in particular.

Candide furnishes an interesting example. The scenario of the novel is, as it were, thrust upon Voltaire in advance; his imagination is sure to work along the lines where he will find everything in readiness. I cannot say that any one novel is the source of the setting and of the general structure of *Candide;* but, after reading nearly all the novels produced during the thirty or forty previous years, I can say that the source of the scenario of *Candide* is the whole mass of a certain part of these productions—novels of adventure and of imaginary travels, in which the plots follow an unalterable plan and the itineraries can be unerringly predicted. It matters little whether Voltaire chooses to ridicule

---

[1] I quote here some lines by Morel as defining clearly a few of the problems met with in all investigations of sources: "We ascertain the 'written' sources, the influences, the identical conditions of mind; the unexpected developments from very small beginnings; we run through the entire gamut of the voluntary or involuntary deformation that ideas undergo in passing from one mind to another. The spoken word is more expressive than the written. Diderot, holding forth upon the *Interprétation de la nature* (published in 1754), must have surpassed his own book: affirming instead of assuming; above all, introducing the problems and perhaps the solutions to be found in a later work. Still, it would be a dangerous method to substitute, for the book actually in our possession, a hypothetical, spoken book" (p. 119).

them or to make use of them: it is here that he finds his background ready made, from which he can hardly escape. Just before *Candide* appeared, a critic made fun of the fiction of the day:

What is there in any novel? Thwarted love affairs, brutal fathers, quarrelsome relations, formidable rivals, jealous rages, kidnapings, sword-thrusts and pistol-shots, dangerous illnesses, unhoped-for recoveries, unexpected meetings, touching recognition scenes, virtuous young girls, women who are far from virtuous, superannuated husbands deceived by their 'better halves,' faithful valets, and chattering chambermaids.[1]

Is not this all there is in *Candide*? The thwarted love of Cunégonde and Candide; the brutality of M. de Thunder-ten-Trunck; Don Fernando, the formidable rival; the jealous rages of Don Issacar; the kidnaping of his beloved; Candide transfixing the baron; Pangloss's illness, and his unhoped-for recovery after the crucial incision and the dissection had been begun; the wildly improbable meetings (in Venice, in Buenos Aires, in Holland, in Paraguay); the duped inquisitor; the "faithful Cacambo"; and the pretty maidservant? Open at random; look down the table of contents; turn the pages: characters, itineraries, incidents and adventures, catastrophes and wonders—their cues are numbered by tens and hundreds. There are the conventional development and the inevitable background (London, Portugal, Venice, Constantinople, Amsterdam). Corsairs abound. Throughout is the same succession of captures, abductions, recognitions, escapes; throughout, journeys to Lisbon, America, Paris, to the carnival at Venice. This inexhaustible rubbish was brutally ridiculed in the brilliant pages of *Candide*; nevertheless, *Candide* is what it is only because all the

---

[1] *Année littéraire*, Vol. V (1757), p. 70.

rubbish existed before it,—in short, this material must be considered one of its sources.

6. *Sources of inspiration.* In contradistinction to the sources that, whether unique or composite, affect only the detail of a work are others that may be called generative sources.[1] They supply the writer with either (1) the initial idea, (2) the subject, or (3) the setting and contexture of the work. The following examples are chosen from many.

a. *A source that accounts for the very existence of a work.* An author's acquaintance with a certain work may stimulate in him the desire to produce a similar work, transformed and adapted to suit the needs of another public and another time. Already he may have had some vague project, which perhaps would have taken years to materialize, if it had materialized at all. It is then that some book takes effect; it spurs the author, crystallizes his ill-defined aspirations and uncertain plans. He begins to write, and, following his model more or less closely, produces the new work.

Such is the case with *La Deffence et illustration de la langue françoise* by Joachim du Bellay. Before Villey's discovery[2] the ideas and theories brought forward by Du Bellay were thought to spring from the deep-seated tendencies of the French Renaissance. Doubtless Du Bellay would, in any case, have been heard in the violent debate that stirred literary opinion at this time. Still, who knows how long he might have waited? who knows what form he might have chosen for his book? As it happened, he read

[1] Naturally these two categories are not mutually exclusive: a book that is the source of inspiration for an entire work is very frequently, even usually, the source of many details.

[2] *Les Sources italiennes de " La Deffence et illustration de la langue françoise" de Joachim du Bellay* (Bibliothèque littéraire de la Renaissance). Paris, 1903.

the *Dialogo delle Lingue* of Sperone Speroni (1542). It is safe to say that, whatever he may have borrowed elsewhere, he took from Speroni, at the very least, all the material for the first book of the *Deffence*—not only entire passages but the fundamental doctrines.

Villey thus describes the effect produced upon the accepted theory about Du Bellay by a simple investigation of sources:

> It must be admitted that all his ideas are borrowed, that entire pages are copied. These ideas have generally been considered Du Bellay's principal claim to glory, . . . an eloquence, an enthusiasm, in which it was good to recognize the petulant ardor of a young reformer . . . We must learn to look upon them as merely the contributions of an imitator of Italy, who repeats for our benefit what is said across the Alps . . . To explain the *Deffence*, it is no longer sufficient to find in it a reaction against the *Art poétique* of Sibilet, and to assert its novelty: the essential point is to reëstablish its connection with an Italian movement of ideas; to trace in it the reflection of Italian theories.

b. Suggestion for the subject. It is always interesting and sometimes very illuminating to discover the origin of the subject itself of a work—of a play, poem, or novel. Often this discovery requires little effort. Mythology and Greek, Roman, and Biblical history have supplied French literature, as they have every other, with subjects that for centuries have been chosen and rechosen, treated and treated again. In such a case, unless we are able to find the intermediary directly used by our author, it is hardly possible to speak of a source in the true sense of the word. We should try especially to determine whether or not the treatment of the subject is original and to give the work its precise position in the general evolution of the legendary or historical theme. This research is, however, no longer a study of sources.

On the contrary, there are many cases where we can witness the very creation of the work. We discover the reading, the association, the impression, that set the author's creative faculty in motion and decided the direction of his thought or fancy. In this case precise investigations and definite solutions are possible.

We shall frequently see some trivial anecdote, some dull, colorless newspaper article, some quotation, become as it were the spark that kindles the great blaze—material often coarse, neglected or unknown, transformed by the genius of a great artist into something precious.

The poets who are worthy of the name are those to whom it matters little whence they gather the wood for their edifices, and this wood is not always cut in the forest. It may have been used several times in former structures. The virtue of these poets is that they demolish the hovel that they rob; above all, it is that they perceive their material where the mass of readers, before and after them, have seen and will see nothing worth gathering and using.[1]

I might enumerate several hundred articles or books where examples of this kind abound; I have space for but two or three.

(1) The typically 'romantic' subject of Victor Hugo's *Ruy Blas*[2] is well known: the valet, Ruy Blas, is in love with the queen of Spain; Don Salluste, whom the queen has sent into exile, thirsts for revenge; he passes Ruy Blas off as a noble, Don César de Bazan, and orders him "de plaire à cette femme et d'être son amant". Ruy Blas obtains power, distinctions, and honors until such time as Don Salluste considers his vengeance ripe; then, enticing the queen into the

---

[1] E. Dupuy, quoted by J. Giraud in *Œuvres choisies de Vigny*, p. xxx.
[2] 1838.

most abominable trap, Don Salluste hurls at her this vile insult: "Ah! vous m'avez banni. . . . Moi, je vous ai donné mon laquais pour amant!" A romantic scenario of incredible unreality, which has been the butt of many critics.

Lanson proves[1] irrefutably that this "improbable" subject, "this love affair of a domestic, not with a queen, it is true, but with a famous woman, is taken from real life, from history."

It is an episode in the life of Angelica Kauffmann, the artist, an episode that the *Biographie nouvelle des contemporains*[2] summarizes as follows:

An English painter whom she had refused to marry revenged himself in a manner unworthy of a gentleman. He chose a good-looking young man of the lower classes, dressed him magnificently, and had him taught the customs and speech of men of the world. The fellow, introduced to Angelica under the name of Count Frédéric de Horn, succeeded in imposing upon the ingenuousness of the young artist. . . . Hardly had the marriage taken place when the painter revealed the trick.

The adventure is related in the notice on Angelica published, in the *Galerie des contemporains*,[3] by A. Rabbe, a great friend of Hugo; later, in Léon de Wailly's novel *Angelica Kauffmann*, which came out only a few weeks before Hugo began to write *Ruy Blas*. A comparison of the detail of the three works is amusing. In Wailly's novel the characters have already become dramatic, the dialogue gives certain cues to *Ruy Blas*, the character of Don Salluste is seen emerging. From this anecdote, then, unearthed in biographical dictionaries, Hugo took the subject of *Ruy Blas*.

[1] "Victor Hugo et Angelica Kauffmann," *Revue d'histoire littéraire*, 1915, pp. 392–401; supplemented by H. C. Lancaster, "The Genesis of Ruy Blas," *Modern Philology*, Vol. XIV, March, 1917.   [2] 1823.   [3] 1828.

Lanson sums up with precision the degree of certainty reached in his conclusions.

(*a*) It is *beyond doubt* that the unfortunate marriage of Angelica Kauffmann to the false Count de Horn furnished the subject of *Ruy Blas*.

(*b*) It is *almost as certain* that Victor Hugo knew the novel by Léon de Wailly founded on this incident.

(*c*) It is *not improbable* that Hugo became interested in the actual event through an account by the historian Rabbe.[1]

Lanson's short article is an excellent model for any treatment of the 'sources of inspiration' of an author.[2]

(2) The same might be said of Berret's *Le Moyen Age dans La Légende des siècles*.[3] With immense learning, as well as with unfailing psychological perspicacity, Berret describes Hugo as the latter selects and works into shape the subjects of his "little epics of *La Légende des siècles*". Through a study of the poet's life, through an analysis of his mental and emotional condition, the critic reconstructs the general trend of Hugo's tastes and prejudices at any given moment. In Berret's pages we watch the poet falling under the influence of some reading—a magazine article, a fragment from a dictionary—which, just at that time, offers him a subject, a setting, a scenario, through which he can give vent to his seething thoughts and tormenting emotions. We observe the decisive effect of an article by the popularizer Jubinal, "Quelques Romans chez nos aïeux," printed in the *Journal du dimanche* of November 1, 1846. The article crystallizes

[1] P. 400.

[2] Lanson points out also (*Revue de Paris*, March 1, 1913, p. 32) that Alfred de Musset's *Fantasio* is inspired by the marriage of the Princess Louise, daughter of Louis-Philippe, to Leopold I, king of the Belgians.

[3] See the interesting review by H. Potez, in *Revue d'histoire littéraire*, 1912, pp. 455-457.

tendencies, desires, plans, until then confused and uncertain in Hugo's mind. Page 6 of the *Journal* strikes him particularly; he cuts it out; in the margin he jots down some lines suggested by the text; he groups other quotations and extracts around this first document. As Berret says, this page is "the infinitesimal source of the immense work". Proceeding farther with the special study of each piece in *La Légende*, he points out, for instance, that "Le Mariage de Roland" and "Aymerillot" take their subjects from the same article by Jubinal; "Le Cirque de Gavarnie" from the *Guide Richard*, which Hugo carried in his pocket when visiting Spain in 1843; the pursuit of Angus in "L'Aigle du casque" from the pursuit of Ernaut in *Raoul de Cambrai*, again in Jubinal's article.

(3) Alfred de Vigny was subject to influences in much the same way, though his reading is often of a more dignified sort than Hugo's. The researches of Dupuy, Baldensperger, Masson, and J. Giraud, of which I have already spoken, show in many instances the initial sources of his inspiration. *Éloa* was suggested to him by reading Klopstock, Byron, and the *Loves of the Angels* by Thomas Moore. *La Neige* is derived from the little-known *La Gaule poétique*, by Marchangy; *La Maison du berger* from a fragment of Book X of *Les Martyrs*, by Chateaubriand; *La Mort du loup* from Byron and from a page of Macaulay's *Lays of Ancient Rome*; *Le Mont des Oliviers* from a part of *Jean Paul's Dream*, translated by Mme de Staël in *De l'Allemagne*; etc.

In treating cases of this kind we should never forget that the important point is not to give an exact reference to an initial text or document but to show how and why the text has played so stimulating a part in the artist's inner life; how and why this harmony between two writers has been established—this mysterious and fruitful collaboration that resulted in a masterpiece. Once more, what erudition discovers is and should be only another step toward a thorough psychological and æsthetic acquaintance with a great author.

c. A source that furnishes the setting or the contexture of the work. We have seen that a literary tradition may furnish the essential elements of the scenario of a novel. In certain instances, of course, a precise source exists. A writer wishes to voice opinions, passions, ideals, all of which are personal to himself; but he borrows the background from someone else,—a series of events, an arrangement of the plot, into which his sentiments and his ideals fit quite naturally, through which they find expression.

Few novels are more personal than *Dominique*, exquisite and profound pages where Fromentin has set down his doubts, his bitterness, his disillusionment. Apart from this strictly personal side, however, there exist in the novel a background, a contexture, a series of incidents and scenes, taken by Fromentin from Mme de Duras's novel *Édouard*.[1] It is to *Édouard* that he owes the general outline of *Dominique*. A study of his indebtedness throws light upon the part in Fromentin's genius played respectively by his creative imagination and his powers of analysis.

7. *Graphic and plastic sources.* The enumeration of the various categories of sources must be completed by one last class, to which sometimes not enough attention is paid: the graphic and plastic sources—sculpture, paintings, engravings, book illustrations. Many writers, poets and novelists in particular, have a powerful visual imagination. Their eye is caught by a painting, or by an illustration in a book. Often this is enough to produce a lasting reaction made use of later by their creative genius.

---

[1] G. Pailhès, "Le Modèle de *Dominique*," *Revue bleue*, March 13–20, 1909.

When I was looking up the sources of *Candide*, I could not imagine where Voltaire had found the word *mitre* to describe, in the chapter on the Inquisition, the headdress of his hero, nor where he had run across several other details in the scene of the *auto-da-fé*. At last I discovered that they were due to the impression made by four picturesque engravings in Dellon's *La Relation de l'inquisition*.[1]

In a recent article on *La Sensibilité plastique et picturale dans la littérature du XVIIe siècle*[2] the author has attempted to show the close relationship between many pages of the great classics and the artistic productions of their time— painting, architecture, landscape gardening, and interior decorating. These comparisons are judicious; they would be more valuable if on certain precise points we could be sure of a direct source of inspiration. Much still remains to be done in this field. In 1668 La Fontaine began to publish his *Fables*; from 1667 to 1674 the labyrinth of the gardens at Versailles was being ornamented with motifs in sculpture taken from the *Fables* of Æsop: is this merely a coincidence? For La Fontaine's description of Night in *Le Songe de Vaux* his inspiration is the painting by Le Brun on the ceiling of Fouquet's gorgeous château: is this the only definite example that can be mentioned?[3]

When writing *Le Déluge* Alfred de Vigny was not unmindful of *L'Inondation* by Poussin nor of *Le Déluge* by Girodet; it is possible that Tony Johannot's illustration for *The Pilot* of Fenimore Cooper suggested to him several details in *La Frégate la Sérieuse*. As inspiration for *La Colère de Samson* and *Le Mont des Oliviers* Milton, J. P. Richter, and others should be named. Another fact, however, must

---

[1] Plates reproduced on pages 45 ff. of my edition.
[2] P. Dorbec, *Revue d'histoire littéraire*, 1919, pp. 374–395.
[3] See Lafenestre, *Artistes et amateurs*. 1900.

not be overlooked: while in England, at Lady Blessington's, Vigny saw two masterpieces by Mantegna, since then added to the National Gallery. One is called *Samson and Delilah*; the other, *The Agony in the Garden.* Dupuy shows how much the opening lines of Vigny's *Mont des Oliviers,*

> . . . La nuit n'a pas calmé
> La fournaise du jour dont l'air est enflammé,

recall the little canvas, "where what catches the eye is the stormy, unforgetable sky, streaked red and black".[1]

Lastly, in Berret's investigations of the sources of *La Légende des siècles* he repeatedly dwells upon the rôle played by an engraving, a picture, an illustration, as exciter of the poet's imagination. Hugo owed the vision that forms the subject of "Montfaucon" to an engraving by Daubigny, in the last chapter of *Notre-Dame de Paris,*[2] representing a gallows with a flock of birds disappearing toward the horizon. A part of "Ratbert" was suggested by an engraving of *Les Crimes des Papes,* by La Vicomterie,[3] that Hugo had at Guernsey; from it he took several of the attitudes, tortures, and scenes of debauchery described in the poem. In "L'Aigle du casque" certain details come from armorial designs that Hugo had seen in *Debrett's Peerage* of 1826, a volume he undoubtedly utilized.[4] In "Plein Ciel," Hugo's *aéroscaphe* is taken from an illustration accompanying an article by Théophile Gautier in the *Presse*[5]: "Victor Hugo, as happened often, was struck more with the picture than with the text."[6]

---

[1] E. Dupuy, *Alfred de Vigny; II. Son Rôle littéraire,* p. 357. See also P. Buhle, *Alfred de Vignys biblische Gedichte und ihre Quellen,* Rostock, 1908.

[2] Garnier edition, 1844.   [3] Paris, 1792.

[4] Berret, *Le Moyen Age dans La Légende des siècles,* pp. 67, 355, and passim.

[5] July 4, 1850.

[6] Berret, in *Revue d'histoire littéraire,* 1902, p. 601. See also Berret's edition of *La Légende des siècles,* p. 793.

It is naturally at periods when plastic art occupies a relatively important place in the attention of authors and public that interconnections of this type become more frequent. A. Cassagne, in his book entitled *La Théorie de l'art pour l'art,*[1] cites useful examples. Flaubert, in preparation for *L'Éducation sentimentale,* laid in a store of maps and engravings of the various quarters of Paris in which the story was laid. The first idea of *La Tentation de Saint Antoine* came to him at Genoa while looking at a painting by Breughel. *Hérodias* has as its source of inspiration some sculptures; *Saint Julien l'Hospitalier,* a stained-glass window in the cathedral at Rouen.[2] Théophile Gautier owed to a picture by Fortuny the conception of his poetic ballet *Le Mariage à Séville.*[3] The beautiful *Passion* of Leconte de Lisle was written "at the request of a painter friend" to translate into verse the grouping and the emotional appeal of fourteen paintings of the stations of the Cross.

Brunetière wrote in 1883, "French art in the seventeenth century has not yet been studied sufficiently in its relation to literature". This is true; I should add that French literature has not yet been studied sufficiently in its relation to plastic art. This field of research holds many precious discoveries in store.

The very diversity of the examples that I have just cited, the possibility of multiplying them endlessly, the impossibility of predicting every type of case that may arise, are

---

[1] P. 369. 8vo. Paris, 1906.

[2] Maxime Du Camp, *Souvenirs littéraires* (8vo) (Paris, 1882–1883), Vol. II, p. 541; and J. Giraud, "La Genèse d'un chef-d'œuvre," *Revue d'histoire littéraire,* 1919, pp. 87–93; M. A. N. Gossez, *Le Saint Julien de Flaubert* (Lille, 1903).

[3] Bergerat, *Théophile Gautier,* p. 211 (reference given by A. Cassagne, loc. cit.).

sufficient proofs of how foolish and futile it would be to conclude this chapter by compiling a sort of *Practical Handbook for the Investigation of Sources*, along the lines of a treatise on chemical analysis. Abundant reading, the study of scholarly works taken as models, the comparison of methods that have succeeded with those that have failed, will be the best lessons.

I venture, however, for convenient reference, to give a brief list of the principal fields for the investigation of sources. Perhaps special studies will disclose some not mentioned here. Not every research, obviously, will be productive,—I want simply to show where those who have sought have usually found, if not everything, at least something.

Any investigation of sources, I believe, may profitably include all or several of the following steps, whether each process is pursued to its farthest limit or whether the preliminary soundings indicate that nothing is to be hoped for in that direction :

a. Reconstruction and study of the private library of an author,[1] either in case the books are still together or in case they are scattered where it is possible to trace them. Investigation of the notes, comments, and underscorings, and of dates and other chronological indications that help to place the reading of each work.

b. Information about the periodicals (reviews, newspapers, bulletins) to which the author may have subscribed (see lists of subscribers, catalogues of members of learned societies and academies, etc.).

---

[1] See works on Montaigne's library, and on books annotated by him. See also, for example, P. Bonnefon, "La Bibliothèque de Racine," *Revue d'histoire littéraire*, 1898, p. 169; and the many catalogues of libraries formerly belonging to famous writers, such as the library of Sainte-Beuve, that of Jules Lemaître, etc.

c. Compilation of the reading done by the author from clues given by himself in his correspondence and other writings: references to proper names and typical events, historical allusions, etc. Care should be taken to distinguish between the works that the writer has *certainly* read and those that it is *probable, possible,* or *not impossible* that he has read.

d. Enumeration of the books or documents that a writer working on a given subject at a given time might have consulted. Special attention (1) to intermediaries; (2) to the writer's knowledge of foreign languages.

e. Study of any biographical elements that throw light on the desired sources: friendships, favorite resorts, social, literary, or religious groups; education, and the reading it entails; travel; familiarity with works of art, with certain neighborhoods and scenery,—in short, the immense contributions from life, which often outweigh the contributions from books.

My concluding remarks have already been indicated in the course of the chapter.

1. In the first place, every investigation of sources presupposes on the part of the investigator an extended, profound knowledge of literary environments and traditions. Each month, in the special reviews, a certain number of articles announce the discovery of the source of some important work. When reading them I always think of the satisfaction of those who have made the discoveries. But very often, too often, these so-called sources are only coincidences, without interest or significance. Too often the illusion of the author arises simply because he lacks a general acquaintance with the literary, intellectual, philosophic, or artistic background of the epoch in question. He acts very much like a student of geography who, perched on

a mountain-top above an ocean of clouds and perceiving to left and to right of him a few isolated peaks, attempts to describe the mountain range they belong to. His work will amount to nothing until he sees the whole chain and studies not only the surface but the layers of subsoil. Likewise, we must be judicious enough not to leap from crag to crag with the happy confidence engendered by ignorance or partial knowledge.

2. In the second place, do not suppose that to discover the source is all there is to do. In itself that has no interest. Every investigation of a source should tend toward a definite end: a wider and truer acquaintance with the author, his thought, the evolution of his art, his working-methods, his character, his originality. Under the inviting title *Comment Voltaire faisait un livre*,[1] Lanson, summarizing his search for the sources of the *Lettres philosophiques*, sets forth in a clear and concise form the entire programme and the cautious method required by such an investigation:

It would be interesting to know with precision *how the book grew in his mind*; to be able to refer the various parts to the *various realities* that affected him,—to the *things* that he saw, the *remarks* that he heard, the *books* that he read; to have the power to determine what *outside instigation* and what *reaction of his eager mind* produced each sentence. By watching the author at work, by seizing *events* and *documents* at the moment when they were first known to him, and by noticing what became of them later in his work, we shall, I hope, form a *more exact idea of his literary psychology*, by which I mean the *play* and the *processes* of his faculties as *thinker* and *artist*.

Is not this, expressed in modern terms, just what Montaigne[2] said a long while ago?

[1] *Revue de Paris*, August 1, 1908, pp. 505–533. The italics are mine.
[2] *Essais*, III, 8.

To distinguish in an author the worthiest parts, and those more strictly his own, the strength and beauty of his soul, we must know what is his and what is not; and, in the case of what is not his, how much we owe to him of the selection, arrangement, ornamentation, and language used therein. . . .

On this point, as on so many others, the old *Essais* offer us wise counsel, which here has the practical ring of modern methods.

CHAPTER VI

CHRONOLOGY IN LITERARY HISTORY

I. Importance of Chronology

It would be superfluous to lay stress upon the importance of chronology in all historical studies—literary history included—were it not, unhappily, that experience in teaching proves the need of this insistence. The ignorance and carelessness of students as to chronology are the sources of constant surprises, which would be amusing to their professors and examiners if they were not more often discouraging. Great writers and great works are sometimes assigned dates several centuries wide of the actual dates. As this inaccuracy is not reserved for the history of literature but frequently extends to the history of art and to history in general, it is not surprising that many students are impervious to general ideas and syntheses that require the correlation of several branches of historical science.

Familiarity with chronology is essential to any organized knowledge of the past. When an important historical or literary fact is mentioned, it should be possible to fit it at once into its literary and historical environment. An event or a work must never appear isolated, but must be comprehended in its full relation to contemporary life. For example, Corneille's *Le Cid*, that great landmark, should link itself instantly with other momentous events. *Le Cid* appeared in 1636: now 1635 is the date of the founding of the Académie française; 1636, of the organization of Port-

Royal; 1637, of the publication of Descartes's *Discours sur la méthode*. And in reading the *Histoire de la littérature anglaise* of Taine (1864) would it not be profitable to remember that the French translation of Darwin's *Origin of Species* dates from 1862, Renan's *Vie de Jésus* from 1863, *La Cité antique* of Fustel de Coulanges from 1864, the *Introduction à l'étude de la médecine expérimentale* of Claude Bernard from 1865?

Chronology, however, is not an object of study: I should call it, rather, a habit of mind. Do not suppose that on the day when you become unpleasantly aware of the gaps in your knowledge of dates it is enough to say to yourselves, "Now I am going to take up chronology!" Any such plan would be mere waste of time. The best way, to borrow a famous saying, is "de n'en point parler, mais d'y penser toujours". I mean that during your work, on whatever subject it may be,—literature, history, philosophy, art, or education,—you should constantly make a particular point of impressing on your mind the dates and their mutual relations. This you should come to feel an indispensable part of any intellectual activity. In acquiring the habit you will be aided by taking systematic notes of chronology, often adding to them and rereading them. By this method, with no special effort, you will find yourself at the end of a few months on much firmer ground.

There are several books that will help you, both in learning useful dates and in grouping together dates that belong to different branches of history. Among others are

Putnam's Handbook of Universal History. A Series of Chronological Tables.[1]

DREYSS, C. *Chronologie universelle.*[2]

[1] 16mo. New York, 1914.   [2] 16mo. Hachette, Paris, 1857.

NICHOL, J. *Tables of European History, Literature and Art.*[1]
CIROT, DUFOURCQ and THIRY. *Synchronismes de la littérature française.*[2]

This last work, serviceable and very cleverly arranged, is a valuable implement. Not only does it tabulate in columns all important dates in French literature, but in many cases it presents in parallel columns the coincident dates of political or artistic history.

Nothing, however, can take the place of chronological tables made by yourself. You should become accustomed to using a notebook in which, allowing a page or half a page for each year of the century or period that specially interests you, you will enter in their proper places all the important dates that come to hand: publications of books; births and deaths; significant events in the biography of the great writers; principal facts of contemporary history, including the history of art, of music, or of foreign literatures, etc. As from time to time you read these notes over, you will quickly see, first, that all these dates, or at least the most essential ones, are engraving themselves on your memory; next, that the mere bringing together of dates and facts is surprisingly productive of general ideas and interesting suggestions.

Remember that nothing is accepted so blindly as a date, and be on your guard. You cannot be sure of the correctness of even a standard work where dates are concerned. As a general rule, never construct a theory, never sustain an argument, by propping it up with any date you have not minutely verified.

[1] 8vo. Glasgow, 1884.
[2] 8vo. Paris, 1894. Good Tableaux chronologiques are to be found at the end of both Lanson's and C. M. des Granges's *Histoire de la littérature française.*

Here is an illustration of that sort of danger. I do not take it from the history of literature but from the history of the law. There exists a Roman law, the Lex Aquilia, dating from 468 A. U. C. It happened that in an excellent French manual of the history of Roman law—one of those 'reliable' books that every student consults and robs continually—by a typographical error 408 was printed instead of 468. As dates are accepted with so little question, this carelessness on the compositor's part was enough to establish a kind of tradition. A respectable number of theses or works on law can be found which, placidly accepting the date of 408, have based deductions and theories thereon.[1] Many works on the history of literature expose you to similar perils. Let skepticism and suspicion be your watchwords.

II. PROBLEMS OF CHRONOLOGY IN LITERARY HISTORY

Chronology is as important for the study of literary works as it is for the history of government, diplomacy, or law. Unluckily, its acquisition is not a simple matter of memory and effort guided by caution—a compiling of incontestable lists of dates, with each great literary event in its proper place. On the contrary, even in very recent literature many dates are either unknown, doubtful, or traditionally inexact. The problems that arise in connection with these may be divided into two classes, as follows:

1. *To fix the date of a work.* Until the correct date of a work is fixed, it obviously cannot be given its true place in the biography of the author and in the literary life of his time.

2. *To fix the dates of the various parts of a work.* If a work represents several years of reflection and labor, the

---

[1] Example cited by A. Girard, in *Revue internationale de l'enseignement*, June 15, 1890, p. 621.

date of each part must be known before the progress of the thought, art, intellectual and moral life, of a writer can be traced.

TO FIX THE DATE OF A WORK

1. *By comparison with the manuscript.* Frequently the testimony of a manuscript, unknown or unnoticed before, makes it possible to establish an exact date on which the printed text throws no light. Verlaine's famous poem *Art poétique*,

> De la musique avant toute chose,
> Et pour cela préfère l'Impair . . .,

appeared in 1885 in *Jadis et naguère*; it became the manifesto of the "École symboliste." E. Dupuy, after a study of Verlaine's manuscripts, pointed out[1] that *Art poétique* is one of a collection entitled *Cellulairement*, written by Verlaine while in prison and completed in August, 1874. This fact, had it been known to A. Barre in time, might perhaps have led him to give a less positive form to the phrase with which he begins his otherwise excellent thesis *Le Symbolisme*[2]: "In French literature the symbolist movement dates from 1885."

2. *By historical criticism of documents.* Take a work as important as Corneille's *Polyeucte*. Until a few years ago the exact date of this masterpiece was uncertain. It used erroneously to be assigned to 1640. After Marty-Laveaux's edition it was supposed—again wrongly—to belong to 1643. E. Rigal has now proved[3] that *Polyeucte* was written in the winter of 1641–1642.

He reaches this result by taking, one by one, the facts or the documents on which it had been thought justifiable to

---

[1] "Étude critique sur le texte d'un manuscrit de P. Verlaine," *Revue d'histoire littéraire*, 1913, pp. 489–516. See page 503.　　[2] Paris, 1912.

[3] "La Date de *Polyeucte*," *Revue universitaire*, Vol. II (1911), pp. 29–36.

base the chronology of Corneille's plays, and by demonstrating that these data are either uncertain or wrongly construed. He begins by eliminating the date of 1640.

a. Horace and *Cinna* already belong to 1640—*Cinna* to the second half of the year; it is not likely that Corneille composed three great tragedies in the same year. (This is simply a presumption, not a certainty.)

b. Polyeucte was read at the Hôtel de Rambouillet, and gave offense there. Now, Corneille had no connection with the Hôtel before the last third of 1641.

Rigal next disposes of a letter from an obscure "conseiller au Parlement," C. Sarrau, addressed to Corneille, December 12, 1642:

Ut valeas tu cum tuis Musis scire imprimis desidero; et utrum tribus eximiis et divinis tuis dramatis quartum adjungere mediteris? . . . Inaudivi nescio quid de aliquo poemate sacro, quod an affectum an perfectum sit, quaeso, rescribe.

This text has always been interpreted as meaning that after the "three exquisite and divine dramas" (*Le Cid, Horace, Cinna*) the "sacred poem" *Polyeucte* was to make a fourth. In that case it would be necessary to place *Polyeucte* later than December, 1642; that is, in 1643.

Rigal contends that (1) the expression "three divine dramas" does not necessarily exclude *Polyeucte*; and (2) that the words "sacred poem" do not necessarily allude to it, but much more probably to one of the religious poems that Corneille wrote at all periods of his life.

Finally, a hand-corrected copy of the Abbé d'Aubignac's *Pratique du théâtre*,[1] long overlooked, bears witness that Richelieu, who died in 1642, knew of *Polyeucte* and disapproved of certain scenes.

[1] Paris, 1657.

If you add the fact that Corneille was in Rouen and not in Paris at the beginning of July, 1641 (and, therefore, unable to oversee the staging of a play), you will notice that, little by little, owing to successive criticisms of facts and documents, *Polyeucte* has been inclosed within two chronological limits—the autumn of 1641 and the summer of 1642.[1]

3. *By the combined study of manuscripts, text, and external documents.* A typical problem is that of the date of *Héléna*, a poem by Alfred de Vigny. What are the facts, and how may the problem be stated?

Héléna was published for the first time in an anonymous book of *Poèmes*, in March, 1822. It disappeared from the *Poèmes* of 1829, having been "jugé sévèrement" by its author. It was not reprinted during Vigny's lifetime.

A note from the *Journal d'un poète*, published by L. Ratisbonne in 1867, after Vigny's death, says, "*Héléna* is an essay written at nineteen years of age", which would be in 1816. Now as early as 1864, in a famous article, Sainte-Beuve denied the accuracy of this date:

Alfred de Vigny's début in literature dates from 1822. With his poem *Héléna* he paid enthusiastic tribute to the cause of the Greeks; at the same time, in his *La Dryade* and *Symétha*, he played the flute to the tune of André Chénier, revived and brought into prominence in the last few years.[2] The real date of these Neo-Greek poems of M. de Vigny is that of their publication, and, for the historian of literature who cares for accuracy, there is no occasion to accept the somewhat arbitrary dates that the poet has since felt impelled to assign to them.[3]

[1] See H. Carrington Lancaster, "The Dates of Corneille's Early Plays," *Modern Language Notes*, January, 1915, pp. 1–5; A. L. Stiefel, *Ueber die Chronologie von Jean Rotrou's dramatischen Werken* (Berlin), and in *Zeitschrift für französische Sprache und Litteratur*, Vol. XVI (1894), pp. 1–49; and E. Dannheisser, "Zur Chronologie der Dramen Jean de Mairet's," *Romanische Forschungen*, 1889.   [2] By H. de Latouche's edition (1819).

[3] *Revue des Deux Mondes*, April 15, 1864.

In the last few years the question has been taken up anew, discussed, and, I believe, very nearly decided.[1] Let us see now the importance of the question and the methods used in the discussion.

A. *Importance of the Question*

This controversy is not the outcome of the minute and fruitless curiosity of scholars. Apart from the interest of placing each work in its exact position in the evolution of a great genius, Vigny's very character is at stake. The point to be decided is whether, by deliberately changing the date, he yielded to an artist's petty desire to make his youthful genius seem more isolated and precocious. If so, his memory is tarnished with a 'white' lie. On the contrary, if the poems really belong to the date they bear, it is Sainte-Beuve who must be accused,—who must be blamed for having through ill-advised jealousy formulated a hypothesis so detrimental to the reputation of a great poet.

In addition, the history of André Chénier's influence and of his rôle in the formation of the Romanticists of the first generation is involved in the solution of this question.

B. *The Discussion*

a. "Héléna" dates from 1816: theory of Dupuy. Dupuy supports his chronological theory by three kinds of argument, as follows:

(1) *Arguments deduced from historical allusions. Héléna*, according to Sainte-Beuve, cannot be anterior to 1821, because of allusions to the Greek Rebellion, which did not break out until March, 1821. *Héléna* ends with the capture

---

[1] Besides Sainte-Beuve's article (reissued in the *Nouveaux Lundis*, Vol. VI) see E. Dupuy, "Les Origines littéraires d'Alfred de Vigny," *Revue d'histoire littéraire*, 1903, pp. 373-412 (reissued in *La Jeunesse des romantiques*, 1905); E. Estève, *Héléna*, critical edition (1907), Introduction; P. M. Masson, "L'Influence d'André Chénier sur Alfred de Vigny," *Revue d'histoire littéraire*,

of Athens, which occurred eight months later, and, therefore, must be posterior to this event. Dupuy retorts that actual historical events were not Vigny's inspiration, since the poem, published in March, 1822, contains a description of the taking of the Acropolis, June 30, 1822 : we should have faith in the poet's imagination.

(2) *Arguments deduced from the sources.* Faith is made easier because other imaginative works that depict the Greeks as fighting against their oppressors were written before 1821 : "Byron's *Turkish Tales* and his lyric outbursts are among these". Dupuy points out also that *The Siege of Corinth* (1816) certainly influenced *Héléna.* In this connection, however, he makes the concession that in 1822, just before sending it to press, Vigny very likely revised it, "so as to touch up the coloring and perhaps lengthen the plot".

(3) *Arguments deduced from other facts connected with literary history.* Dupuy adds that it was not in 1819 but toward 1828, and especially in 1832, that Chénier, little known till then, really conquered the generation of Romanticists. Therefore the argument drawn from Chénier's influence is not of great weight.

b. Héléna dates from 1821 : theory of Estève and Masson. To the arguments of Dupuy, Estève, in his edition of the poem, opposes forceful counterarguments.

(1) Vigny calls *Héléna* "an essay written at nineteen years of age", but this is a hasty note of little weight rather than a positive assertion. Besides, as the entry was made long after the event, Vigny's memory may have been at fault.[1]

1909, pp. 1–48; Vigny, *Poèmes,* Baldensperger edition (Conard, Paris, 1914); E. Dupuy, *Vigny, la vie et l'œuvre* (1913); E. Dupuy, in *Revue d'histoire littéraire,* 1915, pp. 602–605.

[1] This would not be without precedent. Thus, in the second preface to the *Poèmes,* in 1829, Vigny says, "When these poems appeared nine years ago. . ." Yet the collection of 1822 had been published not nine, but seven, years before!

(2) Estève does not believe that in 1816 Vigny could have "imagined" the development of the Greek insurrection of March, 1821. The poem gives the impression of having been written on the rebound from the events themselves. It is comprehensible that Shelley, when writing *Hellas* in October, 1821, should mention the capture of several towns that surrendered some months later. In 1821 Vigny could "foresee" the fall of the Acropolis, Athens being already three-quarters conquered; but in 1816 he would have had to predict, not the capitulation of a town that was almost taken, but the whole insurrection.

(3) Byron's influence in 1816 is not sufficient to explain the stand taken by Vigny in the Greek question. As a matter of fact, at that date, in *Childe Harold*, II, and the first part of *The Giaour*, Byron was sympathetically bemoaning the hopeless degeneration of the Greeks. How, then, is it possible to suppose that a young French lad, hardly out of school, could have not merely predicted but pictured as triumphant a revolt which the most ardent friends of the Greeks could not foresee?

(4) Certain definite facts strengthen this opinion. *Héléna* refers to the famous hymn of Rhigas,[1] known in France through Byron only in 1820; to the heroic death of the Suliote women,[2] a fact learned also only in 1820, from the *Voyage dans la Grèce* by Pouqueville; to the abandonment of the town of Parga by its inhabitants,[3] on May 10, 1819.

(5) Lastly, Byron's influence seems an argument against rather than for the theory that *Héléna* was written in 1816. The poem is indeed full of imitations, many of which are direct. But in 1816 Vigny could not have known Byron thoroughly enough to enable us to explain these imitations. His familiarity with the English poet dates no farther back

[1] Bk. I, line 92.   [2] Bk. II, lines 406–414.   [3] Bk. II, line 396.

than the translation made by Pichot in 1819–1820, and more particularly from the article and extracts contributed to the *Lycée français* by Bruguière de Sorsum in August, 1820.[1] Certain lines prove beyond a doubt that Vigny used Pichot's translation.[2] Therefore *Héléna* could not have been written before 1821. In antedating his work Vigny's motive was to pose as precursor of the Philhellenic movement and also to repudiate his debt to André Chénier.

This last point is strongly corroborated by an article of P. M. Masson entitled "L'Influence d'André Chénier sur Alfred de Vigny."[3] Masson uses most precise methods in his search for the sources of Vigny. He brings to light a considerable number of details borrowed by Vigny from Chénier, and finds it impossible to explain even the works that Vigny places earlier than 1819 except on the assumption of a very complete knowledge of Chénier's work published by Latouche in 1819.

c. Héléna is composed of elements belonging to two different dates: result of recent investigations. The arguments presented by Estève and Masson, are, in my opinion, almost irrefutable. Nevertheless, Baldensperger, when publishing his edition of Vigny's poems,[4] contributes a new fact. Authorized to work among Vigny's manuscripts, he detected that the preparatory notes of *Héléna*—the first material gathered by the poet—were written in the same hand as his earliest papers, "an almost childish hand";[5] and concludes that the original plan and idea of *Héléna* belong certainly to 1816 or before, thus confirming the date given by Vigny.

Besides, by an internal analysis, he shows that the original idea of *Héléna* can be satisfactorily accounted for without

---

[1] For details see another contribution by Estève, *Byron et le romantisme français.* Paris, 1907.   [2] See Book II, lines 47–52.

[3] *Revue d'histoire littéraire,* 1909, pp. 1–48.   [4] 1914.   [5] P. 285.

turning either to Byron, the Greek insurrection, or to Chénier: the subject is taken from Corneille's *Théodore*; the orientalism and exotism can be traced to Chateaubriand, Ossian, the Koran, the Psalms, or to some other reading of Vigny's. There is in the poem a 'first layer' dating undoubtedly, or very probably, from 1816 or thereabouts. Thus the idea and the elements of the poem may very well go back to the time when Vigny was nineteen years old.

It is no less sure, however, that the poem itself did not assume its definitive form until after the events of 1821, and until after reading Chénier. Vigny, following his accustomed method, has "touched up and patched up" the original sketch in many places. It must, therefore, be admitted that, in insisting upon 1816 as the date of composition, he yielded to the temptation to deceive his readers, as Masson puts it, by "un geste inélégant et malhabile".

TO FIX THE DATES OF THE VARIOUS PARTS OF A WORK

The problem of fixing the dates of the various parts of a work may be presented in several ways, depending upon whether it is a question of (1) the date of a work composed of fragments, when the chronological order is not fixed by the author; (2) the chronology of a collection when the dates are not correctly or completely given by the author; (3) the date of the composition of different parts of an important work when the preparation and revision extend over a long period of the author's life.

1. *Chronology of a work made up of fragments.* A typical example of a fragmentary work is the *Journal d'un poète* of Vigny, published after his death by Ratisbonne.[1] The *Journal* is a document of capital importance for the study of Vigny's opinions, philosophy, and art. He enters at random,

[1] 1867.

in his notes, projects for poems, reflections on his reading and on incidents in the political and literary life of his time, and many doleful meditations that exhale bitterness and pessimism. Hence the importance of an exact chronology of these fragments. Ratisbonne's edition, however, is full of gross errors, on which even well-informed critics have based their conclusions as to the development of Vigny's pessimism.

In a very good article[1] I. Roney undertakes the indispensable cleaning up and attempts to reëstablish the genuine dates of some important fragments of the *Journal*. His article is interesting as an example of method, for it shows us (1) that flagrant errors have crept into works as recent as the *Journal d'un poète*; (2) that this minute chronological verification is not merely the whim of a scholar but is requisite to any synthetic reconstruction of the evolution of Vigny's philosophy. For instance:

a. The year 1824 of the Ratisbonne edition includes fragments written surely as late as 1829, since in them Vigny alludes to a play produced in 1829; or even as late as 1832, since they mention the destruction of certain poems that he burned in 1832, and also speak of his revising the proofs of *Stello*, published in 1832.

b. These necessary corrections modify to a great extent our views on the origin of Vigny's pessimism. Obviously, if already in 1824, at the threshold of his intellectual life, we come upon dismal thoughts and melancholy reflections, it is. easy to accept the opinion that Vigny was *born* a pessimist and did not *become* one. Today, however, this idea no longer seems in agreement with the facts.[2] Thus, errors in chronol-

---

[1] "Sur quelques erreurs de date du *Journal d'un poète*," *Revue d'histoire littéraire*, 1907, pp. 17–39.

[2] See particularly E. Dupuy, *La Jeunesse des romantiques* and *Vigny, la vie et l'œuvre*, and the Introduction and commentaries of the Baldensperger edition.

ogy have produced others, not in the material detail of Vigny's biography but in the historical, psychological, and moral interpretation of his personality.

Roney's contribution is a concise and exact application of the method that attempts to fix the chronology of a work by the precise examination of historical or biographical allusions and of information of every kind.

2. *Chronology of the various pieces in a collection.*[1] Almost all the large collections of poetry—the odes of Ronsard or Malherbe no less than the lyrics of Lamartine[2] or Hugo —consist of poems written at different periods and gathered into one volume. Although the poet himself frequently dates each piece, experience teaches that the modern critic should not accept these records without suspicion and precaution.

I shall dwell at some length upon H. Dupin's "Études sur la chronologie des *Contemplations*"[3] of Victor Hugo, partly because, as the work of a student, it proves that, by applying sure and rigorous processes to a well-chosen subject, it is possible to reach successful and serviceable results without being far advanced in one's career. The following is an abridged description of its object and method.

[1] As the contents of these collections often change from one edition to another, close attention should be paid to them. This implies a knowledge of the date of each piece. A fine example of such work is P. Laumonier, *Ronsard, poète lyrique* (Paris, 1910). The first part of the volume is devoted to establishing the chronology of Ronsard's *Odes*. See especially pages 26–69 for a model of scholarly discussion. I do not dwell particularly upon this unusually good book, because it is striking more in the excellence of its conclusions than in the novelty of its method.

[2] See, in the Lanson edition of the *Méditations*, the arguments on the exact date of the composition of the first poems.

[3] *Mélanges d'histoire littéraire* (8vo), pp. 41–107. Published under the direction of Lanson, Bibliothèque de l'Université de Paris, 1906.

Elements of the Problem

The dates respectively given in the edition and in the manuscript disagree for one hundred and thirty-seven poems out of one hundred and seventy-eight. As the contents of the book represent twenty-five years of Victor Hugo's poetic activity, an exact chronology is requisite for establishing the true evolution of his ideas, feelings, and style. Moreover, if he altered the dates, we must know why: perhaps the reasons may disclose some traits of his character or genius.

Attempt at Solution

Dupin, having put aside every poem on which manuscript and edition agree, uses three different methods to ascertain the genuine dates of the others.

a. Critical comparison between the dates in the manuscripts and those in the edition. First, for thirty poems the dates found in the edition antedate those of the manuscripts, giving different years but the same month. The manuscripts are certainly correct in these instances—that is, unless the ridiculous hypothesis be admitted that they are subsequent final copies made each time by chance on the anniversaries of the months when the poems were first written!

Next, it is obvious that, in postdating or antedating certain other pieces in the edition, Hugo, having written them at seasons ill-suited to their subjects, wished to substitute more appropriate occasions.

About twenty of the poems are dated as shown in the table on the opposite page.

b. Evolution of Hugo's feeling about love. In studying the diverse forms that love assumes in Victor Hugo's work, from the pure gravity of the *Lettres à la fiancée* to the sensuous gaiety of *Les Chansons des rues et des bois*, Dupin dis-

POEM	DATE OF MANUSCRIPT	DATE OF EDITION	REASON
II. 5. xxiii: " Le vallon où je vais tous les jours ..."	December 17, 1854	April, 1855	A poem full of springtime, for which December is hardly suitable.
II. 6. xxii: "Ne dites pas : mourir ..."	October, 1854	Jour des morts, November, 1854	A time better fitted for meditation on death.
II. 6. xxvi: "L'homme en songeant ..."	October 1–13, 1854	1855	This poem, like several others, voices Hugo's philosophic ' credo ' at this time. He places all such poems in 1855 or in January, 1856, as if written on the eve of publication.
II. 4. vi: " Quand nous habitions tous ensemble ..."	October 16, 1846	Villequier, September 4, 1844	The anniversary of his daughter's death.
II. 4. xiv: " Demain, dès l'aube ..."	October 4, 1847	September 3, 1847	Eve of the anniversary of his daughter's death.

tinguishes three phases: 1819–1823, the love of "one soul for another", pure, serious, often melancholy and "fatal"; 1830–1840, a love still pure, and constantly interspersed with philosophical reflections, yet showing signs of contamination (his inspiration is no longer "la fiancée" but Juliette Drouet); 1840–1865, including *Les Chansons*, the love is no longer an actual experience—it is the ingenious invention of an artist.

Now, the love poems in *Les Contemplations* naturally fall into two groups, of which one belongs with the poems of the period 1830–1840, the other with *Les Chansons*. The dates of about fifteen poems are thus fixed, and in favor of the manuscript.

c. Evolution of Hugo's versification from 1830 to 1854.
By means of exhaustive statistics bearing upon several thousand lines, Dupin determines for different epochs (1830, 1830–1835, 1835–1840, 1854) the proportion of lines that are cut elsewhere than at the hemistich; the proportion of the different *coupes*; the proportion of *enjambements*. Next he examines the poems of *Les Contemplations* and ranks them under the corresponding headings. In this way he finds the dates of the manuscript usually confirmed.

d. Evolution of Hugo's style from 1830 to 1854. Dupin next makes an experiment similar to the preceding one by studying the formation of Hugo's images and metaphors: the proportion of images of immense size; of images that are sensations; of animated and personified objects; of symbols, etc.

It must be admitted that these last two methods (statistics of the characteristics of versification and of style) are not entirely reliable. There is no real determinism or automatism in literary production. Still, I am far from considering these processes negligible, provided they are applied with prudence and sense. Obviously, a particular *coupe* occurring two or three times in a poem is not enough to fix the date. But if, for instance in a piece assigned in the edition to 1840, a division is repeated six or seven times that is absolutely unheard of in Hugo's versification from 1835 to 1845 but is found in five or six per cent of the lines belonging to 1850–1855, we have a fairly weighty presumption. In such a case the increase or decrease of the characteristics laid bare by the statistical method gives important indications as to the evolution of an author's processes and the date of composition. It is merely an elementary precaution not to attribute to these 'charts' the value we ascribe to the 'curves' obtained by a like scientific observation.

In conclusion Dupin draws up a chronological table of *Les Contemplations* which is most useful for the study and explanation of the work.[1]

3. *To fix the date of the different parts of an extended or autobiographical work.* For every work that has been prepared and composed during many years of the author's life, or contains autobiographical and personal material, it is particularly essential to give each section its exact chronological position, for each is a part of the portrait the author wished to leave us. This is true of Montaigne's *Essais*, Rousseau's *Confessions*, Chateaubriand's *Mémoires d'outre-tombe*, Victor Hugo's *La Légende des siècles*, and many other important works.

An excellent illustration is the way in which Villey has succeeded, with as much certainty as the subject permits, in establishing the chronology of Montaigne's *Essais*. His work fills three volumes: *Les Sources et l'évolution des "Essais" de Montaigne*[2] and *Les Livres d'histoire moderne utilisés par Montaigne.*[3]

Importance of the Question

The *Essais* consist of three books, divided into chapters, some very long, some very short, written by Montaigne between 1572 and 1592 and representing without any logical

---

[1] See the use to which these researches are put in an article by P. Berret, "Une Méthode critique pour l'explication des *Contemplations* à propos de leur chronologie," *Revue universitaire*, Vol. II (1913), pp. 48–57. He points out that the printed date is the poetic date on which the author, inspired by certain events, conceived the ideas or opinions to which he gave literary expression ten or twenty years later; the date of the manuscript is that of composition and represents a certain stage in Victor Hugo's artistic development. In a critical study of *Les Contemplations* both these dates should be taken into account after having been duly verified.

[2] In 2 vols., 8vo. Paris, 1908.   [3] In 1 vol., 8vo. 1908.

sequence the results of his reading, reflection, and personal thoughts. The problem is to establish the exact chronology of this intellectual activity. Thus we shall avoid "falling into the traditional error of mistaking a transient opinion for the final expression of his personality, and, through the confusion of dates, of introducing contradiction and incoherence into his ideas".[1] Furthermore, we shall learn how his inner life has developed.

His life and his books deposit on his mind successive 'strata' of experience. From each stratum he attempts to learn some lesson, and, each time, the succeeding stratum shows him the insufficiency of his ideas and raises the problem again. . . . It is this romance of an intellect that fascinates and instructs the psychologist. To trace it we need as many dates as possible.[2]

First Chronological Data

It is known, before any detailed research, that Montaigne withdrew to his château and began working on the *Essais* in 1571; that Books I and II appeared in 1580; that Book III and about six hundred additions came out in 1588; that, beginning in 1588, correcting and enlarging a copy of the 1588 edition, Montaigne was preparing a new edition, which his death, on September 13, 1592, prevented his issuing. We possess this copy ('Exemplaire de Bordeaux'). It served as the foundation for the edition published in 1595 by M[lle] de Gournay.

Up to this point it is evident that ninety-four essays are anterior to 1580, that thirteen were written between 1580 and 1588, and that the additions to these one hundred and seven were prepared between 1588 and September 13, 1592.

<hr>

[1]Vol. I, p. 281.   [2]P. 282.

But we must go farther. Each group must be taken separately, and an attempt made to place chronologically every essay that it contains.[1]

Processes and Methods Employed

In order to assign a date to each of the *Essais*, Villey resorts to three sources of information: (1) allusions to precise facts of which the dates are known; (2) allusions to Montaigne's reading whenever it is possible to fix the date; (3) possibility of dating certain essays by their relation to others.[2]

a. Allusions to precise facts. Villey collects every allusion to events of known date. He reaches results that vary in certainty.

(1) *Precise date.* "Only fifteen days ago", says Montaigne,[3] "I completed my thirty-ninth year." Therefore the essay was written March 15, 1572.

(2) *Approximate date.* Montaigne speaks[4] of the battle of Lepanto (October 7, 1571), and adds that "it was won a few months ago against the Turks". Therefore the essay belongs to the first months of 1572.

(3) *Double limit.* The study of allusions proves, in quite a number of cases, that the essay could have been written

---

[1] Villey points out that the question is especially important for the period 1571–1580. After 1580 Montaigne changes less, develops less definitely,—the *genre* of the essay is established.

[2] Is it necessary to call attention to the formidable mass of reading and erudition represented by such research? A minute knowledge of sixteenth-century history, a practically exhaustive perusal of everything printed before 1592, a familiarity with all the works of Greek, Latin, and Italian literature, not only through their texts but in the various annotated editions published in the sixteenth century,—this is what Villey has acquired and accomplished. His effort will appear far more splendid, and his example more inspiring to our young workers, if they know that he has been blind since early childhood.

[3] I, 20.   [4] I, 32.

neither anterior to a certain date nor posterior to another. It is thus inclosed between two chronological limits.

(4) *Single limit*. Lastly, several chapters, from their allusions, cannot be anterior or cannot be posterior to a given date—nothing more.

In these last two instances, (3) and (4), the approximation arrived at through the allusions may be narrowed down by other sources of information.

b. Allusions to reading whenever it is possible to fix the date. As to Montaigne's reading, Villey's researches rest upon the following facts:

(1) We have in our possession today a considerable number of books owned by Montaigne. Several bear the date of reading, and precious annotations in his hand.

(2) Montaigne made great use of his books, and when he borrowed from them it was often verbatim. This last fact is particularly important with regard to ancient authors or translations. Whenever Villey is able to decide which sixteenth-century edition Montaigne used,—and he decides this frequently,—he knows that Montaigne cannot have borrowed prior to the publication of the edition.

(3) We learn from Montaigne himself that the books he read are of two sorts.[1] On the one hand, there are those few that he makes constant use of (Virgil, Horace, Lucian, Seneca, Amyot's translation of Plutarch),—books "that it would be harder to dispense with than any others". Borrowings from these books occur in the three editions and are of slight account for chronology. On the other hand, there are the books that he studied for a time and then allowed to sleep in peace in his library,—those, he says, "that I want to use only once". On these he "had a habit of recording the date on which *he* finished them, and *his* judgment of them as a whole".

[1] III, 5.

These various indications enable Villey to reach a certain number of definite conclusions.[1] For instance:

(1) *Julius Cæsar*. The library at Chantilly contains the copy of Cæsar read by Montaigne, with the manuscript note that he read it "from February 25 to July 21, 1578". The essay[2] entitled "Observations sur les moyens de faire la guerre de Julius Cæsar" includes many facts borrowed from the *Commentaries*, and criticisms directly developed from the jottings with which Montaigne has crowded the margins of his copy. This essay, therefore, dates from 1578, or at the latest from 1579.

(2) *Guicciardini*. Villey begins by determining every passage incontestably borrowed by Montaigne.

There is a good chance that all these passages were entered in Montaigne's pages at about the same period: Guicciardini is one of the authors whom he studied "only for a time". The chapters in which they occur must, therefore, be very nearly contemporaneous, "forming a cluster".

If it is possible to date one of these chapters by means of some allusion or statement, we shall learn the approximate date of the whole cluster.

Now in the chapter "Des Livres" we find this sentence: "Here is the entry that I wrote in my Guicciardini about ten years ago". And we know, by other means, that this chapter belongs to 1580.

Therefore the six essays in which Montaigne makes use of Guicciardini were probably written in 1571.

c. Essays dated from their relation to others. On the one hand, certain essays allude to others. For instance, Montaigne, in Book II, chap. 10, mentions that "*he* has an in-

---

[1] The first part of Villey's book (Vol. I, pp. 50–242) is given up to establishing the chronology of Montaigne's reading.
[2] II, 34.

tense curiosity to become acquainted with the soul and the inmost opinions of *his* authors", and adds that "*he* has said this elsewhere". The remark is found in chapter 31 of the same book, which, in this wise, is proved to have been written before chapter 10.

On the other hand, we may draw conclusions from the relative positions of the different essays and from their character. The dates that are conclusively established show how frequently essays belonging to the same epoch are arranged consecutively. Without believing this rule infallible, we may take for granted that an undated essay is probably of the same date as those adjoining, if it is like them in conception or structure. In this way we reach not a certainty but, in many cases, a plausible presumption.

Criticism and Limitations of this Method

With fine scientific loyalty Villey himself points out the objections to his method and conclusions.

(1) To chapters written long before, Montaigne, on completing some new reading, may have added certain passages. If so, the reading is unavailing in dating the chapter.

Answer. First, we must often be resigned to remain in doubt. Next, many essays placed by this means belong unmistakably to the beginning of Montaigne's literary activity and cannot have been composed much before the reading in question. Finally, a conclusion should be thought decisive only when the chapter is built round the reading, or, in other words, when the reading has obviously been the occasion not of ornamenting nor of amplifying the chapter but of writing it as a whole.

(2) Several years after reading some work a long-forgotten phrase or idea may have recurred to Montaigne.

Answer. Apart from the fact that this is not characteristic of all that we know of Montaigne, and that in many cases it is sufficient to place the essays within approximately three or four years, Villey shields himself from this objection by taking into account only such passages as Montaigne borrows word for word—those that imply that he has the book open before him, and never those that contain more or less inexact reminiscences.

(3) It is arbitrary to decide which authors Montaigne really read only once. In spite of his own testimony, he may perfectly well have turned to them again when his train of thought suggested them.

Answer. This objection is indeed strong; but it may be avoided by resting the demonstration, as far as possible, upon the books for which we can incontestably establish the date of reading and by rejecting those that may have been used more customarily and permanently.

"Therefore", concludes Villey, "we should not lose sight for a single instant of the doubts that assail us. Nevertheless, if our results are not characterized by absolute certainty, they reach a high degree of probability"[1]—and, as far as that goes, the results are considerable.

Results

The conclusion of this vast investigation is the establishment of a 'Table chronologique des *Essais*,' where each of the one hundred and seven chapters is given its proper place in Montaigne's life and in the growth of his ideas. This chart is completed by synoptical tables showing the connection between Montaigne's reading and the composition of the *Essais*.

[1] P. 285.

These results are set down in the second volume, where Villey examines "L'Évolution de la pensée de Montaigne," following, epoch by epoch, the development of this "romance of an intellect", but treading now on firm ground.

This last instance[1] illustrates the close coördination and dependence between the work of general synthesis and philosophical interpretation, on the one hand, and, on the other hand, these patient, thorough, often dry researches that furnish material for the former and are their essential condition.

[1] The examples studied in this chapter may be supplemented by many others, in particular by the following: P. Laumonier, *Tableau chronologique de l'œuvre de Ronsard* (1911); P. M. Masson, "Questions de chronologie rousseauiste," *Annales Jean-Jacques Rousseau*, Vol. IX, p. 37; E. Rigal, "Sur les *Contemplations* de Hugo," *Herrig's Archiv*, Vol. 116 (1906), p. 327; F. A. Blossom, *La Composition de Salammbô d'après la correspondance de Flaubert, avec un essai de classement chronologique des lettres* (Elliott Monographs, No. 3) (Baltimore, 1914).

CHAPTER VII

PROBLEMS OF AUTHENTICITY AND ATTRIBUTION

Modern literature is less fertile in problems of authenticity and attribution than are the literatures of antiquity or of the Middle Ages. The circumstances attending the publication of most of the important works are known beyond the possibility of doubt or discussion. If anyone were to dispute the authenticity of Racine's tragedies, Balzac's novels, or *Le Génie du christianisme*, he would be subjected to the sort of ridicule that greeted the paradoxical critic who wrote a book to prove that Napoleon I had never existed.

However, such problems do arise even for relatively recent works.[1] Rabelais, Montaigne, Pascal, Molière, Bossuet, Voltaire, Rousseau, Diderot, are involved, not to mention a great number of authors of memoirs and of correspondence. Sometimes it is a question of ascertaining whether the work handed down under a writer's name is not purely and simply an imposture (question of authenticity);[2] sometimes, of determining whether a work until now accredited to a certain author should not be reassigned to another (question of attribution). In the last few years these questions have many times been asked and answered in regard to important

[1] For example, the discussion about the little book *The Young Visiters*, by Daisy Ashford, with a preface by J. M. Barrie (1919).

[2] By way of introduction to the subject, read the chapter "Critique de provenance," in Langlois and Seignobos, *Introduction aux études historiques*, pp. 66–78. Some curious examples of falsification are found in E. Bernheim, *Lehrbuch der historischen Methode*, pp. 204–256.

works of French literature. The best lesson in method is
to examine the elements of the problems and the processes
employed to settle them.

I. THE AUTHENTICITY OF THE *PARADOXE SUR LE COMÉDIEN* BY DIDEROT

We have in the question of the *Paradoxe sur le comédien*
one of the most curious among these problems of authenticity. Because of the variety of the arguments hurled into
the discussion, because of the psychological elements brought
to light in the controversy, and, finally, because of the success of strictly critical methods in arriving at the truth, this
question is well worth a detailed analysis.

HISTORY OF THE QUESTION

The *Paradoxe sur le comédien* is published for the first
time in 1830—forty-six years after Diderot's death (1784)
—by the Parisian publisher Sautelet, from a copy made at
St. Petersburg of one of Diderot's inedited manuscripts.[1]
Other of his works bought by Sautelet (the *Correspondance
avec M*ᶫᶫᵉ *Volland, Le Rêve de d'Alembert*, etc.) have the
same origin. Until 1902 the little work is reprinted in the
various editions of Diderot without exciting any doubt as to
its authenticity; it is read, admired, spoken of as a gem.
The style is praised as brilliant and spirited. Diderot is
recognized in all his glamor of new, arresting ideas, originality, and wit.

Now in one of those picturesque cubby-holes that line the
old Paris quays, Ernest Dupuy has the good fortune to
stumble upon a thin notebook, which is nothing else than

---

[1] Diderot's personal library was bought by Catherine II, and after his
death his unpublished manuscripts were sold to her by his daughter Mᵐᵉ
de Vandeul.

the manuscript of the *Paradoxe sur le comédien*, not in Diderot's hand but in that of Naigeon, his friend, client, quasi-assistant and secretary, with whom Diderot, on his departure for Russia, left instructions to publish his inedited works in case he himself should die on the journey.

Up to this point everything is quite natural; but now the trouble begins. "The manuscript", says Dupuy, "although very neat in certain spots, in others is covered with erasures and with words written in above the text; the margins of some of the pages are almost completely filled with additions to the original version. After studying the manuscript closely, I was convinced that I had before me a revised text by Naigeon." Indeed, its aspect is disquieting: these additions, corrections, and alterations in the detail of the style and expression could not have been made by a copyist. It is certainly a 'working-copy,' an author's manuscript,—and the *Paradoxe sur le comédien*, hitherto supposed to be a masterpiece by Diderot, appears to be the work of an impostor.

Not entirely; for the *Paradoxe* is only the development of an article published by Diderot in the *Correspondance de Grimm*,[1] under the title "Observations de M. Diderot sur une brochure intitulée Garrick ou les acteurs anglais,"—an article incontestably authentic. Yet everything added to the *Observations* in composing the *Paradoxe* must be Naigeon's; of the *Paradoxe*, says Dupuy, "the greater part is grossly interpolated, the remainder as lacking in taste as in accuracy".

Dupuy exhibits his discovery in a critical edition of the *Paradoxe*,[2] where, in parallel columns, he gives the text of the *Observations* and the text of the Naigeon manuscript. In his Introduction he indicates the sources that the 'inter-

---

[1] October 15, 1770.
[2] Diderot, *Paradoxe sur le comédien*, critical edition, with Introduction, Notes, and Facsimile, by E. Dupuy, 8vo, xxxiii + 179 pp. Paris, 1902.

polator' has drawn from, pointing out that he has stolen from Grimm, Rousseau, and many others—and particularly from Diderot himself. He believes he has discovered that certain of these additions are taken from works, such as *De l'art de la comédie* by Cailhava or the *Mémoires* of Mlle Clairon, that did not appear until after Diderot's death. Therefore there is no longer room for doubt: the whole 'fabrication' of the *Paradoxe* is disclosed to us; Naigeon is caught red-handed; and the *Paradoxe*, that masterpiece by Diderot, is not by Diderot and is not a masterpiece.

THE CONTROVERSY

Immediately great agitation and excitement prevail in the camp of scholars and men of letters. During the next few months articles for and against appear in quick succession. Certain details in this battle are both instructive and amusing.[1]

1. First, there is the attitude that Bédier calls "provisional doubt". This attitude Lanson adopts on the day after Dupuy's publication. In his article in the *Revue universitaire* he enumerates the reasons for agreeing with Dupuy's argument. The aspect of the manuscript, above all, is disturbing. Still, in many passages that Dupuy assigns to

[1] The essential contributions are Lanson, "Le Problème des œuvres posthumes de Diderot," *Revue universitaire*, May 15, 1902, pp. 460–465; and articles by G. Larroumet, in the *Temps*, September 1, 1902, and by Faguet, in the *Journal des débats*, September, 1902,—the first favorable to Dupuy's theory, the second adverse to it. In the *Revue d'histoire littéraire*, July–September, 1902, articles by Brunel (for Dupuy); M. Tourneux (against Dupuy); Dupuy (against Tourneux); Tourneux (answering Dupuy's reply); G. Grappe, "A propos du *Paradoxe sur le comédien*," *Revue latine*, October 25, 1902 (against Dupuy); E. Faguet, "Diderot et Naigeon," *Revue latine*, December 28, 1902 (against Dupuy); A. Aulard, two articles in the *Révolution française*, August 14, 1902, and January 14, 1903 (favorable to Dupuy); R. Doumic, "Les Manuscrits de Diderot," *Revue des Deux Mondes*, October 15, 1902 (for Dupuy); J. Bédier, "Le *Paradoxe* est-il de Diderot?" in *Études critiques*, pp. 83–112.

Naigeon, Lanson recognizes the 'touch' and the art of Diderot. Moreover, the argument based on the fact that everything that the *Paradoxe* adds to the *Observations* of 1770 is merely Diderot chopped up and then patched together may be reversed; as we know that Diderot frequently repeated and copied himself, comparisons with his other works might prove the authenticity as well as the falsity of the *Paradoxe*. However, Dupuy seems to have established with certainty that passages have been borrowed from works published after Diderot's death—a very strong argument, so long as it cannot be proved that Diderot may have been acquainted with them before their publication. "What has resulted", Lanson concludes, "is our inability to feel confident that we are reading pure Diderot when we read the *Paradoxe*: all is doubt and suspicion."

2. Next, there is the camp of those who seem to say, "I told you so!"—those who, in spite of the general admiration aroused for nearly a century by the *Paradoxe*, affirm that they always have thought "something was the matter with it". Larroumet recalls that quite a while before he spoke disparagingly of its artistic worth. Another says:

> This celebrated work bristles with inaccuracies, improprieties, incoherences, which strike me only now that they have been pointed out to me. But, in truth, I have always considered it diffuse, tedious, overrated, and, to be frank, I am thankful that I shall no longer have to blush for my lukewarmness.[1]

All these writers accept Dupuy's theory with satisfaction and do not hesitate to cross the *Paradoxe* off the list of Diderot's works.

3. At the other extreme is the camp of the "irreconcilables"—those who, whether for Diderot's sake or for Nai-

---

[1] Brunel, in *Revue d'histoire littéraire*, 1902, p. 500.

geon's, refuse to believe in the fraud. There is Tourneux, Diderot's well-informed and discriminating editor, who sets forth his arguments in the *Revue d'histoire littéraire*. Passing in review the history of Diderot's manuscripts, he tries to prove that the process of borrowing from himself is habitual with Diderot, and that his borrowing from books such as the *Mémoires* of Mme de Vandeul or of Mlle Clairon is far from being certain, or, if so, can be accounted for. Finally, in order to 'explain' the famous manuscript, Tourneux goes so far as to suppose that Naigeon made a copy duplicating every detail of Diderot's manuscript, putting the additions in the margins and reproducing and then erasing the passages written and then erased by Diderot himself. In short, he is convinced that the *Paradoxe* belongs, and can belong only, to Diderot.

The same conclusion is reached by Grappe, who is especially desirous to rescue the memory of the unfortunate Naigeon. He suggests that Naigeon wrote at Diderot's dictation, which would explain the aspect of the incriminating manuscript.

4. The quarrel is prolonged by an article by Faguet.[1] His fifty pages of criticism, common sense, and prudent, judicious reasoning, full of wit and malice, add to the debate a distinctive contribution of arguments from taste—the most delicate and unerring taste. In literary criticism I know few cleverer or more ingenious pages.

He wishes, as he says, to "filter" the whole discussion, and "to classify the arguments for and against in the following fashion: (1) arguments from fact; (2) arguments partly from fact, partly from taste; (3) arguments from taste".[2]

---

[1] In *Revue latine*, December 25, 1902.
[2] P. 706.

Arguments from Fact

First argument. The condition of Naigeon's manuscript. Tourneux's hypothesis does not hold. The idea of dictation is far from probable. The manuscript has still to be explained. Dupuy's position is very strong.

Second argument. "The *Paradoxe sur le comédien* abounds in passages borrowed by Diderot from several of his own works. 'Proof that it is not his', cries Dupuy. 'Proof that it *is* his', cry Tourneux and, with less assurance, Lanson and Brunel. Ah! Ah! This is becoming diverting."[1] After discussing this argument Faguet concludes that, since Naigeon as well as Diderot is imbued with Diderot's ideas and writings, the fact that a work is stuffed full of Diderot proves that it is either Diderot's or Naigeon's; if the question is to decide between the two, the fact proves absolutely nothing.

Third argument. The passages taken from the *Mémoires* of Mlle Clairon or Mme de Vandeul—or even from the *Correspondance* of Meister, with which Diderot is not acquainted. This is the pivotal point of Dupuy's demonstration. Here Faguet, after a detailed examination, reaches the following conclusion:

Since the manuscript sent to St. Petersburg in 1785 agrees with the Dupuy manuscript, it is clear that the latter was written before 1785. Therefore borrowings that cannot be explained by attributing the *Paradoxe* to Diderot are no less inexplicable if it is attributed to Naigeon. The argument would be tenable only if based upon a passage borrowed from some work that appeared between July 30, 1784 (death of Diderot), and October, 1785 (date of sending the manuscript to Russia), by an author personally unknown to Diderot. Proof of such a passage is lacking.

[1] P. 711.

Arguments Partly from Fact, Partly from Taste

"Every idea contained in the *Paradoxe* is already in the *Observations*", says one of the partisans of Dupuy's theory.[1] "The *Paradoxe* is only a paraphrase in dialogue form, amplified almost exclusively by means of examples." "That is not so", Faguet retorts. By a close analysis of the ideas in the *Paradoxe* he shows that there are several found nowhere in the *Observations*—fresh, interesting ideas, disproving the statement that the *Paradoxe* is simply a dilution of the former writing.

Next, it is said that "the *Paradoxe* bristles with inaccuracies and carelessness of style". "This is not quite exact", replies Faguet. Considering one by one every criticism of the style, he points out that some of the inaccuracies are so slight and insignificant as not to justify attributing the *Paradoxe* definitely to Naigeon;[2] again, that there are no more inaccuracies in the *Paradoxe* than in any other of Diderot's writings, which statement he puts to the test by opening a volume of Diderot—as he assures us—"quite at random". Inaccuracy is the penalty Diderot pays for his offhand, improvised style.

Arguments from Taste

There would be no need to appeal to arguments from taste, according to Faguet, if the arguments from fact were conclusive, but they are not. In this contingency arguments from taste are perfectly legitimate. He uses these arguments in two ways:

[1] Brunel, in *Revue d'histoire littéraire*, 1902, p. 501.

[2] Example: "Diderot, it is said, would never have written, 'une portion de votre habileté'. It is not good. It should be 'une part'. But to affirm that Diderot was incapable of using *portion* instead of *part*, absolutely incapable of using *portion* instead of *part*, so incapable of using *portion* instead of *part* that a work containing *portion* instead of *part* cannot be by Diderot—that seems to me too arbitrary." (P. 720.)

First, by means of examples thoroughly and shrewdly criticized, he demonstrates that the *Paradoxe* is neither desultory nor incoherent. He sees in the free, delightful swing of the dialogue Diderot's mind functioning quite characteristically; he sees him turning once more to the *Observations*, warming up, extracting new ideas, and arranging them not in cold, logical array but in their natural, vivid sequence.

Next, he shows that many of the alterations introduced into the text of the *Observations* by the *Paradoxe* are very happy ones, which perceptibly improve the text.

Finally, in the last and most striking pages of his article, he passes judgment on the *Paradoxe* as a whole. "They insist", he says, "that the *Paradoxe* is so badly written, is so devoid of taste,—in such poor taste! Diderot's? Never! Naigeon's? No difficulty there!" To this Faguet retorts that almost invariably the *Paradoxe* is very well written and full of taste of the best kind. Still, the real question at issue he defines as whether it is possible that Naigeon wrote it,— whether Naigeon was capable of writing it. Then, for about fifteen pages, Faguet quotes, in turn, long fragments of the *Paradoxe* and passages from Naigeon's genuine writings— the sparkling, sprightly, witty, brilliant pages of the *Paradoxe* and the insipid, tame, dull, heavy pages of Naigeon. Each time he maliciously adds: "This is how Naigeon writes when he writes the *Paradoxe*"; "This is how he writes when he signs himself Jacques-André Naigeon". He winds up ironically:

Thus there are two Naigeons: one, who is ridiculous writing as himself; the other, who is admirable writing as Diderot. The idea of producing something by Diderot exalts him to such a degree that he is transformed, and confers upon him, in their perfection, qualities precisely the reverse of his own. This is a very unusual phenomenon!

In conclusion, Faguet asserts that

a. The *Paradoxe* is not by Naigeon, because Naigeon was incapable of writing it.

b. The *Paradoxe* has "Diderot" stamped on almost every line.

c. The *Paradoxe* is by Diderot, or by someone equally skillful, possessed of his ideas, of his manner of exposition and turn of phrase.

d. In the *Paradoxe* what is of doubtful authorship amounts to about three pages out of sixty.

This is all very well. But the manuscript? "I do not try to explain it", says Faguet: "I pause before it. The arguments pointing to Diderot as the author of the *Paradoxe* have more weight with me than those based upon the Naigeon manuscript."

This, then, is where Bédier finds the question when in his turn he undertakes to explain the famous manuscript. Without recourse to history, bibliography, or arguments from style or taste, he is going to probe the manuscript for its secret.

"The dispute must necessarily centre round the Naigeon manuscript", says Dupuy; "that is the crux of the affair." Therefore Bédier concentrates upon it his attack, using for his preliminary study only the six pages reproduced by Dupuy in facsimile. On January 20, 1903, in his seminary at the École normale supérieure, he examines them closely with his students. His examination results in three observations and a hypothesis:

First observation. Every page is covered with erasures. The document looks like the manuscript of an author who has had difficulty in expressing his thought. But in the frequent additions in the margins there are no erasures. "What is this favorable influence that margins exert on Naigeon's talent?"

Second observation. There are many corrections or additions written in over the text between the lines of the manuscript. The lines themselves are, therefore, constantly crossed out, but the corrections or additions between the lines never show an erasure. If Naigeon has trouble in finding a definitive form for his idea while he is writing *on* the line, he discovers it immediately when he begins to write *between* the lines. What is this magical effect of interlines?

Third observation. There are numbers of corrections but never any *repentirs*; that is to say, Naigeon invariably writes a complete word or sentence before he corrects it. He fills his sheet first with an unbroken text, showing no indecision; then he scratches out certain words or parts of sentences and between the lines substitutes others, which also run off his pen without the least hesitancy. A weird and almost pathological way of working!

Thus Naigeon "is revealed to us as a writer who never decides upon a correction until he has filled out his line to the end; who is often dissatisfied with his first wording but delighted with the second; and whose style improves when he writes on the margins". How can these marvels be accounted for? By a very simple hypothesis.

Hypothesis. The manuscript is not the work of an author but of a copyist.

Naigeon first makes a copy of the *Paradoxe*. Later he becomes possessed of a second text of the work, revised by Diderot. "He might have written out a brand-new copy . . . [but] he notices that the alterations can be made on the copy he already has without damaging it too much. To save trouble he dispenses with rewriting the whole, and, minutely erasing letter by letter the readings that Diderot has sacrificed, he contents himself with correcting."

Thus everything is clear:

"Why should Naigeon, alone among writers, never correct in the lines but always between them?" Because the lines represent the first text; the additions above the lines, the second.

"Why should Naigeon, alone among writers, never correct himself twice?" Because his variations represent only the second form of the text.

"Why should Naigeon, alone among writers, never correct the marginal additions?" Because they reproduce the readings of the second text that were too long to fit between the lines.

You must bear in mind that Bédier forms his hypothesis solely upon the six pages of facsimile in Dupuy's edition. Therefore, in forming it, he makes "a triple wager that never in the thirty other pages of the manuscript will there be found (1) an erasure in the margins; (2) a double correction in the interlines; (3) a *repentir* that may not and should not be explained as an accident in copying".

Corroboration of the hypothesis. The next day, January 21, Bédier goes to the Bibliothèque nationale to see the manuscript, which Dupuy has deposited there. What answer does the manuscript give to these three questions?

1. Are there erasures in the marginal additions?—Never.
2. Are there double corrections in the interlines?—Never.
3. Are there any *repentirs*?—Never, except a few tiny mistakes that can be only slips of the pen.[1]

Moreover, the manuscript strengthens the hypothesis in an unlooked-for manner: the text in its original form is writ-

---

[1] As a matter of fact, there is one *repentir* or, at least, a correction having the appearance of one. For the sake of brevity I have not reproduced Bédier's discussion, which is a masterpiece of ingenuity and discernment. For the details, see *Études critiques*, pp. 93–94 and 102–107.

ten from beginning to end with the same ink; everything inserted above the lines, and all the marginal additions, are written with another, paler, more diluted ink.

Conclusions. The conclusions are various and precise.

1. The Dupuy manuscript furnishes no argument that casts a doubt on the authenticity of the *Paradoxe*. Bédier's contribution leaves things just where they were before its discovery.

2. Diderot, the 'improviser,' could on occasions remodel the same work three separate times; here he has been caught in the full swing of composition and revision.

3. Naigeon is reinstated and "amends [are] made for [his] having been considered for several months an 'audacious hoaxer', an 'impudent plagiarist', and a 'stupid forger'". His reverence for Diderot and his probity as an editor are made evident.

The *Paradoxe*, therefore, is restored to Diderot, no longer by reason of disputable impressions as to style but by a minute and exact critical process. We shall see that in many other cases the means of proof are far less precise and that we must turn almost entirely to external evidence. But the affair of the *Paradoxe* is so typical an example, and so clearly brings to bear every argument possible to employ in such a quarrel, that it deserves analysis.[1]

[1] An analogous question of authenticity, over which the discussion has been prolonged not for three months but for three centuries, is that of Book V of Rabelais. The question will repay a careful examination. The principal texts with which to begin the study are the following:

MARTY–LAVEAUX's edition of *Les Œuvres de Maistre François Rabelais*, Vol. IV, pp. 309–314. 1870–1903.

BIRCH–HIRSCHFELD. *Das fünfte Buch des Pantagruel*. Leipzig, 1901.

LEFRANC and BOULENGER. *L'Isle Sonnante*, text of 1562 (published by the Société des études rabelaisiennes) (8vo). Paris, 1906.

TILLEY, A. "The Authorship of the Isle Sonnante," *Modern Language Review*, 1906–1907, pp. 14 and 129; and many other contributions found in the *Revue des études rabelaisiennes* or in the *Revue du seizième siècle*.

CONS, L. "Le Problème du Ve livre de Pantagruel," *Revue bleue*, April 25, 1914; and the discussion in *Revue du seizième siècle*, 1914, pp. 273 and 279.

II. Problems of Attribution solved through Bibliographical Evidence

Problems of attribution are often solved by means of an attentive study of bibliographical evidence. In these cases it is hardly possible to speak of method: it is merely a question of exactness in research, of minute sifting of material, with an element of luck sometimes thrown in that enables us to lay our hands on an unnoticed bibliographical fact. Such evidence occurs oftenest in connection with short pieces—in prose or in verse—that make part of a collection. Whether owing to the error of a copyist or the negligence of an editor, whether from ignorance or from a wish to deceive the reader, writings are introduced under an author's name and afterward included in his collected works until such time as the necessary cleaning up shall be effected.

This process is carried out in one of the following ways:

1. Through the discovery and study of manuscripts hitherto unknown or overlooked, leading to the definite naming of the author of a work of uncertain origin.

2. Through a minute comparison of editions, leading to the recovery of the forgotten original printing of the piece that is handed down under the wrong author's name.

3. Through a close scrutiny of the collections brought out so frequently up to the end of the Romantic period, where many short writings, especially poems, appear before being incorporated, rightly or wrongly, in some author's works.

4. Through a search in correspondences, memoirs, literary or critical miscellanies, in which many small works see the light before being given to the public.

There is hardly an editor of the literature of the fifteenth, sixteenth, or seventeenth century who has not had to make restitutions by one of these means. Kervyn de Lettenhove, when publishing the *Œuvres de Georges Chastellain*,[1] one of the fifteenth-century *rhétoriqueurs*, attributes to Chastellain certain rondeaux that H. Guy returns to their rightful authors, Guillaume de Bissipat and Jean Marot.[2]

P. Jannet includes[3] in his edition of Marot's works a poem called *Douleur et volupté*, which Guiffrey's edition reproduces[4] among the pieces "falsely attributed to Marot", without, however, assigning to it other parentage. Guiffrey rests his decisions on personal impression. He feels that neither the pure Platonism of the little poem, the style, nor the meter is in the least "marotique". The true authorship remains in doubt until F. Gohin finds in the Bibliothèque nationale a manuscript of the poem, under the title *Epistre d'un amant prisonnier à s'amye par la Maison Neufve*. Now "la Maison Neufve" is the other name of the poet Antoine Heroet, whose whole work, in tone, ideas, and workmanship, resembles exactly *Douleur et volupté*.

Laumonier, in preparing his edition of the *Œuvres* of Ronsard, has to set many things to rights. The sixth volume[5] contains a group of poems "attributed to Ronsard", with notes giving the principal reasons for accepting or rejecting them. Two cases deserve special mention: the *Dithyrambes*,[6] which the former editors, Blanchemain and Marty-

---

[1] In 8 vols., 8vo. Bruxelles (Vol. VIII in 1866).

[2] *Histoire de la poésie française au XVIᵉ siècle* (8vo), Vol. I (*L'École des rhétoriqueurs*), § 40, p. 30. 1910.

[3] Vol. I, p. 117.

[4] Vol. II, p. 503. Villey, in his "Tableau chronologique des publications de Marot," *Revue du seizième siècle*, 1920, pp. 46 and 206, restores to Clément Marot, by the same kind of bibliographical evidence, several poems that are really his, and discards others that have been wrongly attributed to him. See also the articles by J. Plattard, "De l'authenticité de quelques poésies inédites de Clément Marot," *Revue des études rabelaisiennes*, 1912, p. 68, and *Bulletin de la société de l'histoire du protestantisme français*, 1912, p. 278.

[5] Pp. 447 ff. 8vo. Lemerre, 1914–1919.

[6] Ibid. pp. 182 ff.

Laveaux, denying to Ronsard, ascribe to Bertrand Berger, and Laumonier restores to Ronsard; and, on the other hand, three sonnets and an elegy of three hundred and thirty lines by Amadis Jamyn, which Blanchemain and Marty-Laveaux have incorporated in Ronsard's works.[1] The restitution of the first two sonnets is a good example of the rôle that a minute study of editions can play in these questions of attribution.

III. *OPUSCULES* AND *FACTUMS* OF PASCAL

In 1657, after the eighteenth *Provinciale*, Pascal suddenly breaks off the series of letters. This cessation is explained by historians to their own entire satisfaction—even by those most familiar with the heroic period of Jansenism—on one of the following grounds: Pascal renounces literary glory; he gives in to the prayers of the friends that keep preaching the spirit of charity to him; he has heard the voice of God himself in the miracle of the Holy Thorn, etc.

In reality, on March 17, 1657, the Assembly of the Clergy decrees the strict enforcement of the bull of Pope Alexander VII which declares open war and no quarter on Jansenism and its supporters and obliges every priest to sign a formula pledging himself to adhere to the formal condemnation of Jansen. This is what so brusquely stops the sequence of the *Provinciales*. The time has gone by for discussing whether or not the Jansenists are heretics. It has become a question of transferring the struggle from the theological to the judicial field: of prevailing upon the Parlement to refuse to register the bull on the plea of the legal nullity, as

[1] See the Introduction of Laumonier's critical edition (Société des textes français modernes, 1914), p. xiv, and, for details of the facts and arguments, his article "Trois pièces attribuées à Ronsard, restituées à Amadis Jamyn," *Revue d'histoire littéraire*, 1906, pp. 112 ff.

regards France, of the new pontifical act—"to shield the Jansenist doctrine behind Gallican liberties".

At this crisis[1] appears the *Lettre d'un avocat au Parlement à un de ses amis, touchant l'inquisition que l'on veut établir en France à l'occasion de la nouvelle bulle du Pape Alexandre VII.* Who wrote it? Lanson discusses and establishes the authorship in an article in the *Revue d'histoire littéraire.*[2]

PREVIOUS ATTRIBUTIONS

Early evidence is contradictory. Nicole is said to have attributed it to Pascal; Périer assigned it to Antoine Le Maître. Again, in a manuscript used by Faugère for his edition, the *Lettre* is inserted as a continuation of the eighteen *Provinciales*. To sum up, the attribution was uncertain, but the choice lay between Pascal and Le Maître. What are we to think?

INDICATIONS GIVEN BY AN ANALYSIS OF THE PIECE

1. *General indications.* The letter is full of canon law, which fact points to the lawyer Le Maître but does not exclude Pascal, who shows in the *Provinciales* that he can make a fine display of learning, authorities, and references.

2. *Particular indications.* Lanson first irrefutably establishes that two pages, at least, belong to Pascal. He discovers in the *Pensées* some notes that are clearly a rough draft, a skeleton, developed in the *Lettre*. Moreover, in the manuscript of the *Pensées* these notes are crossed off, which with Pascal is an habitual reminder that the material thus scored has been used elsewhere. Comparisons between other pages of the *Lettre* and notes in the *Pensées* prove that Pascal certainly wrote at least four or five pages of the work.

---

[1] June 1, 1657.
[2] "Après les *Provinciales*," *Revue d'histoire littéraire*, 1901, pp. 1-34.

3. *Arguments from style and skill.* "It is here," says Lanson, "that arguments based on style and on the general arrangement of the material, *which are valueless when they stand alone*, may reasonably be invoked. . . . If a single page is by Pascal, the entire letter is by him, because of the perfect unity of tone, taste, and movement." Lanson is to prove this by a detailed analysis of the artistic processes used in the letter.

He remarks that these arguments from taste have here a special force, for it is a question not of fleeting effects but of a method personal to Pascal, which his friends at Port-Royal could never have employed. If, therefore, in addition to the indisputable comparisons mentioned above, it is evident that the same literary and artistic processes are used throughout the *Lettre*, its attribution to Pascal is fairly well assured.

Now the *Lettre* shows

a. Fictitious characters introduced as spokesmen for his arguments;

b. The irony, so familiar in Pascal, so foreign to the staid gravity of the *Messieurs* of Port-Royal;

c. The logic of his opponent used to reach an absurd and revolting conclusion;

d. The same characteristics of style as in the *Provinciales.*[1]

The *Lettre d'un avocat* can thus with full security be assigned to Pascal.

It is important to notice, in the second half of the article, how Lanson applies the same method to the nine *Factums* of the "Curés de Paris" addressed to the "Vicaires géné-

---

[1] An argument that would be unconvincing, according to Lanson, if it were an anonymous work that was being assigned to Pascal, but one that has value because the choice lies between Le Maître and Pascal.

raux" against the *Apologie des casuistes* by the Père Pirot.[1]
The authorship of the *Factums* had been long disputed,—in
fact, since the seventeenth century. Some said that these
short pamphlets were "the work of Arnauld, Nicole, and
Pascal"; others, that Pascal wrote the second, third, and
seventh; Sainte-Beuve, that "Pascal had a hand in all of
them"; still others, that his collaboration was limited to the
fifth and sixth, or included the first.

Lanson, in taking up the question, bases his discussion on
intrinsic proofs. First, he accumulates comparisons of detail, which show that Pascal uses material from the *Provinciales*, from the *Pensées*, or from various notes; next, he
searches for what he calls those "marks of authorship that
are less visible and depend less than the general quality of
the style upon the individual impressions and sensitiveness
of the reader—favorite processes of reasoning, logical treatment, method of proof"; finally, he draws his conclusion
that the first, second, fifth, and sixth *Factums* are by Pascal
and should have a place in editions of the great Jansenist's
works. This short study is a model of rapid, sound, and
convincing discussion.[2]

[1] At the end of the year 1657.

[2] Still more brilliant is Lanson's demonstration, in the *French Quarterly*,
January–March, 1920, that the *Discours sur les passions de l'amour* is by
Pascal. Without going into details here, the essential point that he makes is
this: the *Discours* can belong only to Pascal, because, in comparing it with
the *Pensées*, similarities are found between it and the text that the editors of
the eighteenth and nineteenth centuries took from Pascal's manuscript, a text
unknown in the seventeenth century except to Pascal himself. If the *Discours*
were the work of some imitator of Pascal, it would resemble the text of the
Port-Royal edition; as it reproduces words and phrases not discovered before
the nineteenth century, its attribution to Pascal is the only possible solution.
This solution displeases certains *dévots* of Pascal, and it is indeed amusing to
see them setting forth arguments of mere 'feeling' which, of course, do not
hold against well-established facts.

IV. Problem of the Attribution of the *Discours*
DE LA SERVITUDE VOLONTAIRE

Is the *Discours de la servitude volontaire*—also known as the *Contr'un*—written wholly or partly by Montaigne's friend La Boétie, or is it not? If he did not write any of it, who is the author? If he wrote only a part, who is responsible for the additions and alterations? May it be Montaigne himself? This is the problem raised by a recent polemic.[1]

STATEMENT OF THE QUESTION

The facts are as follows:

1. Étienne de la Boétie dies in 1563, leaving his books and papers to Montaigne.

2. In 1571 Montaigne publishes the *Œuvres diverses* of La Boétie, not including in this edition, however, the *Discours de la servitude volontaire*. He explains that he does not give the book to the public because he finds its "façon

---

[1] The principal documents of the controversy are as follows: The offensive is taken by Dr. Armaingaud, "Montaigne et La Boétie," *Revue politique et parlementaire*, Vol. XLVII (March, 1906), p. 499, and Vol. XLVIII (May, 1906), p. 322. The replies come thick and fast: P. Villey, in *Revue d'histoire littéraire*, 1906, p. 727; P. Bonnefon, in *Revue d'histoire littéraire*, 1906, p. 737, and in *Revue politique et parlementaire*, Vol. LI (1907), p. 107; Strowski, "A propos de Montaigne," *Revue philomathique de Bordeaux et du sud-ouest*, 1907, p. 59 ("Montaigne et l'action politique"), with a rejoinder by Dr. Armaingaud, "Le Discours de la servitude volontaire," same volume, pp. 193 and 303; R. Dezeimeris, "Sur l'objectif réel du *Discours* d'Étienne de la Boétie," *Actes de l'Académie de Bordeaux*, 1907, with a reply by Dr. Armaingaud, "Le Tyran du *Discours de la servitude volontaire* est-il Charles VI?" in *Revue philomathique de Bordeaux et du sud-ouest*, 1907, p. 547. Also an article by Barckhausen, "A propos du Contr'un," *Revue historique de Bordeaux*, March–April, 1909, and a book by J. Barrère, *Étienne de la Boétie contre Nicolas Machiavel* (Bordeaux, 1908). Dr. Armaingaud gathers most of his articles, more or less revised, into one volume, *Montaigne pamphlétaire: L'Énigme du Contr'un* (8vo) (Paris, 1910).

trop délicate et mignarde pour l'abandonner au grossier et pesant air d'une si mal plaisante saison".[1]

3. In 1574 the *Réveille-matin des français et de leurs voisins*, a Protestant polemic of extreme violence and brutality, prints long passages in Latin and in French from the *Discours*.

4. In 1576, thirteen years after La Boétie's death, appears the *Mémoires de l'Estat de la France sous Charles le Neufiesme*, containing in the third volume, complete but still anonymous, the *Discours de la servitude volontaire*.

5. In 1580 Montaigne publishes the first edition of the *Essais*. The chapter "De l'amitié"[2] is a touching and immortal tribute to the tender affection that united him and La Boétie. At the beginning of the chapter Montaigne speaks of his intention to print in that very place the *Discours de la servitude volontaire*, "si gentil et tout plein de ce qu'il est possible". However, after writing his admirable pages on friendship, when on the point of adding the text of the *Discours* he changes his mind and declares point-blank that he is not going to print it:

Parce que j'ai trouvé que cet ouvrage a depuis été mis en lumière, et à mauvaise fin, par ceux qui cherchent à troubler et changer l'état de notre police sans se soucier s'ils l'amenderont, qu'ils l'ont mêlé à d'autres écrits de leur farine, je me suis dédit de le loger ici.

Here we have Montaigne about to print the manuscript and then abandoning his purpose; protesting against the published text and the use it has been put to, yet not attempting to counteract the effect by releasing the correct version; finally, keeping his own counsel as to how a copy fell into Protestant hands.

[1] "Avertissement au lecteur," August 10, 1570.   [2] I, 27.

Such are the historical data. Until 1906 the *Discours* or *Contr'un* is reprinted without question both among La Boétie's works and separately under his name. But in 1906 a revolutionary theory is advanced, defended with learning and eloquence, and the battle begins.

THEORY OF DR. ARMAINGAUD

The theory abruptly brought forward by Dr. Armaingaud may be summarized thus:

1. It is an error to believe, as has always been believed, that the *Contr'un* is simply a rhetorical exercise, an eloquent declamation against tyrants in general, which the Protestants take possession of because they can apply it more or less aptly to the Catholic king, their natural enemy.

2. It is an error to suppose, with the historian De Thou, that the *Contr'un* is a controversial paper written by La Boétie against Montmorency and Henri II on the occasion of the revolt of the Bordelais in 1548.

3. The truth is that the *Contr'un* is a political pamphlet explainable only if it is considered as directed against Henri III, king of Poland in 1573, king of France in 1574.

4. Therefore the most important pages of the *Contr'un* cannot be the work of La Boétie (this is the negative side of the thesis).

5. The alterations in the text, the inflammatory additions to La Boétie's vague schoolboy eloquence, are the work of Montaigne himself (this statement, subversive of every tradition, is the positive side of the thesis).

IMPORTANCE OF THE QUESTION

Is it necessary to dwell upon the importance of the question? If this daring thesis can be justified, all our ideas of La Boétie and of Montaigne must be revised. La Boétie must be stripped of his chief claim to glory,—the pages that have found an echo in France whenever the people have made a stand for liberty against an increasingly tyrannical autocracy.

Worse than this, Montaigne's image, the product of three centuries, must ruthlessly be effaced. We have thought of him, not as indifferent to truth, but as possessing a slightly skeptical and detached wariness which held him aloof, unscathed by the fray; respectful to the established government and to the State religion; not antipathetic to the persecuted Protestants, but hostile to the idea of taking part in the fight. Now we discover him actively involved in the political and religious struggles of his time, aggressive and in fighting mood, indignant at the massacre of St. Bartholomew, violently aroused against the "tyrant" and ready to proclaim his contempt,—to incite the people of France to revolt, if not to regicide.

Our idea of Montaigne's personal character as well is hopelessly upset. The delightful chapter on friendship,— "Je l'aimois parce que c'était lui, parce que c'étoit moy",— filled with a charm so touching that few read it without tears, cloaks one of the basest acts that a writer can commit. If Dr. Armaingaud's theory is correct, Montaigne, with craft and dissimulation, charges to the account of a friend, for whom he professes the warmest and most delicate affection, passages that he himself has written, and that at the time cannot help injuring his friend's reputation. He combines deceit with baseness.

It is easy to understand the excitement caused by such hypotheses, the violence with which Montaigne's friends contradict and fight them. Let us see how Dr. Armaingaud presents and sustains his position.

ARGUMENT OF DR. ARMAINGAUD

The negative part of the thesis consists in proving that the allusions contained in the *Contr'un* apply, and can apply only, to Henri III. To this end Dr. Armaingaud chooses first the important and celebrated passage of the *Discours* in which La Boétie describes the tyrant:

Voir un nombre infini . . . souffrir les paillardises, les cruautez, non pas d'une armée, . . . mais d'un seul, non pas d'un Hercules ni d'un Samson, mais d'un seul hommeau, et le plus souvent du plus lasche et du plus femelin de la nation : non pas accoustumé à la poudre des batailles, mais encore à grand peine au sable des tournois ; non pas qui puisse par force commander aux hommes, mais tout empesché de servir vilement à la moindre femmelette.

This portrait suggests to him a remark and a question : It is far too detailed to be a portrait of the traditional tyrant. If it is the portrait of an individual, whose portrait is it?

It cannot be, as De Thou will have it, an allusion to Henri II, a cruel but brave prince, a gallant knight, intrepid in tournaments, who by his amours with Diane de Poitiers and others gives the lie to the last trait mentioned by La Boétie. However, "there is a Valois in whose character all these blemishes are found—Henri III".[1] Hereafter Dr. Armaingaud, in his efforts to prove that every important allusion can refer only to Henri III and to his reign, finds two fields of investigation open to him :

1. "An analysis of the qualifications by which the author characterizes his tyrant, and a comparison between them and the well-known moral and physical traits of the Duc d'Anjou, later Henri III."[1]

2. An application of the same method to the deeds, events, and policies that the tyrant is responsible for.

[1] *Revue politique et parlementaire*, Vol. XLVII, p. 504.

This task Dr. Armaingaud undertakes equipped with a sound knowledge of history. At the end of his long pages of proof, the details of which it is useless to reproduce here, he is satisfied that he has established his thesis.

Up to this point, in the negative part of the thesis, Dr. Armaingaud applies only the entirely natural method of historical allusions.[1] In establishing his positive thesis that every passage denied to La Boétie must be attributed to Montaigne, he uses in succession three sorts of arguments:

a. Arguments of psychological probability drawn from the conditions of the publication of the "Contr'un." Dr. Armaingaud finds Montaigne's attitude suspicious and his sincerity open to doubt. Montaigne is La Boétie's heir, the trustee of his thought. He denies having had anything to do with publishing the *Contr'un*; but can he implicate himself without danger of death? His testimony is, then, valueless; his volte-face in the course of the chapter on friendship is disquieting. Besides, argues Dr. Armaingaud, no one else alludes to the *Discours* until 1574, no one except Montaigne knows of its existence, no one possesses the text; if, therefore, the text is given to the Protestants, who can have given it to them? If it contains incendiary passages that La Boétie cannot have written, who if not Montaigne can have written them?

b. Arguments of psychological probability drawn from Montaigne's political attitude. Dr. Armaingaud attempts to place the personal character and political record of Montaigne in such a light that what La Boétie cannot have written in the *Contr'un* only Montaigne can have added. The latter is in Paris, after the peace of Saint-Germain, from August, 1570,

---

[1] He does add one appeal to reason: The *Discours*, as De Thou says, violently roused its contemporaries. Would this be possible for a writing that dealt with the preceding reign, with events of sixteen years before?

to March, 1571; at court he finds tolerance in the air; he is ready to accept honors, perhaps a place in the government. Then suddenly he leaves the court and Paris for the solitude of his château in the heart of Périgord. Why? Is it not because he foresees the end of this tolerant policy, the approaching triumph of the fanaticism of Catherine de Médicis? In 1572 the Saint-Barthélemy, and the terrible massacres of Bordeaux and of Guyenne almost under his château windows, are sinister justifications of his move.

Again, what at this date are Montaigne's affiliations? Who are his associates? Protestants or 'tolerants.' Dr. Armaingaud carefully makes out a list with descriptive details.

Now at this moment (as Dr. Armaingaud explains) the Protestants are pulling themselves together, multiplying their appeals against tyranny. The *Contr'un*, one of their appeals, —a polemical treatise against the reigning tyrant,—appears anonymously when Montaigne, sole possessor of the text, is precisely in the frame of mind to write such a paper. What follows if not that Montaigne, sick at heart, rebellious, sympathizing with the vanquished, takes the occasion to publish La Boétie's dissertation touched up to further the desired end? In this way he can without too much risk express his feelings and serve the cause that is secretly dear to him, "mais jusqu'au feu exclusivement, si je puis", as he liked to say.

c. Arguments taken from Montaigne's personal attitude. Dr. Armaingaud believes that Montaigne gives us good reason to doubt his veracity.

(1) Montaigne tells us some fine tales about his ancient lineage, and certain episodes of his travels in Italy.

(2) He contradicts himself as to La Boétie: he first says that he composed the *Contr'un* at the age of eighteen, but later he corrects this to sixteen.

(3) The very way in which Montaigne announces that he is going to publish the *Discours de la servitude volontaire*, and then that he has changed his mind and is not going to publish it, is "an evident, intentional contradiction implying lack of sincerity".

(4) If it is true that the *Contr'un* has been published "à mauvaise fin", and that the work is of a sort "à troubler et changer l'état de notre police", Montaigne finds himself in the following dilemma: if at any time during the ten years from 1571 to 1580 he intended to publish the *Discours* in his book, it can have been only "à mauvaise fin" and in order to cause a disturbance; if he had no such intention, he deceives us by saying that he had and that he renounced it later.

Finally, if the text of the *Discours* has been mixed with "autre farine, altéré, falsifié", Montaigne's plain duty is, by publishing the genuine text, to reëstablish the facts. By not publishing it he defames the character of La Boétie, and out of this discreet, respectful magistrate of the established order he makes the revolutionary that posterity has thought him.

GENERAL CONCLUSIONS OF DR. ARMAINGAUD

1. The essential parts of the *Contr'un* are not by La Boétie.

2. That Montaigne has an understanding with the Protestant editors of the *Contr'un* is evident—not that he adopts the new religion, but that, after the massacre of St. Bartholomew, touched by "the unhappy and desperate cause", ill-content to "look on with an ironical smile", he actively enters the political arena.

3. Montaigne rewrites the *Contr'un* to make sure that La Boétie says nothing that he does not want him to say.

THE COUNTERATTACK

Such a theory is bound to stir up vehement opposition, which comes without delay. I need not go into details here. What interests us especially is not the contents of these articles but the methods we find in them; it is on this aspect only that I shall dwell.

1. *The reply of P. Bonnefon.* The adversaries of Dr. Armaingaud naturally attack each half of his thesis separately, in order to prove, first, that the *Contr'un* is not aimed at Henri III, and, next, that Montaigne cannot be held responsible for the additions and alterations imputed to him. Bonnefon replies to Dr. Armaingaud with the following arguments:

a. No established fact justifies the affirmation that the tyrant in the *Contr'un* is Henri III rather than any other contemporary prince—rather than the traditional tyrant. Dr. Armaingaud, becoming hypnotized by certain tempting resemblances, wants to twist everything to fit his hypothesis. Doubtless the *Discours*, infected with the general tone of the collections in which it has been published, has been open to interpretations and in places takes on a precise and specific sense; it is possible to read into its lofty pages an appeal against the power of the Valois; but it must be *proved* that these pages can be aimed at Henri III only, that they refer to events posterior to 1574 only. This, according to Bonnefon, Dr. Armaingaud does not do. He confuses possible applications of the text to certain historical events with indisputable allusions to these events.

b. As a matter of fact, the passages against the tyrant seem on close analysis like a rhetorical exercise conforming exactly to school traditions; the famous sentence supposed to describe Henri III is nothing but a long balancing of antitheses, where each clause suggests another. The literary analysis of the text, if carried out without prejudice, goes against Dr. Armaingaud's thesis.

c. If the Protestants add the *Contr'un* to their literature, it is as a piece of polemic against tyranny in general. They rearrange and elaborate the text but slightly here and there. If they wished, and if Montaigne wished, to make the *Contr'un* a deliberate attack against a given person, they would not fail to accumulate definite grievances, allusions clear enough to be understood by everyone; it is not effective propaganda to make allusions so vague that it is necessary to wait three hundred years—until the coming of Dr. Armaingaud—to discover in them open attacks on the king of France then on the throne! Probability, logical and psychological, is against Dr. Armaingaud's thesis.

d. Nor is strict chronology favorable to him. He continually mentions the *Contr'un* as a work published "in 1574 and 1576",—which, broadly speaking, is true. But we know definitely through other channels that the *Réveille-matin*, containing the famous sentence about the tyrant, the corner-stone of Dr. Armaingaud's entire argument, is printed before March 22, 1574. Thus every allusion must pass muster not only for Henri III but for the Duc d'Anjou, as he is known before that date,—and such is not the case. Before March, 1574, the Huguenots do not show any special hatred for the Duc d'Anjou, who has not yet mounted the "tyrant's" throne; on the contrary, they base their hopes on him. Chronology is, therefore, against Dr. Armaingaud's thesis.

e. Montaigne's contradictory statements, his volte-face, which seem so suspicious to Dr. Armaingaud, remain to be explained. In the collection of La Boétie's *Œuvres* that Montaigne publishes he is reluctant to include the *Contr'un*, whose dangerous nature he recognizes; he intends to join it to the beautiful chapter consecrated to the memory of his friend and withholds both chapter and manuscript until the first volume of the *Essais* shall be published. This day comes (1580); but, as the *Contr'un* has already been printed by the Protestants, Montaigne, vexed, refuses to harbor it in his book. The chapter, however, is already written and well written; the plan of it pleases him; and so he leaves it just as it is, explaining in a few additional lines why he does not keep his promise. In the *Essais* there are other instances of this practice; there is no need to look for diabolical or Machiavellian intentions. "The text", as Bonnefon wisely remarks, "makes perfectly good sense without distortion; the best thing to do is to stick to it, and not to search too curiously for all sorts of cabalistic meanings. Sometimes we are tricked through fear of being tricked."

2. *The reply of Villey.* To these common-sense and scholarly arguments Villey[1] adds others of even greater force, which once more show his fine critical sense. He aptly defines the attitude of mind of scholars who, like Dr. Armaingaud, have but "one idea": "They accumulate a mass of insignificant facts which, crystallizing round their ruling idea, give it apparent solidity." This is an excellent suggestion of method.

Like a clever lawyer, Villey, in the statement of his thesis, makes all possible concessions to his adversary:

Either La Boétie's text has not suffered glaring corruption, or else Montaigne is the author of the interpolations or a party to them. Let us accept the latter conclusion: if indeed there are in the *Contr'un* important additions directed against Henri III, Montaigne is responsible. But it is just this first point that has not been established: nothing shows that La Boétie's text has been fundamentally altered, metamorphosed by the first editors.

[1] *Revue d'histoire littéraire*, 1906, pp. 727–736.

a. Criticism of the allusions. Villey begins by attacking
the point that Dr. Armaingaud finds most striking: "non
pas qui puisse par force commander aux hommes, mais tout
empesché de servir vilement à la moindre femmelette". No
one but Henri III, according to Dr. Armaingaud, can be intended; on this assumption he builds his proof. "The language of the sixteenth century", Villey replies, "leads the
most wary into temptation"; Dr. Armaingaud, yielding to
the temptation, has mistranslated. *Empesché de* does not
mean "incapable of", but "engrossed by", "absorbed in";
other examples prove this. The question is settled, however,
by the Latin translation, published simultaneously with the
text: "qui impudicae mulierculae servitio totus addictus sit".
Thus Henri III is eliminated; the argument built on the
supposed allusion is unsupported. Dr. Armaingaud next
ransacks the character of Henri III for every other feature
of the portrait; doubtless with diligence some of them can
be found, but all are found with equal or greater certainty
in the traditional idea of the tyrant. The real sources of the
Contr'un are not the life or the reign of Henri III: they are
Rome, Greece, the Orient.

One by one, Villey discusses the different allusions tracked
down by Dr. Armaingaud, showing either that they do not
tally with history or that they would have been unintelligible to the public—which in a polemical pamphlet is un-
heard-of. Since all portraits of tyrants are alike, it is possible
for the Protestants of 1573 to appropriate La Boétie's *Discours*. "But we must not conclude that, because it is applicable to one epoch, it is inspired by the events of that
epoch. The multiplicity of the possible allusions proves that
there is no precise allusion to be found."

b. Uncertainty of its attribution to Montaigne. To demolish Dr. Armaingaud's second position Villey uses methods

of great interest, founded upon a detailed comparison of the language and the habitual processes of Montaigne with those of the author of the *Contr'un*. Villey proceeds as follows:

(1) When Montaigne quotes Plutarch, whether or not verbatim, he uses Amyot's translation; when the author of the *Contr'un* quotes Plutarch, which he does frequently, he never uses Amyot.

(2) When Montaigne cites the Latin poets he gives the exact Latin text: he never translates; above all, he could not have brought himself to translate into verse, for he cannot, as he says, "se souffrir en vers". In a parallel case the author of the *Contr'un* translates into French verse.

(3) Montaigne preserves the Latin form of ancient proper names: he writes "Darius", "Caecilius", "Pyrrhus", "Tacitus" or "Cornelius Tacitus"; "he does so on principle". The author of the *Contr'un* follows an exactly opposite principle: he writes "Daire", "Cécile", "Pyrrhe", "Tacite".

Dr. Armaingaud has the "impression" that the *Contr'un* is written in the same style as the *Essais*. Villey does not claim that his counterarguments are "absolutely decisive"; "nevertheless", he says, "placed in the opposite balance, I think they outweigh the argument that Dr. Armaingaud bases on a very subjective impression". To me they seem to sink the scales unhesitatingly.

I should be sorry not to quote here the last lines of Villey's article, in which he puts us on our guard, for delicate questions like these, against brilliant but precipitate hypotheses, and daring but ruinous conclusions.

If, with all his learning, Dr. Armaingaud has been able to advance so far without encountering a single obstacle that shatters his ill-founded hypothesis, do we realize with what circumspection we should test the ground we build on, and make sure of our corner-stones?[1]

[1] *Revue d'histoire littéraire*, 1906, p. 736.

I shall break off my account of this endless polemic at what I believe to be the victory of the Bonnefon-Villey party. The dispute spreads over more than three years, without contributing anything really new, without having recourse to any method that deserves careful consideration.[1]

V. Methods in Questions of Authenticity and Attribution

How shall we define and classify the methods and processes that we have seen operating in the solution of these widely different problems? "The instinctive tendency of the human mind is to pin its faith to any existing sign of authorship."[2] A name on a title-page, an attribution in a catalogue, are strong inducements to accept the authorship or the attribution without further discussion. Naturally, it would be ridiculous to doubt for an instant a work whose genuineness is beyond question; but when it is a matter of secondary works, unknown works, posthumous works added to the writings of an author long since dead, works published anony-

---

[1] To all the examples discussed here, add among others the following: H. Chamard, "La date et l'auteur du *Quintil Horatian*," *Revue d'histoire littéraire*, 1898, p. 54; P. Martinon, "Note sur le *Philandre* attribué à Maynard," ibid. 1908, p. 495; C. Beaugrand, "Est-ce un madrigal de Bossuet?" ibid. 1901, p. 35; G. Ascoli, "Bayle et l'*Avis aux réfugiés*," ibid. 1913, p. 517, an excellent article in which the discussion of the various internal and external proofs is managed with much skill. Finally, quite recently in an article in the *Temps* (October 16, 1919) Pierre Louys, the author of *Aphrodite* and of the *Chansons de Bilitis*, defended the thesis—unexpected, to say the least— that Corneille is the author of most of Molière's great comedies. His arguments do not seem to have made much impression on the world of scholars; nevertheless, it is interesting and amusing from the point of view of method to follow the discussion that this question provoked. See, in particular, A. Poizat, in *Revue bleue*, 1919, p. 682; P. P. Plan, in *Mercure de France*, Vol. CXXXVI (1919), p. 603; H. Lyonnet, in *Nouvelle Revue*, May 1, 1920, p. 33; H. Bidou, in *Revue critique des idées et des livres*, Vol. XXVII (1920), p. 1.

[2] Langlois and Seignobos, *Introduction aux études historiques*, p. 67.

mously or pseudonymously, our first attitude should be one of prudence if not of mistrust. If we look at the subject as a whole, the analyzed examples teach us certain definite lessons.

1. Beware of evidence too hastily gathered; do not announce a victory too soon; avoid premature conclusions: on a first reading, the famous Naigeon manuscript, for example, apparently leaves no room for doubt; Dr. Armaingaud's arguments have a disturbing force. Besides, do not statistics prove that attempts to deprive an author of some work that is universally attributed to him often result, when all is said, in restoring it to him with doubts removed?

2. In every case confine yourself to the text, without preconceived ideas, without the desire to prove at all costs its authenticity or lack of authenticity. You have watched Bédier, Lanson, Villey, and the rest reach their most decisive conclusions solely by close application to the text.

3. The process that seems to recommend itself in problems of this kind is the following: (1) after separating the facts sharply one from another, analyze and arrange them (compare Bédier's statements about the Naigeon manuscript, and Villey's study of the working-methods and mannerisms of the author of the *Contr'un*); (2) form a hypothesis as to the authenticity of a part or of the whole; (3) verify the hypothesis by returning to the text—the hypothesis, if correct, should allow you to explain every fact singled out in your preliminary work.

The arguments that arise in these problems in literary history resemble those found in the critical investigations of general history. They are of two sorts: arguments from internal analysis; arguments from external analysis.[1]

---

[1] See *Introduction aux études historiques*, chap. iii, "Critique de provenance," pp. 66–78.

INTERNAL CRITICISM

1. For such problems internal criticism or analysis consists first in collating all indications, information, and evidence bearing on the author and the origins of his work: the handwriting; the manuscript itself (its appearance, its peculiarities); the first edition or any interesting reprints,—in short, all bibliographical evidence as defined in another part of this chapter.

2. Next should follow the arguments we call 'philological': arguments based on the language, the vocabulary, the syntax; on mannerisms of expression and of style. Every great writer—often in proportion to his greatness—has turns of phrase, of expression, that belong only to him; personal tricks of style that may be sufficiently marked to enable us to identify him. Again caution is needed: a few isolated facts prove nothing; peculiarities may be seized upon by someone else and successfully imitated. Under the title *A la manière de* . . . two humorists have published a collection of *pastiches* of the best French writers, into which all the tricks of these writers are cleverly introduced; Voltaire knows so well how to imitate the style of one of his enemies that in after years the latter is deceived himself. Moreover, the language and the style of a writer are not fixed; in an early work they may not be definitely formed. At times the style varies with the work: Montaigne's *Voyages* seems in many places to be by a different hand from the *Essais*. Accumulated in sufficient numbers, however, these philological arguments, carefully studied and criticized, have great weight.

3. A third class of argument is drawn from the facts or names mentioned in the work—the allusions of every kind that it contains (we have seen such an argument used in the quarrel over the *Contr'un*). Chronology is of powerful as-

sistance here, not infrequently betraying the forger or the untrustworthy editor. Nevertheless, once more you must guard against unjustified conclusions: an historical allusion that chronologically cannot be attributed to a writer may reveal an interpolation, an addition, without condemning the whole work; allusions to works published after the one under discussion may mean only that the books mentioned were known and read before their publication, as often happened a few centuries ago.

4. It is only if we can produce some dependable arguments from internal analysis that we may safely add to them considerations of taste or personal impression. The latter should not be neglected: they may reënforce the proof (though they do not furnish it). Faguet guesses correctly about the *Paradoxe sur le comédien,* but others are deceived about Book V of Rabelais and about Montaigne. The best writers have their off moments, in which they produce pages unworthy of themselves. Or they may systematically affect different mannerisms (compare Montesquieu's style in the *Lettres persanes* with his style in some parts of the *Esprit des lois*). Finally, a writer may try to disguise his own style. In no case should the reader's subjective impression decide a question of attribution.

EXTERNAL CRITICISM

To the arguments from internal analysis should be added the information gained through external criticism.

a. The connection between the work and the life of the author, studied particularly in his correspondence and autobiographical documents.

b. The conditions under which the book is printed: if there is an editor, his worth and personality, the degree of confidence he inspires, etc.

c. References made to the document by contemporary witnesses or subsequent writers. This testimony should be criticized and studied with an eye to whether it follows a single tradition or represents different sources.

Rare are the texts that, subjected to an impartial examination, do not eventually give up their secrets. In every case the methods used in problems of attribution or of authenticity are those that need the keenest critical sense, those that connect most closely the historical study of literature with general history and its successful processes.

CHAPTER VIII

QUESTIONS OF VERSIFICATION

To describe in detail the methods used in the study of versification a thick volume would be needed: metres and rhythms constitute nowadays just as special branches as language or as literature itself, requiring a careful, complete technical preparation. If this preparation is too much to expect of a young student, he should at any rate gain a certain familiarity with the domain of versification—ground often touched upon by the works of literary history and sown with difficulties and obstacles. He should be able to prepare an intelligent commentary on a poem, to write without absurd heresies a chapter on the versification of an author, or to supply the introduction and annotation to a critical edition of a poetic work. The aim of the following pages is to help him in these undertakings.

The important and valuable aid furnished today to the study of versification by experimental phonetics will not be included. This, again, is a field for trained specialists working with an equipment and along lines of which it is impossible to give here a detailed account. Those who desire to initiate themselves may read with advantage works such as G. Lote, *L'Alexandrin français d'après la phonétique expérimentale*[1]; E. Landry, *Théorie du rythme*[2]; P. Verrier, *L'Isochronisme dans le vers français.*[3] They will find in them descriptions of instruments, and accounts of experiments and of the resulting conclusions.

[1] 2d ed., 3 vols. Paris, 1914.   [2] Paris, 1911.   [3] Paris, 1912.

For our purpose it will suffice, first, to make known the implements, the works essential to an understanding of the structure and the artistic elements of French poetry; next, to draw up an outline of research, a list of questions to be raised in studying a text in verse. By this means it will be easy to find the points that call for remark or discussion and to reach the literary and æsthetic conclusions that are their natural consequences.

I. Implements

The acquisition of bibliographical information regarding French verse is greatly simplified today by Hugo P. Thieme, *Essai sur l'histoire du vers français*.[1] The title might have been more judiciously chosen: it should be, rather, *Introduction bibliographique à la versification française*. The work has obvious faults, which the reviews in the special periodicals have emphasized without mercy. Indeed, there is little of importance in the first two hundred pages, which, commenting upon the references given in Part II, merely rearrange them; but in this second part there is a valuable and systematic enumeration of everything or almost everything that has been printed on French verse and related subjects. First, there is a comprehensive Bibliographie chronologique et analytique, extending from the documents of the early fourteenth century to works published in 1914, and completed by references to periodicals in every language, from the *Journal des savants* in 1665 up to 1914. Next follow Tableaux analytiques, where all references given elsewhere are reassembled under such headings as "Accent," "Alexandrine," "Assonance," "Ballad," "Cæsura," "Rhyme," "Enjambement," "Ode," "Quarrels and polemics," "Sonnet."

[1] 8vo. Paris, 1916.

Lastly, an Index chronologique arranges each text in its place in the bibliographical history of French verse. A few moments spent in glancing through this book will give an idea of what a help it may be. As has been justly said of Thieme's *Guide bibliographique*, it will always be possible to indulge in criticizing it and pointing out its errors, but it will never be possible to do without it.

For some of our students, nevertheless, Thieme's book has another shortcoming, for which the author this time is not responsible. He takes for granted that the reader knows the essential principles and terminology of versification as well as the allied problems of metre and rhythm. For those who feel this drawback the following works will serve as the necessary preparation:[1]

1. GRAMMONT, M. *Petit Traité de versification française.*[2]

LE GOFFIC and THIEULIN. *Nouveau Traité de versification française.*[3]

These two treatises are elementary but full of information and general ideas. They supplement each other so satisfactorily that to read them is an excellent initiation to the study of French verse. In Grammont's book the best chapters are those on rhythm (pp. 47–66) and harmony (pp. 104–125), and the conclusion (pp. 127–133)—a short but keen analysis of the evolution of French poetry from its origin. In the *Nouveau Traité* I recommend the chapters on the counting of syllables (pp. 10–31), on rhyme and its varieties (pp. 41–68), and on poems of fixed form (pp. 106–131). Perhaps it is well to warn the reader of the slightly oversystematic tendency of some of Grammont's opinions, especially concerning the rhythms of the classic Alexandrine (pp. 60–61).

---

[1] Here it is a question of versification only after the beginning of the sixteenth century.

[2] Paris, 1908.   [3] Paris, 1890.

2. DORCHAIN, A. *L'Art des vers.*[1]

Dorchain's book is an exoteric work, but intelligently exoteric and written by a poet. The general rules of versification are clearly set forth, and the artistic value of French verse is analyzed with finesse and simplicity. It forms an excellent introduction to the subject.

3. GRAMMONT, M. *Le Vers français. Ses Moyens d'expression, son harmonie.*[2]

The *Petit Traité* by the same author, mentioned above, is only a summary of this important work. Owing to the abundance of examples, the clearness of arrangement, the precision of analysis, Grammont's *Vers français* is the *vade-mecum* for every study of versification, especially for rhythms and the expressive value of vowels and consonants. As was the case with the *Petit Traité*, one should distrust certain narrow or too systematic views of the author on the rhythm of classic lines or the expressive value of sounds, and understand that his theories are neither definitely established nor universally accepted. It is also well to remember that Grammont's *Vers français* should be read in the *second* edition, much enlarged and improved.

4. BECQ DE FOUQUIÈRES. *Traité général de versification française.*[3]

If Becq de Fouquières's book contained only his ingenious but unfounded hypotheses concerning the origin of the Alexandrine, it would not be worth recommending. But once the first chapters are left behind, there follow the most able, the most artistic, analyses of rhythmic accent, with long series of well-chosen, well-arranged examples. In this respect he completes, and on many points helps to modify and correct, Grammont's conclusions.

[1] Paris, 1905.   [2] 2d ed. Paris, 1913.
[3] Paris, 1879.

5. TOBLER. *Vom französischen Versbau.*[1]

Tobler's *Versbau* is a standard work, not because it is perfect but because of its clear treatment of the metrical mechanism of French verse. On this point it is still of great use, although in the treatment of rhythms the two works just mentioned completely supplant it.

6. KASTNER, L. E. *A History of French Versification.*[2]

Although Kastner's work is slightly out of date on questions of rhythm, its chapters on the counting of syllables, on rhyme, and on fixed forms of poetry should be highly recommended. The great number of examples given makes it particularly valuable.

It should be well understood that these few references are intended merely as an introduction to the questions of versification. They will acquaint the student who has had little or no experience in this field (1) with the terminology[3] and (2) with the principles, and the technical and artistic processes, of French verse.

II. PLAN AND METHODS OF THE STUDY OF VERSIFICATION

"We are always compelled, we Frenchmen, to tell foreigners, confident of their learning and judgment, that there are some things in the French language and in French literature that only a Frenchman perceives, and that only he is qualified to appreciate."[4] It is certain that to understand French poetry, and, above all, to feel with precision its rhythm and harmony, presuppose an intimate familiarity

---

[1] 1st ed., 1880; 5th ed., 1910; French translation, 1885.

[2] Oxford, 1903.

[3] See Kastner, "Histoire des termes techniques de la versification," *Revue des langues romanes*, 1904, pp. 1–28.

[4] Lanson, preface to Hugo P. Thieme's *Essai sur l'histoire du vers français*, p. ix.

with the very spirit of the language; and it is unhappily certain also that many works on French versification written by foreigners show, together with much conscientious labor, a sad if not a ridiculous inability to grasp what constitutes French poetry. This remark should not be the cause of discouragement but of prudence. I fully believe that an American student can acquire a deep feeling for the beauty of French poetry and can comment upon it with insight and accuracy. Experience has proved this. Two indispensable conditions, however, are implied: first, the precise, technical apprenticeship already insisted on; next, and even more necessarily, a long training of the ear, a practiced sense of the harmonies and the accents of the French language. Without this training he runs the risk of preparing dry, tedious, profitless statistics, like those Germans who count rhymes and cæsuras in Antoine de Montchrestien or fill over a hundred pages with charts of Rostand's rhymes in *Cyrano de Bergerac*; or perhaps—and this is even more to be feared —he exposes himself to random conclusions about things he cannot understand.

Let us suppose, then, that the necessary preparation is completed. How should a study in versification be carried on? What questions should be raised? What arrangements chosen?

A general division should first be laid down: (1) Each line should be studied separately, and (2) the lines should be considered in their mutual relations.

There will remain a third series of questions,—the most important of all,—those on the relations between the poetic expression and the subject treated.[1]

[1] The plan of study outlined here seems, barring certain more or less fundamental modifications, to be generally adopted in recent works on versification. Here are varied examples, chosen from many, that may be examined

LINES CONSIDERED SEPARATELY

Each line taken by itself gives rise to three sorts of remarks, varying in importance with the instance.

1. *Syllabic structure: description of the line.* How many syllables has the line? Should it be given a particular name? A word or a figure usually suffices to answer these questions. The only point that may present any difficulty is the number of syllables. Lines exist where either the presence of a mute *e* or of a word in which the number of syllables is uncertain raises a problem. It is, however, almost always simple to collect the material and examples necessary for the kind of historical or logical explanation required.[1]

2. *Rhythmical structure.* It is when undertaking the commentary on rhythm that the real perplexity of the student is likely to begin. It is here, besides, that he specially needs definite ideas. The treatises and manuals, in offering him information, are liable to confuse him further. In them occur the words "cæsura," *coupe*, "pause," "rhythm," "ac-

and discussed before undertaking researches in this field: L. Clément, "La Versification de La Fontaine," *Revue universitaire*, Vol. II (1892), pp. 282–302; M. Souriau, *L'Évolution du vers français au XVIIe siècle* (Paris, 1893) (see Brunetière's critical contribution, in *Revue d'histoire littéraire*, 1894, p. 497); P. Nebout, *Le Drame romantique* (1895) (interesting for the study of the influence on versification exerted by the new dramatic forms); M. Souriau, "La Versification de Lamartine," *Revue des cours et conférences*, Vol. VII (1899), pp. 841–860; A. Beaunier, "Le Vers libre," *Mercure de France*, 1901, pp. 613–633; Jasinski, *Histoire du sonnet en France* (Douai, 1903); Chatelain, "Le Vers libre dans *Amphytrion*," *Mélanges de philologie offerts à M. Brunot* (1904), pp. 41–55; A. Cassagne, *Versification et métrique de Ch. Baudelaire* (Paris, 1906); D. Mornet, *L'Alexandrin français dans la deuxième moitié du XVIIIe siècle* (Toulouse, 1907); A. Rochette, *L'Alexandrin chez Victor Hugo* (Paris, 1911); P. Martinon, "La Versification de Corneille," *Revue des cours et conférences*, Vol. XXII (1913), pp. 198–205.

[1] See Thieme, p. 372, for references on the question of the mute *e*, and the opening chapters of Le Goffic and Thieulin or of Kastner for those on the number of syllables in doubtful words.

cent," "measure," defined in twenty ways—sometimes differentiated, sometimes used nearly synonymously. He will
find contradictory interpretations and theories; he will see
that German scholars have based on syllabic quantity and
on accent a theory of rhythm in French verse that French
theorists have in general energetically disclaimed. Among
French theorists themselves there are as many doctrines as
treatises; the same line, quoted as an example in two works,
may be scanned in different ways. If he opens the *Vers
français* of Grammont, he will read a very acceptable theory
of the Romantic trimeter and, in turning to Rochette's thick
volume entitled *L'Alexandrin chez Victor Hugo,* he will notice
that the author practically denies the existence of this trimeter. The *Réflexions sur l'art des vers* of Sully-Prudhomme,
who was a good poet, is radically contradicted by the writings
of Verlaine, Gustave Kahn, Souza, and many other poets
belonging to the younger schools. Even the so-called scientific conclusions of experimental phonetics do not seem to be
unanimous: Landry, in concluding his enormous *Théorie du
rythme,* apparently reaches a definition on an essential point
—the equality of the intervals between stresses—that dis-
agrees with that reached by Lote at the end of his still more
gigantic work entitled *L'Alexandrin français d'après la phonétique expérimentale.* Indeed, "grammatici certant . . ."[1]

Face to face with this chaos of definitions, of ideas, and
of doctrines, nothing can equal the bewilderment of the student who is obliged to handle these questions, unless it is that
of the professor whose duty it is to explain them to him.
And this is precisely the difficulty that delays us now.

It would be unacceptable dogmatism to set up one more
system and to attempt to thrust it upon my readers. Doubt-

[1] An idea of the complexity of the question may be had from Thieme's historical outline of it, chap. ix, pp. 154–196.

less it seems to me that a certain number of points have been established, on which I base comments in the classroom and opinions as to my personal reading. I follow the majority of the theorists of the present day in believing that poetic rhythms may be defined as the recurrence at approximately regular intervals of stress, or rhythmic accent. I believe that, through a gradual evolution, French verse, purely syllabic at the start, with pauses or cæsuras in fixed positions, has progressively grown into a verse whose artistic effect is based on a rhythm produced by accents, or stress. The duration of the rhythmic measures varies only slightly; the number of syllables contained in these measures may vary considerably. It is necessary, then, for the delivery to be retarded or hastened so that the last tonic syllable of the group inclosed in a measure shall coincide with the stress that marks the end of the measure. If to this we add the expressive, melodic, and harmonic value of vowels and consonants, we have every element necessary to the analysis and æsthetic appreciation of French verse. The existence of the trimeter, which, although found in all our great poets since the sixteenth century, is called Romantic—a line of three metrical units instead of the four contained in the so-called classic Alexandrine—seems to me an established fact. It must be understood, however, that this, as well as many other details that might be added, is neither indisputable nor universally admitted.

How, then, shall the student be guided and advised? His effort, it seems to me, should be successively directed toward three points: first, the acquisition of an intimate familiarity with French poetry; next, the building up of a technical knowledge of the various terminologies and doctrines offered to him; lastly, the adoption of a personal attitude that will enable him to judge, feel, and comment intelligently.

I do not hesitate to insist once more upon the necessity of a personal and prolonged acquaintance with French poetry before attempting either commentary or discussion. It is the same with poetry as with music: ear-training is the indispensable preliminary condition of any technical apprenticeship. It is superfluous to teach harmony or counterpoint to someone who does not know whether a chord is in tune or a measure in time. Although it is true that Beethoven became deaf, he was not deaf during the years when his genius was forming. When the ear feels the rhythm of the line, then, and then only, is it possible to theorize and to comment on this rhythm.

Next, the student must look up the question of terminology and the principal systems involved in the discussion. Many of the obscurities that he encounters come from the fact that the same word is used for different things: "cæsura" is a good example of this. If the cæsura is defined as "a rest for the voice, marked in the interior of the line by a tonic syllable more strongly accented than the other tonics in the line",[1] this definition, which is exact for the ancient French line, is found to be already less applicable to many of the classic lines, and difficult to apply at all to Romantic verse. If it is defined as synonymous with the rhythmic *coupe*, this explains neither the ancient line nor the classic Alexandrine. The student should, then, first of all be clear in his own mind, and oftener than not it is the history of French verse that will enlighten him. What was the condition of versification at a given epoch? What were its canons and its technique? In what sense would the poet he is studying have understood the terms that seem to him vague and confused? It is his own affair, through research and reading, to form a technical vocabulary in which each word shall finally assume

[1] Le Goffic and Thieulin, *Nouveau Traité de versification française*, p. 69.

a distinct value; this is why I refrain, in these questions of rhythm, from giving any ready-made definitions.

The same may be said of systems and doctrines. Through reading, reflection, attentive and open-minded study of the texts, the student who at first will feel at sea, and buffeted about from system to system, will notice that gradually certain ideas are taking shape in his mind. By using elementary works as a starting-point, verifying definitions, distinguishing from among the different theories those that are dangerous hypotheses, excessive systematization, or the exclusive creed of a single school, he will succeed in constructing a system for himself, not original, of course, but coherent, clear, well-assimilated. And on this foundation he will base his personal studies and commentaries.

Thus, when the occasion arises, he will possess the elements with which to answer the necessary questions as to the rhythmical structure of a line:

a. Where do the rhythmic accents occur?

b. From the number and place of these accents how should the line be described? For instance, if it is an Alexandrine, is it a tetrameter or a trimeter? Is the *coupe* usual, rare, traditional, original, etc.?

c. What is the æsthetic and expressive value of the rhythmic structure in this line? What effect is produced (majestic slowness, balance, rapidity, lightness, etc.)?

Is it necessary to add that it is, above all, in this commentary on rhythm that the student's accuracy of ear and depth of artistic feeling are disclosed?

3. *Harmonic structure.* There remains to be studied the question of "sounds considered as means of expression".[1] Without doubt, in the work of real poets there is a relation between the sound of the words and the ideas or the feelings

[1] Title of the second part of Grammont's *Vers français* (2d ed.), p. 193.

they express. Poetry has analogies with music: "Vowels are kinds of notes." Combined with consonants they form groups of sound whose tone, brilliance, softness, and duration are infinitely varied. Assonance, repetition, alliteration, skillfully used and artistically combined with certain sounds, are the means that poets use to give their lines melody and harmony. These delicate shades are brought out, analyzed, and explained by the study of the poetic text.

Now into the study itself must be put much delicacy and many shadings. There is great risk of drying up everything that is touched and of crushing the poem under a weight of commentary. Such clumsiness gives rise to a certain ironic skepticism in regard to minute studies of this kind. We hear people say: "Do you suppose that the poet thought of all those things when he wrote his lines? Do you believe that he said to himself: 'Here I am going to use alliteration with *m*; here, multiply the *gr's* and *cr's*, so as to obtain a harsh effect; here, construct my line on the sound of *é* to make it clear and light'? You do not give him credit for spontaneous inspiration."

To this objection the reply is simple. On the one hand, it is primarily a question of explaining the why of the impression produced in a line: as sounds have much to do with that impression, it is legitimate to analyze the sounds. "It is these details", said Théophile Gautier, in his study on Baudelaire, "that make poetry good or bad and that make a poet good or bad". On the other hand, I am convinced that frequently these effects are intentional on the part of the author: he is well aware of the expressive value of sounds and wants to profit systematically by them. The best proof of this is found in his corrections in the manuscript. It is there that we trace the effort to interweave the sounds little by little so as finally to express the inner melody heard by the poet. One day José-Maria de Heredia, commenting to a friend on an admirable sonnet that he had just written, said: "Here I first put *je ne sais*; but how much better *j'ignore* is! How well that *o* sounds with the other *o's* in the next line!" In many cases it is not defaming a poet to credit him with very definite intentions, even when the perfect, easy form of the finished line seems to exclude all idea of preliminary reflection.

Therefore the harmonic structure of each line may—indeed, should—be studied with minute care. On this point the best guide seems to me to be Grammont, whose analyses are extremely detailed and are followed by abundant examples. If you make allowance for his too great love of systematizing, you will learn easily from him how to establish with accuracy this important part of the commentary.

GROUPS OF LINES

When the commentary on each separate line has been completed, the lines must be studied in their mutual relations and groupings. Three series of questions arise here: rhyme, enjambements, arrangement of lines in strophes or in poems of fixed form.

1. *Rhyme.* The study of rhyme offers no great difficulty, after the few technicalities connected with it have been thoroughly mastered: the difference between assonance and rhyme; the various sorts of rhyme (poor, sufficient, rich); the various possible arrangements of rhyme (*rimes continues, plates, croisées, embrassées, tiercées, mêlées,* etc.).[1] You will have treated the subject amply in a given poem if you have defined the quality of the rhymes used, the arrange-

[1] Questions relative to rhyme are treated with special clearness by Le Goffic and Thieulin and by Kastner.

ment adopted, and lastly—when occasion arises—the artistic effects produced by their combination.

2. *Enjambements and rejets.* Enjambement and rejet are not two different things: "When a phrase is begun in one line and ended in the next, without completely filling the second, we call this 'enjambement,' and the end of the phrase that has run over into the second line is the 'rejet'."[1] Attention should be paid to the following points: (1) the frequency of the enjambements and their proportion to the total number of lines in a poem; (2) their purpose and the effects produced by them. Enjambement is one of the details of French versification that have varied most in the course of time: rare in ancient poetry, used with growing discrimination in the fifteenth and sixteenth centuries, forbidden by Malherbe and by Boileau, it assumes new importance with Chénier and becomes one of the favorite means of expression of the Romanticists, especially of Victor Hugo. It will be wise, therefore, in commenting on the *rejets*, to state what is the usage of the poet compared with the general usage of his time.

3. *Grouping of the lines.* The rhythmical combinations according to which lines may be grouped remain to be considered. Three cases occur:

First, there may be a succession of lines of the same kind; if so, the question is much simplified. How does the poetic phrase develop? What advantage has the poet taken of the rhythmic resources of his line? Has he framed long periods that spread over several lines, or does he cut the monotonous cadence by frequent, unexpected, bold breaks? In short, the adaptation of the poetic form to the general movement of inspiration and thought should be described.

[1] Grammont, *Petit Traité*, p. 20.

Next, the text may be what is called a poem of fixed form: *rondeau, ballade, chant royal, lai, virelai, villanelle, sonnet,* etc.[1] In this case it is important first to gain a clear idea of the rules and traditions of the form used and then to decide to what extent the text conforms to accepted canons or breaks away from them. The form chosen may, besides, be well or ill adapted to the feeling or the thought that the poet wishes to express—and this suitability should be closely analyzed.

Lastly, lines may be grouped in strophes. The ground here is more difficult; the student may come face to face with somewhat contradictory definitions and theories. He will find a wise guide—though one not always easy to follow—in the huge work by Martinon on *Les Strophes.*[2] An historical introduction treats the development of every variety of strophe since the time of Marot. There follows a detailed study of each strophe, with many examples; finally, a *Répertoire général des strophes* makes comparison easy by giving with the necessary references a list of the poets who have used each form of strophe. The general method adopted by Martinon points the way for special studies on the strophes of a given author or work. We see that there are three series of questions to ask: (1) the number of lines (the most evident and superficial characteristic); (2) the order of the rhymes (the arrangement determines what may be called the rhythm of the strophe, and clearly indicates the type of the strophe in the category to which its length assigns it); (3) the nature of the lines that make up the strophe, and the order in which they are arranged—whether

---

[1] Le Goffic and Thieulin, as well as Kastner, explain with precision and simplicity the various poems of fixed form. In Thieme, pp. 359–387, will be found the essential bibliography for each form.

[2] P. Martinon, *Les Strophes. Étude historique et critique sur les formes de la poésie lyrique en France depuis la renaissance* (8vo). Paris, 1911.

one kind of line only is used (*strophes isométriques*), or whether there is a combination of lines of various lengths (*strophes hétérométriques*). Thanks to Martinon's list and tables, it will always be simple to classify any variety of strophe. The use to which the poet has put his means of expression will remain to be shown.

ÆSTHETIC COMMENTARY

All that has been said up to this point is but the technical study preliminary to what should be the real and essential aim of all commentary on versification—the artistic and æsthetic analysis. The line is only the harmonious covering for thought and emotion; it is the delicate instrument touched by the true poet, whose music in its turn touches our hearts. But the poet succeeds precisely because he employs the processes that we have just been studying. Therefore how and why he succeeds must be made clear. I do not refer to declamatory effusions full of vague admiration. Nothing is worse. I ask, first, that the student understand and feel, fully and sincerely, what the poet has in his mind or in his heart; that he share these ideas and feelings; then, that he trace the poet's attempts at expression, through rhythms, harmonic values, interplay of rhymes, *coupes,* and strophes; that he show whether the poet, through inspiration or through patient toil, has indeed found the most expressive, the most suggestive, the most moving forms. In this way he will have accomplished a task infinitely more worth while than the piling up of laudatory epithets and exclamation points. He will have learned to understand, to appreciate, to feel.

CHAPTER IX

TREATMENT OF BIOGRAPHICAL MATERIAL IN THE HISTORY OF LITERATURE

There is scarcely a work on the history of literature that does not devote a certain space to biography. In a monograph on a writer its place will be large. In the study of some particular work, even of some *genre* or of some current of ideas, biographical elements of varying importance must often be introduced. Indeed, the relation between a book and the personality of its author is of necessity so close that a knowledge of the work presupposes complete acquaintance with the antecedents and the life of the writer. It is therefore indispensable to reflect for a time upon the treatment, and more particularly upon the collecting and selecting, of biographical material in literary history.

I purposely restrict myself to this aspect of the question. It is the province of special books to develop a theory of biography and to analyze its principal characteristics and regulations. My aim is to point out to the student from what angle, in a literary essay, it is well to treat biography; what type of material is especially suitable; and on what features it is important to throw the strongest light.[1]

---

[1] An excellent treatment of the question discussed in this chapter is found in D. Mornet, "Les Méthodes de l'histoire littéraire étudiées à propos d'une œuvre: *La Nouvelle Héloïse*," *Revue des cours et conférences*, Vol. XXII[1] and XXII[2] (1913–1914). But a familiarity with Sainte-Beuve's works is undoubtedly the best training in the handling of literary biography. Some pages of great interest are found in *Nouveaux Lundis*, Vol. III, article on Chateaubriand; *Portraits littéraires*, Vol. I, pp. 29 ff.; *Port-Royal*, Vol. I, chap. i. See also the following works dealing with Sainte-Beuve's methods: Faguet,

In one of Pailleron's comedies an author, engaged in preparing a book, takes every occasion pompously to announce
its title: "Murillo: sa vie, son œuvre." Life and Works—how
many theses have been ruined in advance by the adoption
of this stereotyped plan, which, by arbitrarily separating
the biography from the historical and critical study of the
works, condemns the author either to a series of useless and
fatiguing repetitions (if he wishes to refer to the biography
in his explanation of the works) or else to a biographical
narrative in which the facts and dates, isolated from the
study of the works, lose a large part of their interest!

For the historian of literature the final and essential aims
should be the interpretation of the literary work and the
analysis of the literary personality of the writer. These aims
determine the spirit in which the biographical researches
should be undertaken: they should be the means not of
satisfying a predilection for anecdotes but of elucidating the
writer's work and personality. William Mathews has written a clever page denouncing the futility of these infinitesimal researches on which the efforts of biographers are often
expended—a page that doubtless was not hard to write or
to make entertaining. "What matters", he says, "if a book
charms, inspires, or instructs us, whether the author smoked
or drank stimulants; or borrowed money, or forgot to pay

Politiques et moralistes du XIXe siècle (third series, 1900), pp. 185 ff.; Lanson,
Avant-Propos of *Hommes et livres*. It will be helpful to read F. S. Stevenson,
Historic Personality (London, 1893); L. Stein, "Zur Methodenlehre der Bio-
graphik," in *Biographische Blätter* (herausgegeben von A. Bettelheim, Berlin),
1895, Vol. I, pp. 22–39; L. Arnould, "La Méthode biographique de Sainte-
Beuve," *Correspondant*, December 25, 1904, and his "La Méthode biographique en critique littéraire," which prefaces the volume *Quelques Poètes* (Paris,
1907); S. Lee, *Principles of Biography* (Cambridge, 1911); W. H. Dunn, *English Biography* (London, 1916), especially chap. ix, "Problems and Tendencies
of the Present"; W. R. Thayer, "Biography in the XIXth century," *North American Review*, May–June, 1920, and published in book form (New York, 1921).

his tailor and his washerwoman; whether he quarreled with his wife, separated from his wife, was divorced from his wife, or kept out of the matrimonial noose altogether? To know the vices and weaknesses of a great writer, his oddities and eccentricities and manner of life; to know that Pope had a voracious appetite for stewed lampreys, Dr. Parr for hot lobsters with shrimp sauce, and Johnson for a leg of mutton; . . . that Byron shaved his brow to make it look higher, and found his inspiration in green tea, tobacco, and semi-starvation; that within the Chateaubriand of *Atala* there was an obscene Chateaubriand that indulged in the coarsest talk,—to know all these petty details is pleasant, and gratifies a natural curiosity; they give picturesqueness and charm to biography; they may help occasionally to explain the growth and prominence of some idiosyncrasy, or some characteristic sentiment or idea; but how a knowledge of them is necessary to a just estimate of the literary productions of these authors, it is hard to see."[1] This is, however, too casual a dismissal of the question. If the biographer has the "exquisite tact" and the "appreciation of nuances" so dear to Renan, he will know how to discriminate and choose; he will know how to show that many of these details, which are so easy to make fun of, are very useful, if not indispensable, for a just estimate of the character and the art of the writer. After all, a knowledge of Lamartine's pecuniary difficulties explains many shortcomings in his style. Victor Hugo's walks on the rocks at Guernsey, La Fontaine's habit of taking daily strolls, help to explain their feelings toward nature. And to know when and how Alfred de Musset began to drink is not superfluous for fathoming his later works. Even if it is quite true that we can "pronounce upon the beauty and

---

[1] Introductory essay to the translation of a selection of Sainte-Beuve's *Causeries du lundi* ("Monday Chats"), pp. lviii–lx. Chicago, 1877.

perfume of a rose without analyzing the soil whence it sprang", it is no less true that the real rose-lover, he who wants not only to enjoy the flower momentarily but to know all about it and, if need be, to reproduce it, must consider the question of the soil and will not be satisfied until he has solved it. Of this sort is the legitimate curiosity of the historian of books and authors: he realizes that he can understand neither the book nor the author if he separates his life from his work.

There are, besides, excellent reasons of another kind for adopting this policy. Numerous examples remind both the historian and the critic of the wise rule that biographical precision should be the basis of psychological conclusions. He knows that the most ingenious analyses, the most seemingly logical deductions, may be shattered by fresh biographical details duly established. He thinks of the number of pages that become obsolete as more accurate information brings out salient biographical facts. Are examples necessary? Take Molière and *Tartuffe*: the biographical documents unearthed within the last fifteen years have certainly changed the traditional interpretation of the comedy. And how about Molière's distant ancestor, the Pierre Gringore whose legendary figure fills the pages of *Notre-Dame de Paris* and Banville's delightful play? Up to within a scant dozen years it has been difficult to think of Gringore in any other light. But historians have been at work; successively Oulmont and Guy, stripping the legend from Gringore, have disclosed the real man.

It is indeed regrettable that the real Gringore bears no resemblance whatever to the Gringore conceived by the Romanticists. Nothing in him recalls either the proud, independent artist with heroic, chivalrous soul that Théodore de Banville has drawn, or the starving "Gringoire" in *Notre-Dame de Paris*. . . . Yes, picture to yourself a person no longer young, lacking in enthusiasm, a stodgy, humdrum bourgeois, a Joseph Prudhomme armed with proverbs, a petty official reflecting the opinions of his superiors, a model of circumspection, a dealer in poetic wares who never leaves his counter,—and you will see before you the real Gringore.[1]

There has been the same readjustment of ideas relative to the poet Nicolas Gilbert. In his case it is not only Vigny's touching pages but the entire tradition that had to be revised when well-informed biographers brought to light, in place of the romantic Gilbert dying on a straw pallet in an unheated garret, "au banquet de la vie infortuné convive", a poet in easy circumstances, possessed of a fairly disagreeable nature and a knack of finding useful patronage.[2]

Finally, much that has been written about the exotism of Chateaubriand in his rôle of traveler, his powers of observation, and the sincerity of his descriptions, was seriously impaired when Bédier's precise researches[3] established, for the writer's stay in America, his itinerary almost day by day. Was it not Stendhal who remarked that the cleverest and wittiest man alive stands agape before the blockhead who knows a date?

Such is the vital importance of biographical precision in the deductions of literary history. How can it be attained? I believe that here we can find, if not rules and recipes, at least a trustworthy, attractive guide—I mean Sainte-Beuve. There is no surer training than to read and reread the best

[1] H. Guy, *Histoire de la poésie française au XVIe siècle*, Vol. I, pp. 278 ff. See also C. Oulmont, *Pierre Gringore* (1911).

[2] See, on the one hand, Alfred de Vigny, *Stello*, chap. xi, "Un Grabat"; and, on the other hand, H. Potez, *L'Élégie en France avant le romantisme* (1897), or Johann Weiss, *Nicolas Gilberts Satiren* (1896), corrected by the documents published by H. Druon, in *Correspondant*, August 25 and September 10, 1897, and by Laffay, *Le Poète Nicolas Gilbert* (1898).

[3] "Chateaubriand en Amérique," *Études critiques*, 1903.

of his *Portraits littéraires* or of his *Causeries du lundi,* with attention to the way in which he makes biographical information the very basis of his literary criticism. Little by little the true technique of literary biography evolves itself, made up not of mechanical devices but of a combination of curiosity, perspicacity, and intuition that no one has achieved in the same degree as Sainte-Beuve. First of all, he defines with force both the aim and the difficulty of the biographer's task.

We should invade an author; take up our abode with him; set him in motion under various conditions; make him live, act, speak, as was habitual to him; penetrate as far as possible into his inner and domestic life; attach him on all sides firmly to that earth and to those daily habits upon which great men no less than others depend. . . . We should study an author; revolve him round and round; question him at our leisure; or persuade him to pose before us. One at a time the features are added and fall automatically into place in the physiognomy. . . . With the vague, abstract, general type by degrees is blended and fused a concrete individuality. *We have found the man.*[1]

In this extract an entire programme is contained, which presents at least two distinct parts: (1) collection of biographical documents; (2) treatment, arrangement, and interpretations of these documents.

I. Collection of the Documents

The sources of information naturally vary with the writer, his epoch, the place of his activity, and the social class to which he belongs. Yet, in a general way, it may be said that the principal fields to be explored are the following:

1. Archives and official documents of every kind: manuscript and printed genealogical records, public and private;

---

[1] *Portraits littéraires*, Vol. I, p. 29.

attorneys' files; parish and civil registers (*dossiers de no-taires, registres de paroisse, registres d'état-civil*).[1]

2. Works by the author himself, with particular insistence upon his correspondence and upon all works directly or indirectly autobiographical in character.

3. Literature relative to the author: contemporary memoirs and correspondence; allusions to the author in other literary works; newspapers and reviews; works of erudition and research, among which books edited in the heart of the provinces, or the smaller, local reviews, though difficult in many cases to find in even the best-equipped libraries, should not be neglected. A fact to be remembered is that the enormous series Ln[27] of the *Catalogue de l'histoire de France* at the Bibliothèque nationale is devoted to *Biographies indivi-duelles*. Interesting data may often be found by glancing through the tables of the *Catalogue des manuscrits des bibliothèques des départements*. Lastly, the contributions of all local and provincial societies are also important.[2]

4. A visit to the spot where the writer has lived may leave a valuable impression. To become familiar with the house where he was born and brought up, the landscape at which he gazed (especially during his childhood); to be a Breton with Chateaubriand or Renan, a Genevese or Savoyard with Rousseau; to seek Pascal in the valley of Port-Royal, Voltaire at Ferney, or Lamartine by the Lake: this is not merely to accomplish a pious literary pilgrimage—it is to fit ourselves, as well, to understand and know these men more thoroughly.

---

[1] The *Manuel de bibliographie historique*, by Langlois, gives detailed descriptions of these various sources and tells how and where to find them.

[2] An essential work for references of this kind is R. de Lasteyrie and A. Lefèvre-Pontalis, *Bibliographie générale des travaux historiques et archéo-logiques publiés par les sociétés savantes de France* (4 vols., 4to (1888–1905), and a continuation).

5. In the case of many modern authors the oral tradition should not be overlooked. Descendants, collaborators, friends, more or less direct witnesses, may furnish helpful information, provided the facts thus obtained are carefully verified and accepted at their true value.[1]

II. Treatment of Documents—Essential Points of Literary Biography

Now, with attention to exactness and authenticity, we must learn how to use and combine the documents in constructing a biography. It is at this point that the special characteristic assumed by biography in literary history appears most clearly. It is not, so to speak, disinterested biography; the aim is not to find as many facts as possible and to weave them into an appealing, moving, brilliant narrative. The aim is to shed light upon the development of the author's literary personality and the inspiration of his work. There are, then, special points—doubtless attractive to any biographer—that become real centres of interest to the historian of literature. Sainte-Beuve will still be our guide in enumerating the following topics of paramount importance:

1. Native country, physical environment, scenery of childhood and youth.

2. Racial conditions and general heredity.

3. Ancestry, both direct and collateral, as far back as it can be traced. Sainte-Beuve rightly dwells on the importance and the influence of the mother, "the most direct and certain parent". He also advises that if there are brothers and sisters they receive special consideration, believing that in

---

[1] With all the documents assembled, and according as the biographical research advances, every incident in the author's life should be recorded on a series of cards, as on a calendar, day by day, week by week, or month by month, as suits the particular case.

them the hereditary strain and family traits will be disclosed, undimmed by the disturbances of genius. "We discover in these relatives", he says, "some essential lineaments of character that in the great man himself are often masked through extreme concentration or a too intimate union with other qualities. The elements of the man are exhibited in his kindred with less concealment and less disguise; we profit by an analysis that nature alone has been at the pains of making."[1]

4. Formation of personality through education and study: early education in the family; schools or colleges; masters and fellow students; curricula of instruction; certain or probable reading; general tendencies of the education received (for instance, the Jesuitical leaning toward Latin, the Greek bias of Port-Royal, the influence of some eminent teacher).

5. Physical and physiological conditions active in moulding a writer: scientific data as to his health, physical defects or weaknesses, etc. This is a field fertile in interesting and curious discoveries, but dangerous for the layman who trusts himself to use a medical vocabulary and to deal with the results of medical experiments. On this question books such as Toulouse, *Émile Zola*,[2] Dumesnil, *Flaubert, son hérédité, son milieu, sa méthode*,[3] or Lauvrière, *Alfred de Vigny*,[4] may be profitably studied.

6. Moral and intellectual environment: his friends and comrades; the groups or sets among which he reached maturity.[5]

---

[1] *Nouveaux Lundis*, Vol. III, article on Chateaubriand.

[2] Paris, 1896.   [3] Paris, 1905.

[4] Paris, 1910. Researches of the same kind are found in his *Edgar Poe, sa vie et son œuvre* (2 vols.) (Paris, 1904).

[5] There are talents that partake of several groups at once, and never stop traversing successive surroundings, perfecting, transforming, or deforming

7. Publication of the first masterpiece or of the first work of real importance. Sainte-Beuve sees in this the "essential point" of a great author's life; he wants to "seize, comprehend, and analyze the entire man at the instant when, by a more or less gradual coöperation, his genius, education, and circumstances have combined in such a fashion that he produces his first masterpiece".[1]

8. Publication of each work, with its date and all pertinent biographical details.

9. Period of deterioration, at times of decadence, during which the writer evidences an exhausted or deflected inspiration; causes, personal or historical, psychological or physical, immediate or indirect, of this sterility or deviation.

Such in outline are the tactics to be followed when we would "lay siege" to an author. We must now, to continue Sainte-Beuve's military metaphor, launch the attack and storm the position.

"It is impossible", he says again, "to try too many ways of becoming acquainted with a man, which means something very different from becoming acquainted with a pure spirit. So long as you have not asked yourselves a certain number of questions about an author, and answered them, if only for your private benefit, and *sotto voce*, you cannot be sure of possessing him completely. This is true, even though these questions seem altogether foreign to the nature of his writings. What were his views on religion? How was he affected by the spectacle of nature? How did he behave in regard to women? in regard to money? Was he rich or poor? What was his daily mode of life from the standpoint of hygiene?

---

themselves. It is important to note, even in these slow or rapid variations and conversions, the hidden, unalterable spring, the persisting motive power. —Sainte-Beuve, loc. cit.

[1] *Portraits littéraires*, Vol. I, p. 31.

Lastly, what was his besetting vice or weakness? Every man has one."[1]

You should, therefore, in the course of your researches keep ever before your mind this list of questions suggested by Sainte-Beuve. You should be fired with the tireless curiosity that never deserted him; you should force yourself to develop a little of his extraordinary psychological finesse and divination. You will then see the results of your biographical quest take shape almost automatically: your analysis will lend to each detail psychological significance at the same time that its own foundation is rounded out and solidified by every added fact.[2]

It is especially on the arrangement of these biographical elements that a work of literary history depends for attraction, interest, and charm. There is no field, however, that demands more intelligence and skill.

---

[1] *Nouveaux Lundis*, Vol. III, article on Chateaubriand.

[2] For examples of French biography, I should first have to cite, with few exceptions, Sainte-Beuve's complete works. Besides these there are biographies of every length, of every type, of every style, from the eight volumes in which Desnoiresterres traces Voltaire's life, to the sixteen pages in which Baldensperger, prefacing his edition of Vigny, has condensed into definite and vivid form all that is essential in the poet's career. It is solely as samples, and knowing well that for each of these titles another might be substituted, that I mention here a few works that will repay a close study : E. Biré, *Victor Hugo avant 1830*, *Victor Hugo après 1830*, distinguished by admirable documentation but marked hostility to the poet; E. Dupuy, *La Jeunesse des romantiques*, and other works on Vigny, models of intuitive, artistic biography; E. Faguet, *Vie de Rousseau*, a perfect example of the way to disentangle complicated questions; G. Michaut, *Sainte-Beuve avant les ".Lundis,"* an interesting study on the formation of a great writer, but heavy and inartistic; G. Rudler, *La Jeunesse de Benjamin Constant*, containing irreproachable documentation, which, however, slightly overbalances the book; P. Courteault, *Blaise de Montluc, historien*, alert, lively, clear, scholarly, attractive biography. Two other useful examples of a happy biographical arrangement are Lanson's *Voltaire* and A. Barine's *Alfred de Musset* in the *Collection des grands écrivains de la France*. W. R. Thayer's little book *Biography in the XIXth century* mentions several of the best biographies written in English during that period.

First to be considered is the delicate question of proportionate importance. The space that should be allotted to the life as compared with that devoted to the works varies greatly and depends obviously upon the closeness of the relation that exists between the two: the biography of a Rousseau or of a Chateaubriand is more essential to the complete comprehension of his works than is that of a Boileau or even of a Montesquieu.

It depends also upon the particular goal in view: the life of a writer may be made the pivotal point in the treatment of his work, or preference may be given to the literary examination of his books. What is indispensable in each instance is a clear statement and justification of the attitude adopted. P. M. Masson purposed, in dealing with Mme de Tencin, to recount "a woman's life in the eighteenth century", and he has succeeded admirably. Doubtless, he has not exhausted everything that literary history could find to say about Mme de Tencin. She played a rôle in the development of the sentimental or historical novel of the eighteenth century that Masson has not completely studied; he does not take up the history of the origins and evolution of the *genre*; he makes no attempt to define the exact place of the author of the *Mémoires du Comte de Comminges* and of *Le Siège de Calais* among the other novelists of her time. Why should we reproach him? It would be as unjust as to criticize the historian engaged on a history of the eighteenth-century novel for not entering into the details of Mme de Tencin's life as a *femme d'intrigue* and a more or less unscrupulous adventuress. In the vast field of literary studies each critic treats the subject that interests him from the angle that he prefers. Nothing is more profitable than the sort of checking up that consists in concentrating on one detail a number of individual researches with different starting-points and different objectives. Reviewing Masson's excellent contribution, Mornet[1] remarks that in it he has woven a solid warp; another writer, treating the question from a more strictly literary angle, will some day furnish the woof; and, as the threads cross and recross, the power of resistance will be doubled— that is to say, the facts will be substantiated by a double current of investigation.

A second requirement in the treatment of biographical material, though not peculiar to literary biography, assumes such importance in this field that it is well to emphasize it. This is the feeling for life, and especially for the supple, complex continuity of life. There is always a temptation to divide a 'life' into two, three, or four periods, set apart by prominent dates or works. This process is convenient, because usually conducive to clearness and precision, but it is almost always artificial and often quite misleading. The old-time critic is still held up to ridicule who found in the development of Racine's career three epochs, "that in which he was inferior to himself; that in which he was equal to himself; that in which he was superior to himself". It is to be feared that more recently, when Faguet[2] discovered "three successive Chéniers", and in his poetry a "first manner, a second manner, and a third manner", he was merely perpetuating, under a more scientific and modern guise, the ancient methods.

There are rarely sharp turns in the lives and careers of famous writers, any more than there are leaps in nature. Doubtless we find crises, crucial periods, but if we look closely and push our analyses far enough, we discover that there have been slow, obscure, progressive preparations. We perceive the seed, the underground sprout, which often

[1] *Revue d'histoire littéraire*, 1909, p. 627.
[2] *André Chénier* (in *Collection des grands écrivains*). Paris, 1902.

abruptly bursts forth, giving an illusion of entire novelty. We must discover all this mysterious and invisible preparatory work. It is thus that certain biographical and literary studies of a more exact and extensive kind have shown that neither Voltaire's stay in England, Victor Hugo's exile, nor the episode of the oak of Vincennes in the life of Rousseau, nor even the 'conversion' of Pascal, justifies any ruthless division under the headings "before" and "after."[1]

Lastly, neither the most scrupulously arranged documents nor the most thorough researches suffice to make a biography *living*. The resurrection of a literary personality calls for a higher art; it belongs indeed to the realm of creative literature rather than to that of mere scholarship. Many excesses and errors have been perpetrated in this regard: witness the 'Molierists,' the 'Rousseauists,' or the 'Stendhalians,' who, in their respectable adoration of their idols, have frequently confused limitless scholarly curiosity with real biographical sense. It is not by the accumulation of documents in the text of a biography; it is not by the multiplication of footnotes, by the reproduction of insignificant papers, that the characteristics of an author are necessarily illumined. Material must be sifted and sacrifices made; it is in this that the critical and artistic sense of a biographer is put to the test. It is shown also in the effort to infuse through his style the youth and freshness of life into dead, dry documents; in the skill with which material is incorporated and merged into the narrative itself; finally, in the gift, possessed by Sainte-Beuve to a superlative degree, of knowing first how to choose, and next how to emphasize, the trait that adds color and life.

[1] Here again, it is a question of caution, tact, and fine distinctions. These crucial moments may serve as natural dividing lines in a biography, on condition that we do not neglect to bring out the preparations and continuity.

This entire programme, or rather this ideal, is expressed with great skill in an unfamiliar page by Taine,[1] which will be the best possible conclusion to these remarks.

To paint is to make others see, and it is a special art to make others see people of a bygone age. Anyone who tries it should be fitted for this artist's work by an artist's apprenticeship: he should in his youth have been a novelist or even a poet, that by just right he may perceive easily and spontaneously the slightest distinctions and the most fragile ties of sentiment; that, little by little, the advancing years and the intimate communion of reflection may add to the artist in him the psychologist; that . . . the scholarship of the nineteenth century, the epicurism of curiosity, the knowledge of man and of men, may impart to him an exquisite and unique tact. Thus endowed and thus equipped, . . . he should flit round his personage, noting with a word each attitude, each gesture, and each look; he should retrace his steps, shading his first colors with new, even paler, tints; he should thus work by touching up and touching up again, never tired of pursuing the complex and changing contour, the faint, fleeting light, that are the sign and, as it were, the bloom of life.

---

[1] This page in which Taine draws Sainte-Beuve's portrait was included in the preface to the first edition of the *Essais de critique et d'histoire*, and afterwards omitted. V. Giraud reprints it in his *Bibliographie critique de Taine*, and in his *Maîtres d'autrefois et d'aujourd'hui* (p. 109).

CHAPTER X

QUESTIONS OF SUCCESS AND OF INFLUENCE

"Biographers of great men", said Renan, "are as a rule satisfied to recount the life of their subjects while on earth, but usually another life should be added. . . . This is their life after death, their influence on the world, the varied fortunes of their writings, the turn given by these writings to other minds, . . . the impetus they have added at different times to the thoughts of men."[1] In these lines, written in 1845, Renan has traced the complete curriculum of a study in which the exigencies of historical methods are multiple and insistent. It is no longer acceptable to 'conclude' a monograph, a study of the life and works of some author, be he of the first or of the tenth rank, by a few scintillating pages of eloquent but vague declamation on his 'influence,' as has been done in hundreds of Ph.D. theses the world over. On the contrary, in treating the fortunes and influence of a work or a doctrine a certain number of definite questions should be considered: What sort of success has the work enjoyed? When, how, why, did the success begin and end? Did it correspond to a real and durable influence? On what types of readers was it exerted, to what degree, and in what fields? How have the work and the author been interpreted by each generation? Why has the work affected foreign countries differently from the country of its origin? Why are certain works, after conquering their own countries and even the whole of Europe, dead and gone

---

[1] E. Renan, *Cahiers de jeunesse*, p. 134.

today? Such questions are of great importance but their complexity is almost infinite.

Indeed, it is more difficult to define a cut-and-dried method for this type of problem than for any other. Each student must map out his own, applicable to the particular case. Therefore this is not in any sense a chapter on method, but rather a list of suggestions; and it will accomplish its aim if, far from simplifying the question, it shows its complexity and difficulty.[1]

DISTINCTION BETWEEN SUCCESS AND INFLUENCE

The first precaution is to distinguish clearly between success and influence. Doubtless they are not always opposed, —sometimes they are even inseparable,—but oftener than not they are independent of each other. For an author's name or a book title to acquire lasting or passing fame is not the same thing as for it to possess the vitality that assures continued action.

Success is, in sum, a sociological fact, to which the artistic, literary, or philosophical value of a work too often contributes nothing. Success means simply that, from a number of causes,—fashion, advertising, an accord with the aspirations

---

[1] In connection with this chapter the following works may be read: F. Baldensperger, *La Littérature* (Paris, 1913), pp. 180–286; G. Renard, *La Méthode scientifique de l'histoire littéraire* (1900), chap. vi, pp. 76 ff., "Recherche des effets produits par une œuvre littéraire"; P. Stapfer, *Des Réputations littéraires* (2 vols.) (Paris, 1901); G. Lanson, "L'Histoire littéraire et la sociologie," *Revue de métaphysique et de morale*, 1904, especially § 6, p. 640, Loi de l'action du livre sur le public; P. Hazard, "Les Récents Travaux en littérature comparée," *Revue universitaire*, 1914, pp. 112–124 and 212–222 (good suggestions as to method); G. Rageot, *Le Succès* (1906); A. Ferrière, "La Psychologie bibliologique," *Archives de psychologie*, Vol. XVI, pp. 101–132 (analysis of the way a book penetrates into the public mind); G. Tarde, *L'Opinion et la foule* (1901) (accurate psychological observations on the public as a social fact).

and requirements of a certain social group,—a work has momentarily become the 'rage.' This phenomenon the historian should try to interpret. "Every literary success", wrote Sainte-Beuve, "has a reason, good or bad, that explains it, excuses it, or at least saves it from absurdity. This should be taken into account."

Schopenhauer divides all writers into three groups—the "shooting stars", the "planets", and the "fixed stars". The first produce vivid and startling effects of short duration: we behold them; we cry, "Look!"—and they are gone forever. Yet even if the literary historian finds no influence to trace, it devolves upon him to give a plausible reason for the success itself. He must, then, in each instance ask some such questions as these:

1. What was the strange suitability of the work to its public? How did it fill the needs of its readers more satisfactorily than other contemporary works of superior artistic and philosophic value?

2. What part did fashion play in this success? If a fashion in literature really existed at this date, in what way did the author cater to this transient taste? Does his desire to please suffice to explain the popularity of the work, and, when the fad had passed, its abatement?

3. How fully was the success heralded and prolonged through articles before and reviews after its publication,[1] 'booming' of booksellers, conversations of faithful adherents?

4. Why has the success dwindled and then vanished?

If it is indisputable that success is not synonymous with influence, it is no less evident that success is usually the

---

[1] "The people", said Diderot to Falconet, "in the long run are only the echo of a few men of taste. In a sense, we critics and historians give God's true verdict."—SAINTE-BEUVE

starting-point of influence. Success proves the adoption of a work by a social group, which finds in it an answer to its aspirations, an expression of its unanimous opinion. By this adoption the group is modified; a new element enters into the intellectual, moral, or artistic life of the community and makes its action felt. Thenceforth influence exists.

DEFINITION OF INFLUENCE

It is not enough to draw an exact line between success and influence. We must be yet more definite: a certain number of actions and reactions are often collectively called influence which in reality should be clearly differentiated.

The influence of a work is something more than its general diffusion. There may be acquaintance and curiosity without the real permeation that is influence. This is particularly true of the work of a foreigner.

Nor is influence imitation. Needless to say, if at a given moment imitations of some writer or of some literature spring up on every hand, especially if they continue during a protracted interval, these imitations may be taken as manifesting a genuine influence. And yet textual borrowings may have no bearing whatever on the inspiration or its artistic elaboration.

Influence is, in truth, something more profound, and generally something less tangible. "When", said Lanson, "it chances that neither previous tradition nor individual originality accounts for a sudden modification, and that the introduction of a fragment of the soul or of the taste of another nation is the only explanation of the tendency or the form that has been remarked"[1]; when literary, philo-

---

[1] "Études sur les rapports de la littérature française et de la littérature espagnole au XVIIe siècle," *Revue d'histoire littéraire*, 1896, pp. 45–70. See page 47.

sophic, or artistic analysis reveals the presence of an element that shifts the existing equilibrium and orients anew the activity of writer, *genre*, or literature,—then we may say that influence exists.

Influence by its very nature does not always declare itself by precise and well-defined signs; its study does not admit of the same exactness as, for instance, the investigation of sources. Frequently, it consists in following the capricious, unexpected meanderings of a stream whose waters are led hither and thither by the accidental contour of the ground and take their color from the various tributaries and the soil through which they flow—at times even disappearing from view for a space, to reappear farther on.

I do not recommend to beginners problems as complex and delicate as these; they demand too extensive and advanced a knowledge not only of one complete literature, but of several. Yet the field is so largely uninvaded that it is desirable to see our most promising young scholars actively and courageously working there.

It need hardly be added that the study of influences may accomplish more than its original object and make the student look far beyond the limits of a mere literary problem. To see how a work is judged, received, adopted or adapted, transformed or deformed, to analyze the successive attitudes of the public, the fluctuations of opinion, the reactions and contradictions, is to penetrate far into psychology. It compels us to reconstruct the different social groups, to enter deeply into the personality of those who are the guides or spokesmen of opinion, to piece together all the social, æsthetic, moral, political, or economic elements that, at a given moment, have decided, increased, modified, or stopped some literary influence.

Given the impracticability of laying down rules of method for such a study of influence, it remains possible to group a few remarks as follows:

I. Under what aspects may the history of an influence present itself?

II. What is the mechanism, the mode of action, habitual to literary influences?

III. Do any practical methods of tracing and measuring an influence exist?

IV. Lastly, for this study as for so many others, are there certain special precautions against error and misinterpretation?

I. How may an Influence present itself?

If it is an unthinkable undertaking to enumerate all possible examples of influence, at least it seems possible to define and to classify a certain number of typical cases. Such a classification is not superfluous: it may serve as a sort of formula or questionnaire by means of which to check up the influence of a given work; it may help to fit the book into some of the already analyzed categories.

All kinds of combinations may occur, but two main facts stand out: first, each literary influence passes through successive phases of eclipse and emergence, alternating with an irregular and unforeseeable rhythm; next, each literary influence is forwarded or held back according as it strikes more or less favorable periods.

1. *Eclipse and emergence.* Alfred de Vigny wrote:

> Flots d'amis renaissants! Puissent mes destinées
> Vous amener à moi, de dix en dix années,
> Attentifs à mon œuvre, et pour moi c'est assez.

All literary works have a destiny somewhat similar to that desired by Vigny. Sometimes the eclipse occurs immediately after a writer's death, as if a short period of inaction, a "preliminary sleep", were the first step toward a posthumous existence of the kind that insures influence. Balzac's work lay dormant for a time; then woke to glory twenty-five years later, "ripe", says H. de Régnier, "for the fame that he sadly and magnificently names 'the sunshine of the dead'".[1]

One of the most typical examples of an interrupted and resuscitated influence is that of Ronsard.[2] After the period of apotheosis in the sixteenth century, when everyone went 'Ronsard mad,' the influence of Malherbe and of his school paralyzed Ronsard's almost completely. Not that his works entirely disappeared. Despite their condemnation at the hands of Boileau and Voltaire, they were still included in libraries[3] and anthologies. However, like *Le Roman de la Rose* and other texts of ancient French literature (also to be found in many private or public collections), they were merely objects looked at occasionally with curiosity or respect,—perhaps with good-natured condescension,—but counting no longer as vital, telling elements of literary influence. For this they had to wait until the beginning of the nineteenth century, when a general veering of taste and, above all, Sainte-Beuve's rousing trumpet-call in his *Tableau historique et critique de la poésie française et du théâtre français au XVIe siècle* prepared and announced the resurrection of Ronsard's influence.

[1] Read some delightful pages by the poet Henri de Régnier, in *Figures et caractères* (1901), pp. 94–98.

[2] See Fuchs, "Comment le XVIIe et le XVIIIe siècles ont jugé Ronsard," *Revue de la renaissance*, 1907, pp. 228–238, and 1908, pp. 49–72.

[3] See D. Mornet, "Les Enseignements des bibliothèques privées," *Revue d'histoire littéraire*, 1910, pp. 449–496, especially p. 483.

It is needless to give further examples: no history of influence flows in a continuous current. We must, therefore, in each case 'plot a graph,' determine exactly the periods of eclipse and of resurrection, seek their causes, and discover whether, when the influence declines, the work falls completely into desuetude and disappears from circulation, or whether it merely ceases for a certain time to be in accord with public taste and aspirations.

2. *Assimilation or rejection by the taste of an epoch.* Another very general phenomenon that we encounter is this: literary taste and the public mind have times of greater or less susceptibility to the influence both of previous works and of a foreign literature. Periods of withdrawal and concentration have been justly contrasted with times of lively intellectual 'free trade' among the nations:[1] periods, on the one hand, when a literature seems sufficient unto itself, or at least reduces to the minimum its models and sources of inspiration; and on the other hand, times of vast curiosity for varied or unexpected forms of art and of thought—times when influences repressed hitherto may freely develop and expand. There are four periods in French literature that, for reasons differing in each case, seem to be more impervious to influence than others. These periods are 1660, and the classical era in all its glory; 1800, and the Pseudoclassicism of the Empire; 1845, and the years succeeding Romanticism; 1871, and the aftermath of the Franco-Prussian War. On the other hand, the years from about 1615 to 1640, when Italy and Spain were treasure-houses for the French poets; from 1750 to 1789 and from 1815 to 1840, when cosmopolitan inspiration combined with the revival of many national influences; the later age of universal artistic and scientific curiosity, which is in some respects responsible for

---

[1] F. Baldensperger, *Études d'histoire littéraire* (1907), Préface, p. xxiv.

the literary anarchy of the last years of the nineteenth century,—these are the times when literary influences found the soil more favorable for taking root, spreading, and flowering afresh.

The preceding remarks make it clear that, in general, we have to deal with epochs of success and of failure, with influences that develop or shrink, dart forward, slow up, or stop. Here we find a means of classifying cases and examples.

a. Active influences. (1) The influence no less than the success of a work may originate in propaganda by one or more of the critics. A writer, heretofore quite unnoticed, is launched by some book or article; readers flock to him; authors imitate him or find inspiration in his writings, and works that have slumbered in the undisturbed peace that is so close to neglect become dominant. This happens in every country. Friedrich Logau, the German epigrammatist, is under obligation to Lessing, and Manzoni to Goethe. In France the famous Provençal poet Mistral became an active centre of influence thanks largely to Lamartine. The pessimistic and thoughtful poetry of Mme Ackermann might not have produced the effect that it did had it not been discovered by the philosopher Caro; the critic Scherer performed the same service for Amiel. Again, should not the fervor with which many young writers turned to Maeterlinck as a source of inspiration be dated from an article by Octave Mirbeau in the *Figaro*?[1]

(2) Sometimes a writer acquires no influence in his own country until he has made a detour and passed through an interval of adoption in a foreign land. Germany, for instance, gave to the Frenchmen Gobineau and Claude Tillier the fame that France at first denied them; whereas Hoffmann with his *Phantasiestücke* exerted in France a far wider

[1] Several of these examples are suggested by Stapfer or Baldensperger.

influence than in Germany. At a time when Heinrich Heine could write, "In Germany today Hoffmann has no vogue whatever", all the great French writers of the Romantic period were reading him and were affected by him.[1] Heine himself and Edgar Allan Poe were helped to gain influence in their own countries by recognition in France.

What takes place? Is it not simply that influence presupposes the harmony between the work and the public that we have already spoken of, and that this harmony, nonexistent in the mother country, is found in a group, a public, a literary school, in some neighboring country? This is true of Hoffmann:

His works were published in France at a moment when the public had become sufficiently accustomed to the supernatural to be able to appreciate this element in them; the Romantic doctrines then holding full sway were in perfect accord with these writings. His translators were able and intelligent men who knew how to enhance their compatriots' interest in his works.[2]

Thus an influence was assured. Besides, it usually follows that a work, after its foreign adoption, finds at last in its native country conditions favorable for the spread of its influence.

(3) An influence may be fixed and durably maintained by some established tradition. In each country there are certain national standard works. They form a nucleus for the public libraries; they are kept in stock by booksellers and bought by a wide range of readers; they become part of the literary programmes of schools, colleges, and universities. The last-mentioned fact involves a vitality of influence too often unappreciated. In this connection we must consider

[1] M. Breuillac, "Hoffmann en France," *Revue d'histoire littéraire*, 1906, pp. 427–457. See page 445.
[2] M. Breuillac, loc. cit. p. 457.

the countries, such as France, where a single centralized authority regulates the authors and works to be read and studied. There is no doubt that on the day when Hugo, Vigny, and Lamartine were added to the list of authors required for French colleges and universities their influence on the younger generation was signally increased. A Latin bias is noticeable in all writers formed in Jesuit colleges, whereas the pupils of the Jansenists of Port-Royal lean toward Greece. The history of foreign influences in France is certainly linked with the history of the development of modern languages and foreign literature in the educational institutions. Some definite investigations of these questions would lead to interesting discoveries.

(4) The chief and most frequent cause of influence is the prevalence in the general public or in a social group, at a given moment and for a variable length of time, of a need, a craving, a trend, satisfied by the literary work in question. This is why every study of influence that is not to remain irremediably superficial should be largely a study of social psychology. Why did some book that today seems dead, unreadable, intolerable, to all save historians by profession, have such deep, such powerful effect upon literature, society, and life? Because it appeared at the opportune moment, responded to the call of a public that yielded to its influence without restraint. Even fervent Rousseauists realize that it requires an effort of will to read *La Nouvelle Héloïse* from cover to cover "without the book's dropping from their hands"; yet the six small volumes of 1761 not only enjoyed in their day the most immense success of the century, but their influence was profound, even on the lives of the humblest readers. The reason is that there was an interplay at that date between the public and the new book: every tendency, every emotion, every ideal, formulated in the novel

existed already in the community, but in a nebulous, inar-ticulate state. The literature of the time was incapable of voicing these confused needs. Rousseau comes; to the vague searchings he gives impassioned, eloquent, feverish expression. His pulsating phrases utter all that the souls about him are struggling to say.[1]

He did not create the taste for emotion, but he made it tyrannical. Before him, people persuaded themselves that emotion was one of the legitimate and profound joys of life. After him, they knew that it was the best and only joy.[2]

Lamartine's *Méditations*, as well, came in response to a demand, and its immense influence at the outset was due to its perfect agreement with a public awaiting just such a work.

In other cases a work does not express a wide-felt need but diffuses certain ideas or certain bents hitherto confined to groups of specialists or technicians.[3] A good share of Voltaire's influence on the public of his time arises from this source. There are no economic, political, or social ideas found in his works that many other writers did not voice at

[1] See the article by D. Mornet, "Les Admirateurs inconnus de *La Nouvelle Héloïse*," *Revue du mois*, 1909, pp. 535-554. Mornet, having access to the vast collection of letters written to Rousseau after the publication of his novel, is able to show how fundamentally the influence of Rousseau is bound up with the preëxisting conditions of public psychology. See also his article entitled "L'Influence de Rousseau au XVIIIᵉ siècle," *Annales Jean-Jacques Rousseau*, Vol. VIII.

[2] *Annales Jean-Jacques Rousseau*, loc. cit. p. 52.

[3] Before the time of Rousseau, it was continually said that women should nurse their children; that the study of facts was being obscured by the study of words; that the abuse of Latin made young people stupid; that it was important to open our eyes to the world and to life; and that travel, and the study of the sciences, of physics, of history, or of a trade, were worth more than synecdoches and catachreses. Suddenly *Émile* gave clamorous utterance to the quarrel that until then had stirred only specialists or a few of the more curious.—D. Mornet, in *Annales Jean-Jacques Rousseau*, loc. cit. p. 48

the same epoch; but he knew how to make them active and effective; he knew how to give them an assimilable, attractive, seductive guise. And the public, quite prepared to take an interest in such questions, though until then unsuccessful in making them its own, heard, followed, and adopted Voltaire.

(5) Lastly, the influence of true, irradiating genius must be taken into account, even if the far-reaching influence often exercised by mediocrities or 'minors' proves that genius and influence stand in no invariable relation of cause and effect. There are writers who exert over the public the same magnetism as an orator over his audience. This expansive and all-conquering power writers such as Montaigne, Pascal, Rousseau, and Chateaubriand have imparted to their work. Literary history, says P. M. Masson, would be an inexact science if "it neglected the decisive action of the heroes of literature and the renovating power that their genius possesses. Rousseau is one of the striking examples. He appeared abruptly in a desert solitude; and, nevertheless, below him on every hand it was as if clouds were supporting and impelling him; it was perhaps he who gave French literature its most powerful shock and influence; it was perhaps he for whom French literature had been most continuously preparing."[1]

b. Retarded or arrested influences. (1) There are influences, as well as successes, that last no longer than a shooting star. A book may for several years be widely read and received with warm approval. Its imitators may be numerous; its trace may be clear, and the more easily followed because of its shortness. Whether the demand is a temporary fashion or infatuation, whether the book is soon

---

[1] *La Formation religieuse de Rousseau* (in *La Religion de J.-J. Rousseau*), Avant-propos, p. vi. 1916.

engulfed by a more potent influence, or whether the attachment of the public is only superficial, the book quickly sinks into oblivion. Saint-Évremond's influence was profound, widespread, fruitful, but brief. From 1705 to 1750 the large number of editions and of imitations, the trail of Saint-Évremond's ideas discernible on all sides, bespeak the vigor and activity of his influence; after these forty-five years there was an almost total cessation. The obvious reason is that, beginning in 1750, other works—more especially the *Encyclopédie*—superseded his, and relegated them to the company of those books that are now mere printed pages and no longer quickening and living forces.

(2) A case of frequent occurrence may be termed the retarded influence. It is the converse of the brilliant but fleeting influences of which we have spoken. Very often an author begins by preaching or singing to the desert air. His voice wakes no echo; he is either ignored or slighted. Meanwhile the new truth "goes on quietly working its way and, like an acid, undermining everything around it. From time to time a crash is heard: the old error comes tottering to the ground, and suddenly the new fabric of thought stands revealed, as though it were a monument just uncovered."[1] Such in substance is the history of many influences, even when not so dramatically staged. Many famous writers, and books that have since become immortal, have had to wait their chance; the historian's task is to discover why. He will find in many cases that at the date of publication the necessary harmony between book and public was lacking. It may be a question of closely 'sealed' works, impossible to break open or absorb without effort and silent thought. *Les Destinées* of Vigny was among these; it was not until the begin-

---

[1] Schopenhauer, *The Art of Literature* (London, 1891), translated by T. Bailey Saunders. For the whole passage see pages 119–120.

ning of the twentieth century that the book found a public
ready to assimilate it. Again, it may be a question of works
that in their day answered to no general call: the writer was
in advance of his times; the passing years were needed to
bring him the public that during his lifetime he had never
had. Today in France we consider the *Dominique* of Fromentin one of the three or four great novels of the nineteenth
century. Yet at its publication it was greeted by a mere
handful of discreet admirers. Stendhal with keen vision predicted that his novels would find favor about 1880: he mis-
calculated by only a few years the rise of that 'Stendhalian'
movement whose influence on recent French literature is
considerable. Such works have revived with accrued value,
with fresh power to influence, "like building-lots that profit
by exorbitant advances, much less because of their own soil
than because of the vast development of their surroundings".[1]

(3) We have seen what rôle critics may play in promoting
an influence. Inversely, they may be responsible for its
subsidence or cessation. Exact account must be taken of
these forces of resistance, which may well prove deadly. We
find toward the beginning of the nineteenth century the
Night Thoughts of Edward Young, after a period of amazing
vogue and widespread influence in France, little by little
losing ground; the reason is that Mme de Staël and Chateaubriand by their unsparing criticisms dealt the work a hard
blow.[2] Likewise, in a remarkable article entitled *Rousseau
en Angleterre*,[3] Edmund Gosse points out that Burke's de-
nunciation "prominently brought forward by the first of
English orators, in a work which was read by every educated

---

[1] Baldensperger, *La Littérature*, p. 227.

[2] See W. Thomas, *Le Poète Edward Young* (Paris, 1902), and Baldensperger, *Études d'histoire littéraire* (first series).

[3] *Annales Jean-Jacques Rousseau*, Vol. VIII. Published, in the original English, in *Fortnightly Review*, July, 1912.

man in Great Britain, sapped the reputation of Rousseau
. . ., and led to the gradual decline of his fame in England all
down the nineteenth century". More recently, in France,
we have witnessed a still more characteristic phenomenon:
the novelist Georges Ohnet had an immense clientele, chiefly
through *Le Maître de forges*,—printed in tens of thousands,
—and was beginning to have disciples. An article by Jules
Lemaître,[1] displaying sparkling wit but scathingly caustic,
'killed' Georges Ohnet, and, as has been aptly said, if people
read him nowadays, they do not boast about it.

(4) The opposing force that causes literary influences to
languish or die is found also in events themselves. In the
article quoted above, Edmund Gosse explains that, although
Rousseau's influence managed to survive with a somewhat
precarious existence the attacks of Burke, its destruction
was completed by the social and moral evolution in England,
the sterner code of conduct that came in, "as a reaction to
the swinish coarseness of the late Georgian period". A similar mishap has been remarked in the history of Mme de
Staël's influence.[2] She succeeded in fixing in France a certain idea of Germany, and created the fervent enthusiasm of
the romanticist generations for the country of Werther,
Faust, and Oberon, of Kant, Klopstock, and J. P. Richter.
But in 1840 the Treaty of London opened the eyes of France;
the "Teutomania" was denounced, the thread of enchant-
ment snapped,—and with it the influence of Mme de Staël's
famous book. The World War will be found to have
had an analogous effect upon the influence in France of
Nietzsche and, in fact, of German philosophy and literature
in general.

---

[1] *Revue bleue*, June, 1885, p. 803, and *Les Contemporains*, Vol. V (1889).

[2] J. Texte, "Les Origines de l'influence allemande dans la littérature française du XIXe siècle," *Revue d'histoire littéraire*, 1898, pp. 1 ff.

(5) Lastly, an influence may be obstructed or superseded by other more powerful influences. A typical example is given in the chapter entitled "L'Influence de Voltaire," with which Lanson concludes his admirable little volume on the author of *Candide*. The influence of Voltaire as dramatist is checked, first, by that of the English drama and the *drame bourgeois*; next, during the Revolution and the Empire, by the partisans of pure Classicism, who were opposed to innovating tendencies; finally, by the Romantic drama. As poet, Voltaire could make no headway against Delille in didactic poetry, against J. B. Rousseau in the ode, or against Ossianism and the pre-Romanticists in elegiac verse. His influence as novelist was submerged by that of *La Nouvelle Héloïse* and by the "torrent of sensibility" that swept its readers along. To offset this, as journalist, pamphleteer, and controversialist he has always had a clear field and has won receptive and eager disciples.[1]

c. Special cases and general remarks. (1) The action of a writer is rarely 'single-tracked.' He may make himself felt in several *genres*; he may in the same *genre* have produced widely different works, with widely different effects: *Notre-Dame de Paris* has not the same influence as *Les Misérables*. Again, a writer's personality may be so complex that his influences in various fields are mutually prejudicial: there is Fontenelle the wit; Fontenelle the conscientious scholar; Fontenelle the daring and often original philosopher. Maigron, analyzing Fontenelle's influences,[2] indicates the cleavage between them. He shows that Fontenelle the wit has restricted the influence of Fontenelle the scholar and

---

[1] See Lanson, *Voltaire*, pp. 206–209.

[2] *Fontenelle, l'homme, l'œuvre, l'influence* (Paris, 1906). The chapter entitled "L'Influence de Fontenelle" appeared previously, in the *Revue d'histoire littéraire*, 1906, pp. 193–227.

philosopher, and that, although active on every side, he is paramount nowhere. Influences are often streams, splitting at the delta into many branches, some to water fertile regions, others to be lost in the sand.

(2) A curious case is that in which the name of a writer dominates a given public to the point of leading historians and critics to believe in his influence, when there is doubt that he was even known. Lanson has brought to light an exact instance of this in connection with 'Gongorism' in France. At the beginning of the seventeenth century Gongora was, he says, "the big name, the best-known and most popular writer of Spanish poetry. *Nobody read him*, or knew his genius at first hand. But there was his name; and this name became representative of the thought or the spirit of his country; . . . it epitomized the effect of Spanish poetry upon the *précieux*. . . . 'Gongorism' was made an element of the *précieux* turn of mind."[1]

(3) Finally, we must be on our guard against the 'superstition of masterpieces.' Certain of the most fruitful and dynamic influences have been exerted by obscure, forgotten, mediocre authors,—by those that criticism classifies under the slightly disdainful head of 'minors.' They have repeatedly been the vehicles for ideas,—popularizers and propagandists. Whether because they curried favor instead of triumphantly snatching it, whether because they never exceeded the average level, or simply because our present classification corresponds in no way to that formed by public taste at other eras,[2] many of these forgotten and neglected

[1] "Études sur les rapports de la littérature française et de la littérature espagnole au XVIIᵉ siècle: Gongora," *Revue d'histoire littéraire*, 1896, pp. 321-331.

[2] See H. Rigault, *Histoire de la querelle des anciens et des modernes* (Paris, 1856), p. 300: "Sir William Temple made a list of the most famous authors, Italian, English, Spanish, and French; this is what he compiled: in Italy,

writers were in their own time active leavens. It is idle to suppose that the famous books and masterpieces have exerted the sole or even the principal influence over subsequent generations. In the eighteenth century, the *Essai sur les mœurs* or *Candide, Le Contrat social* or even *La Nouvelle Héloïse*, were not privileged works, shaping more definitely than any others the thoughts and the emotions of their contemporaries: the *Spectacle de la nature* by the Abbé Pluche, *Le Chef d'œuvre d'un inconnu* by Thémiseul de Saint-Hyacinte, *De l'usage des romans* by Lenglet-Dufresnoy, acted for a time, upon certain groups, with an effect at least equal to that of the more enduring works just enumerated.[1] A list of the books read by a woman like Mme Roland or a poet like Lamartine is a convincing proof of this.[2] Nevertheless, in the long run the great works have their revenge: if the minors enjoy for a period a wide influence, it is never durable or deep.

II. MECHANISM AND MODE OF ACTION OF LITERARY INFLUENCES

How is the action of the book (an individual work) established over the public—a social group? How does the public, how do successive publics, take possession of the book? What do they choose? What do they leave? How is the work accepted, transformed, deformed, transfigured, until

Boccaccio, Machiavelli, Fra Paolo Sarpi; in England, Philip Sidney, Bacon, and Selden; in Spain, Cervantes and Guevara; in France, Rabelais, Voiture, La Rochefoucauld, and Bussy-Rabutin. Shakespeare, Milton, Dryden, Descartes, Pascal, Corneille, Racine, Molière, Boileau, La Fontaine, Dante, Tasso, Lope de Vega, Calderón, have no place on his roll of honor."

[1] Mornet, *Revue d'histoire littéraire*, 1910, p. 470.

[2] *Mémoires* (ed. Perroud, 1905), Vol. I, and observations by Lanson, in *Revue d'histoire littéraire*, 1905, pp. 341–342; also Lamartine, *Méditations* (ed. Lanson), Introduction.

its actual influence frequently corresponds in no way to what the author wrote or intended? We have to do, of course, not with a regular chronological evolution, but rather with sundry phases succeeding one another in variable order, and composing a series, complete or incomplete, which may even recur after an interval of time. An analysis of the nature and functioning of such a process may be helpful.

1. *Simplification; elimination; choice.* A preliminary process[1] of simplification and elimination takes place in some such way as this: the social groups on which a literary work may react have, as Baldensperger says, only "a limited memory", incapable of retaining in their entirety the huge structures of many of the important works. Besides the æsthetic or ethical value, a thousand reasons decide which parts are to remain active and which are to sink into sleep and inertia; that there is this choice, however, is a fact. Of Voltaire there remain *Candide*, the *Dictionnaire philosophique*, a selection from his *Lettres*, perhaps a tragedy or two. Yet in his fifty-two volumes are doubtless many pages inferior to these in no respect; it matters little, for the Voltaire who is active is the Voltaire of the works just mentioned. Today do the Abbé Prévost and Lamartine stand for anything more than *Manon Lescaut* and the *Méditations*? Renan goes so far as to say that "after the lapse of a century a genius of the first order is reduced to two or three pages".[2] At any rate, this simplification tends toward a specialization of the line of influence: Taine, the critic; Lamartine, the lyrist; La Bruyère, the moralist,—what could be more simple? What matter that Taine was not merely a critic, Lamartine a lyrist, La Bruyère a moralist?

[1] Well analyzed by P. Stapfer, *Des Réputations littéraires*, and by Baldensperger, *La Littérature*, pp. 268 ff.

[2] *L'Avenir de la science*, p. 208 (English translation, Boston, 1891).

Their influences will flow in the directions assigned to them by the public. This process of elimination may take various forms.

Perhaps a writer's works will not all evince effective action at the same time. Whereas Pascal's *Provinciales* had at first far more influence than his *Pensées*, their rôles were afterwards reversed.[1] Voltaire the pamphleteer continues active; Voltaire the dramatist is almost dead. Finally, for all foreign works, translation is obviously an important, and almost mechanical, element of elimination.

In other cases, following the modification of the environment and the transformation of public opinion, a versatile author will have one part of his work dropped after another. Fénelon's fortunes during the eighteenth century[2] offer a striking illustration of this. At first the 'active' Fénelon was an almost exclusively 'literary' Fénelon, the author of *Télémaque*. His prestige and his irradiation were primarily on the artistic side. When the key to *Télémaque* was better known, people reveled in the eloquent ingenuity of the author. Then attention was drawn to other works, notably the *Dialogues des Morts,* in which the public discovered daring assertions that tickled its fancy and altered the image of the first Fénelon. Toward 1750 the change was complete. The *Directions pour la conscience d'un roi* had just been published; *Télémaque* was decidedly obsolete; the generation that welcomed the *Encyclopédie*, applauded Rousseau's first *Discours*, and was enraptured by Voltaire was not the generation that had known Louis XIV and Fénelon himself. Thenceforth "the controversies of the Jansenists had dropped

---

[1] V. Giraud, *Pascal, l'homme, l'œuvre, l'influence* (Fribourg, 1898), Lesson XIX, pp. 135 ff.

[2] Minutely studied in A. Chérel, *Fénelon au XVIIIe siècle: son prestige, son influence.* Paris, 1917.

into the background. . . . To the eyes of the Encyclopæ-
dists, the seventeenth century derived its greatest glory from
the 'ancestors' of their new doctrines, whom they discerned
in the *grand siècle*. They found in Fénelon one of these
ancestors . . .: he became a 'great man' and the patron
saint of 'Tolerance,' displaying, in the heart of Christianity,
a 'philosophic' charity; he was indulgent to mankind, believing in nature, indifferent to dogmas, interested in the
welfare of the people, hating force in itself and in all its
uses, confusing authority with force only to condemn them
both."[1] Of Fénelon's entire works, after all these elimina-
tions and transformations, but a limited number of texts and
impressions remain,—just enough to inspire the tragedy of
Fénelon, by M. J. de Chénier, and to allow the members of
the National Convention to place the mystical prelate among
the saints of the Revolutionary calendar. The reputation of
Fénelon has become a legend.[2]

In these changes the critics may play an important part.
They may help to fix the traits by which a writer or a work
shall thenceforth be known, and prescribe their choice to at
least a part of the public. Ramsay, in his *Life of Fénelon*,
drew a portrait that the public seized upon. To the generation
of Romanticists, the poets of the *Pléiade* have appeared largely
as Sainte-Beuve depicted them in his *Tableau de la poésie
française au XVIIIe siècle*. Voltaire is to a great extent responsible for the Shakespeare that influenced France during
the eighteenth century. When, in 1873, John Morley published his monograph on Jean-Jacques Rousseau, he decided
in no small measure the aspect under which England from
that date was to picture the author of the *Confessions*.

---

[1] A. Chérel, loc. cit. p. 608.
[2] Compare the history of Pope's influence on French literature as sketched
by G. Charlier, "De Pope à Lamartine," *Revue de Belgique*, December, 1906.

Nothing is more illuminating than to follow these successive oscillations of public opinion, and no better example may be offered than *Goethe en France*,[1] in which Baldensperger shows how, epoch by epoch, French readers have picked from the immense treasury of Goethe's works what best suited their preoccupations. There is the uneasy, depressed generation that adopted *Werther*; the next, that preferred *Faust*, one group more interested in the fantastic, another in the philosophic, element. There is the generation of 1848, under the spell of science and rationalism, which, neglecting the works delighted in by its elders, turned to other sources. There are the impassive Parnassians, whom Goethe satisfied as thoroughly as he did their predecessors, and there are the thinkers of yesterday, who, working often in totally different directions, found a rich harvest in his inexhaustible work.[2]

2. *The image that each epoch or each milieu forms of a work.* Pascal said that "we desire to live an imaginary life in the thoughts of others". His aphorism may be taken almost literally. Writers after their death live a life whose development is unforeseeable and often capricious. The history of an influence is commonly less the history of the ideas of a writer than that of the successive errors and false constructions based on those ideas. There is an incessant phenomenon of 'refraction': a work suffers deformation in passing from epoch to epoch or from one environment to another. This is true not only of literary works in general but of

---

[1] Paris, 1904. See also Estève, *Byron et le romantisme français* (Paris, 1907); Van Tieghem, *Ossian en France* (2 vols.) (Paris, 1917); Tronchon, *La Fortune intellectuelle de Herder en France* (Paris, 1920); J. M. Carré, *Goethe en Angleterre* (Paris, 1920).

[2] See Lanson, "La Fonction des influences étrangères dans le développement de la littérature française," *Revue des Deux Mondes*, February 15, 1917, pp. 800–806.

philosophical or literary doctrines. The Spinoza that possessed a decisive influence over the formation of the French eighteenth century is not the Spinoza that the historian of today discovers in the pages of the *Ethica* or of the *Tractatus Theologico-Politicus*: it is, on the contrary, a Spinoza imagined and constructed by his contemporaries, through accumulated errors and misinterpretations.[1] The same may be said of every system of philosophy,—of Rousseau as of Kant, of Berkeley as of Auguste Comte. "If it is interesting", said Brunetière, "to know what Descartes thought, it is far more interesting to know what his contemporaries believed that he thought. For doctrines and systems act only in proportion as they are understood, and those who adopt them are no less their inventors than those who teach them."[2]

A striking illustration is the religious influence of Rousseau, traced in a masterly fashion by P. M. Masson.[3] The Rousseau who is active after 1778 is entirely different from the true Rousseau whom Masson begins by resuscitating: from that time forward it is "the Rousseau of the public"— a public that is permeated by him. As these people are of infinite variety, their aspirations and their tendencies complex and sometimes contradictory, the natural result is that the influence of Rousseau, separated from Rousseau himself, is diverted into channels complex and contradictory in their turn.

Lastly, the same is true of works that are acclimated to a foreign country.[4] Joseph de Maistre said that "each nation

[1] See Lanson's analyses, "Origines et premières manifestations de l'esprit philosophique," *Revue des cours et conférences*, 1908, pp. 241–254.

[2] "Jansénistes et cartésiens," *Études critiques*, Vol. IV, p. 119.

[3] *La Religion de J.-J. Rousseau*, Vol. III. 1916.

[4] An important place must be given here to translators. The deformations to which they subject a work decide in no small degree its subsequent fortunes. These deformations, caused by religious, political, artistic, or literary scruples, are frequently the very condition of a foreign public's accepting and assimilating the work. See on this subject the judicious remarks of P. Hazard in

is for its neighbors a contemporary posterity". In passing from one country to another, the influence of a work undergoes the same vicissitudes and the same transformations as in passing from one century to the next. Every careful study of comparative literature piles up fresh proof of this. It will suffice here to recall the infinite series of mistranslations and nonadaptations that characterize the history of Shakespeare in France; yet it is this poorly adapted, poorly understood, and even ridiculously caricatured Shakespeare that has been one of the most active leavens in the transformation of the French theatre.[1]

In a wise and stimulating page, which is the best conclusion to the foregoing remarks, Lanson vividly describes the social character of the influence of a literary work:

It is not the author that determines the efficacy of a book. . . . The Descartes or the Rousseau that acts is neither Descartes nor Rousseau, but the personality that the public reads into his book and calls by his name. This personality depends on the public, and changes as the public changes. Each generation . . . makes a Descartes and a Rousseau for itself, according to its own need

his article already cited, in *Revue universitaire*, 1914, p. 213: "There is an underlying reason for the liberties taken by so many translators, liberties at which we rail without understanding their necessity at the given epoch. . . . Translators mar the text because, practically, there is nothing else for them to do. . . . We should be grateful to them for the opportune wisdom that alone has permitted the smooth acclimating of the product of a foreign taste." Du Resnel, the translator of Pope, prides himself on the way he has suited Pope to French taste; Voltaire congratulates Letourneur, the translator of Young, on having "set to rights this collection of high-flown, obscure commonplaces". Hazard hopes that essays on translators will become more numerous: "What changes do they make in the texts? What suppressions and what modifications? Why? Because of what customs, what doctrines? From one translation to the next is there any improvement? At what epoch and under what conditions has an exact decalcomania of a foreign work been made?"

[1] See J. J. Jusserand, *Shakespeare en France sous l'ancien régime* (Paris, 1898); and Baldensperger, "Esquisse d'une histoire de Shakespeare en France," *Études d'histoire littéraire* (second series, 1910), p. 155.

and in its own image. . . . The connection established is not that existing at the time of composition . . . between the work and the author: the work is exclusively connected with the public, which continually retouches, remodels, enriches, or impoverishes it. The author's real intention produces only a part of the total effect, and sometimes almost completely disappears. To follow the fortunes of a work, therefore, is frequently less to watch what happens to an individual thought in the common domain of thinkers than to read by means of some recording device certain modifications in the social environment.[1]

III. Tracing and Measuring Literary Influences

It is always easy to agree that the influence of such and such a writer has been "considerable"; but "how shall we grasp and measure this influence? Above all, how distinguish it from what it resembles and yet is not? How make it evident by incontestable, precise facts? Finally, how define it otherwise than in vague epithets, guided by purely personal impressions and general considerations?"[2] To answer these questions, there are no unfailing rules or processes: there are only certain sources of information that it is advisable to seek; certain directions that it is well to look in; certain fields that will repay attention.

1. *Bibliographical statistics; history of printing; history of libraries; various documents.* Every study of influence should begin with minute statistics of successive editions and reprints, including—whenever obtainable—information as to the number of copies printed and sold. For works subsequent to 1811, consult the *Journal de la librairie.* For all others, information may be less exact but is usually acces-

[1] "L'Histoire littéraire et la sociologie," *Revue de métaphysique et de morale*, 1904, p. 631.

[2] V. Giraud, *Essai sur Taine* (1st ed.), p. 125. Paris, 1902.

sible. The multiplicity of editions, the interruption and re-
sumption of their sequence, are definite points in the 'curve'
of an influence, especially when these data are explained and
confirmed by additional means.

For instance, a fairly accurate idea of the diffusion of
Voltaire's and Rousseau's works, and the number of their
readers, has been formed from statistics given in a *mémoire*
written at the time of the Restoration.[1] To a great extent
it has been possible to follow the sale and the penetration
of Vigny's works, at least during a certain period: figures of
the various printings, of the copies sold, of the rapidity of
the sale, are procurable and have been examined with care.[2]

Ronsard had no edition during the great classical period;
beginning with 1626, certain poems were included in anthologies, which proves that his complete works were no
longer demanded by the public.[3] In the space of ten years
La Bruyère was edited in Belgium six times.[4] Light is
thrown on the history of Fénelon's influence by the bibliographical study of his editions: not to mention the innumerable reprints of *Télémaque*, we find the *Directions pour la
conscience d'un roi* republished at least sixteen times between
1747 and 1789; and, after a long interval (1789–1805)
"during which there was no question of directing the con-
sciences of kings", edited again in 1805, 1806, and 1810.[5]
I need not recall here works such as *La Nouvelle Héloïse* or
Candide, whose diffusion is registered almost automatically

[1] See Lanson, *Voltaire*, p. 205.

[2] J. Marsan, "A. de Vigny et G. H. Charpentier (the publisher)," *Revue
d'histoire littéraire*, 1913, pp. 51–64.

[3] See F. Lachèvre, *Bibliographie de recueils collectifs de poésies* (4 vols.)
(Paris, 1901–1905), and the "Comptes-rendus" of his work in the *Revue
d'histoire littéraire*, 1902, p. 697.

[4] G. Servois, "Les Éditions belges des *Caractères* de La Bruyère," *Bibliographie moderne*, 1908, pp. 5–31.

[5] A. Chérel, *Fénelon au XVIIIe siècle*, pp. 341 ff.

in bibliographical statistics.[1] Is it not instructive to find that *La Princesse de Clèves* enjoyed its greatest popularity in the flood tide of Romanticism?[2]

Although valuable aid can be had from bibliography and from the history of printing,[3] this sort of statistical information should be handled with caution, accepted with reserve, and its value justly gauged.

a. For many modern works, the booksellers' announcements are only fallacious advertising. A comic author once introduced as one of his characters a poet who had had "eleven editions in ten days". This seems hardly an exaggeration when we think of certain statements of present-day booksellers.

b. It is hazardous to make the number of editions a basis for calculating the number of readers. How many books are bought and never read, and, inversely, how many books are read and never bought!

c. A large number of editions does not necessarily mean the distribution of a proportionate number of copies. Of some work perhaps only twenty to one hundred copies de luxe are struck off; of another, as many as twenty or thirty thousand. Mornet points out that the original edition of *La Nouvelle Héloïse* (1761) was of four thousand copies; the edition of 1764, of only seven hundred and fifty.

d. Nor does a small number of editions necessarily mean that no influence has been exercised. On the contrary, the

---

[1] D. Mornet, "Le Texte de *La Nouvelle Héloïse*, et les éditions du XVIIIᵉ siècle," *Annales Jean-Jacques Rousseau*, 1909, pp. 1 ff.; *Candide* (A. Morize edition, 1913), Introduction.

[2] H. Ashton, "Essai de bibliographie des œuvres de Mᵐᵉ de la Fayette," *Revue d'histoire littéraire*, 1913, pp. 899–918.

[3] See Lanson's suggestive "Comptes-rendus" on A. Claudin's *Histoire de l'imprimerie en France au XVᵉ et au XVIᵉ siècle*, *Revue d'histoire littéraire*, 1902, pp. 312–315, and 1905, pp. 522–525.

influence may have been as deep as the material diffusion was limited. Such is the case for Kant:

> The influence of Kant on the French mind escapes the investigator who looks for indications in library catalogues or in the literary columns of the newspapers: its action was deep, not extended; it was none the less one of the most powerful influences manifested during the nineteenth century.[1]

e. Lastly, it must not be forgotten that at certain epochs before the freedom of the press had been achieved, a book might exert an extended influence through its circulation by manuscript.[2]

One interesting source of information is the study of libraries—especially private libraries—at a given date. The collation, the comparison, and the examination of their catalogues, which we possess in great numbers, may, if necessary precautions are taken, lead to stimulating conclusions.[3]

Curious and amusing evidence is often furnished by iconography, the history of caricature, or the history of the *bibelot*. The graphic representations of a great writer help us to grasp the idea formed of him by some generation: Rousseau rusticating among garden or forest foliage; Voltaire fluently descanting, surrounded by an admiring circle; Lamartine on the borders of the "Lac"; Victor Hugo seated

[1] P. Hazard, in *Revue universitaire*, 1914, p. 123.

[2] This is particularly true of the transition period between the seventeenth and the eighteenth century in France. See Lanson, "Questions diverses sur l'histoire de l'esprit philosophique," *Revue d'histoire littéraire*, 1912, pp. 1–29; "It would be worth while for someone to make a list of extant copies, with—when procurable—their dates or the date of the original from which they are derived, thus enabling us to conjecture from the number of copies the possible diffusion of ideas" (pp. 2–3).

[3] See D. Mornet, "Les Enseignements des bibliothèques privées (1750–1780)," *Revue d'histoire littéraire*, 1910, pp. 449–496. This, so far as I know, is the first systematic treatment of the question.

alone, diminutive, on an immense rock, facing the infinite ocean,—these are documents of no mean interest. Even if there is nothing very 'literary' about knowing that at the time of the Revolution Rousseau's bust was used to decorate ink-bottles, or that Hugo was transformed into a pipe bowl, this at least makes it possible in a certain degree to watch the popularization of a famous writer.[1] Again, we find a representation of this kind in plays or fiction where a great writer is given the rôle of hero. Molière, Fénelon,[2] Rousseau,[3]—shall I add Geffroy Rudel, Villon, Cyrano de Bergerac, and George Sand?—and others still, have had that honor. These images, necessarily distorted, are evidences of influence.

2. *Journals and reviews; evidence from criticism; categories of admirers.* We shall next question the periodical press,—newspapers and reviews. They will tell us of the immediate success of a work, of its reception by the public, of the continued enthusiasm or the reaction that increased or decreased its influence.[4] Newspapers possess the double interest of reflecting with considerable accuracy the average opinion of certain social groups, and of showing through the medium of these groups the diffusion and influence of literary works.[5] The power of dissemination of the periodical press is, and always has been, immense. Voltaire speaks of one hundred and seventy-three newspapers that in his day

---

[1] See G. Desnoiresterres, *Iconographie voltairienne* (1879); F. de Girardin, *Iconographie de J.-J. Rousseau* (2 vols.) (1909); H. Buffenoir, *Les Portraits de J.-J. Rousseau* (1913); Beuve and Daragon, *Victor Hugo par le bibelot* (1902).

[2] See A. Chérel, *Fénelon au XVIIIe siècle*, pp. 341 ff.

[3] See A. A. Pons, *J.-J. Rousseau et le théâtre.* 1909.

[4] See, for example, P. Van Tieghem, *"L'Année littéraire"* (1754–1790) comme intermédiaire en France des littératures étrangères. 1917.

[5] See Loth, *La France et l'esprit français jugés par le "Mercure de Wieland,"* 1773–1787. Paris, 1913.

affected public opinion. The number of volumes of journals published from 1750 to 1780 has been computed at fifty thousand; the figures would be no less formidable for the period of Romanticism.[1] This material was "doubtless an obscure mass, and rarely reread; yet, month by month, and fortnight by fortnight, it relentlessly fashioned a multitude of minds".[2] The interest of the newspapers in this respect is heightened whenever we are able to procure a list of subscribers from which to learn the class of readers affected.[3]

Attention should next be directed toward the critics and toward all those who, under whatever title, have expressed an opinion, favorable or unfavorable, upon the work in question.[4] We must weigh their authority, measure their strength as propagandists, and define their rôle in the launching of an author, or in the decline and disappearance of his influence.[5]

We must, moreover, look beyond pure literary opinion and, by describing the various categories of admirers,[6] analyze the reactions of opinion in general. Were the readers of the book men of letters or men of the world? of the middle

[1] See C. M. Des Granges, *Le Romantisme et la critique. La Presse littéraire sous la Restauration.* Paris, 1907.

[2] D. Mornet, "Les Enseignements des bibliothèques privées (1750–1780)," *Revue d'histoire littéraire*, 1910, p. 478.

[3] See, in the *Bulletin de la société d'histoire moderne et contemporaine*, a list of subscribers to the *Mercure de France*. There is a similar list in the *Journal étranger*, 1755.

[4] See the contribution, already cited, of Fuchs, *Comment le XVIIe et le XVIIIe siècles ont jugé Ronsard*; J. Boulenger, "Rabelais à travers les âges," *Revue des livres anciens*, Vol. II (1914), No. 1 ; P. Champion, "Du succès de l'œuvre de Charles d'Orléans" (*Mélanges Picot*, 1913), Vol. I, p. 409; G. D. Morris, *Fenimore Cooper et Edgar Poe d'après la critique française du XIXe siècle* (Paris, 1912).

[5] It may be added here that biographical representations sometimes extend or perpetuate influences. Such is certainly the case with Boswell's *Life of Johnson*.

[6] I borrow the expression from E. Hennequin, *La Critique scientifique*, p. 237.

class or of high rank? women or young men? scholars or ill-educated? of a religious cast of mind or skeptical free-thinkers? Had it admirers in one category only, as the poems of Voiture among the *précieuses*, or was it so varied that its influence extended to many categories, as Rousseau's works found an echo in emotional but unbelieving souls, in Catholics and Protestants, and in the world of the rationalistic and irreligious 'philosophers'? This chapter of our study of influences will certainly be one of the most fascinating and rich.

3. *Biographical information.* The personal activities of a writer, his travels (especially in foreign countries), the part played by him in the literary circles of his time, are often important elements of influence: the visits of Voltaire to England and to Germany, of Dickens and of Turgenev to France, of Chateaubriand to London, of Victor Hugo, and of the other writers exiled after December 2, 1851, to Belgium or elsewhere, certainly quickened their literary action in the countries visited.

4. *Determination of an influence through the study of the sources of later writers.* An obvious means of tracing an influence is through studying the sources of later writers. Borrowings, imitations, and inspirations, admitted or unacknowledged, vague or precise, help to mark the trail that a writer has left through the history of thought and of art. The study of the sources of Ronsard is valuable for the history of Marot's influence;[1] the documents on the sources of Cyrano de Bergerac or of Swift, for Rabelais's;[2] the *Lettres philosophiques* of Voltaire, for the history of English influ-

[1] See H. Guy, "Les Sources françaises de Ronsard," *Revue d'histoire littéraire*, 1902, pp. 217–256.

[2] See P. Toldo, "Les Voyages merveilleux de Cyrano de Bergerac et de Swift et leurs rapports avec le livre de Rabelais," *Revue des études rabelaisiennes*, 1906, pp. 295–334.

ence;[1] the *Profession de foi du vicaire savoyard*,[2] for Descartes, Condillac, and many others; the poems of Vigny, for Chénier[3] or Byron[4]; and Lamartine, for Ossian.[5]

We may include also the cases where a literary work inspires not another literary work but a painting, a piece of sculpture, a musical composition. Pictures, statues, operas, and symphonies frequently reveal an unexpected extension of the influence of a literary masterpiece.

5. *Reaction of foreign opinion.* Investigations naturally should not be restricted to the country to which the work is indigenous. They cannot be complete before answering, as fully as possible, the following questions: How did the work become known in foreign countries? When was it translated? By whom? With what skill and success? Was it commented upon by the press (newspapers and reviews)? Was it read in the original? Was it adapted? If so, in what did the adaptations consist? What sort of deformations or transformations has the work undergone? Has foreign criticism agreed or disagreed with opinion in its native country? Did the work merely arouse curiosity or did it exert a genuine influence? Was it imitated or really assimilated? Translations, adaptations, reactions, and criticisms, —these are some of the subjects on which we should question foreign countries.[6]

---

[1] *Lettres philosophiques* (ed. Lanson). Commentary.

[2] P. M. Masson edition.

[3] P. M. Masson, "L'Influence d'André Chénier sur A. de Vigny," *Revue d'histoire littéraire*, 1909, pp. 1-48.

[4] E. Estève, *Byron et le romantisme français*. Paris, 1907.

[5] P. Van Tieghem, *Ossian en France*, Vol. II. Paris, 1917.

[6] Besides the works already cited (*Goethe en France* etc), see contributions such as Bouvy, *Voltaire et l'Italie* (1898); Kont, *Voltaire en Hongrie* (Congrès d'histoire comparée, 1900); Whibley, "Rabelais en Angleterre," *Revue des études rabelaisiennes*, 1903; Ashton, *Du Bartas en Angleterre* (1908); D. F. Canfield, *Corneille and Racine in England* (New York, 1904); and, in the *Manuel bibliographique* of Lanson, Nos. 5175-5192 ("Molière à l'étran-

6. *Refutations; disputes; negative influences.* An influence is manifested not only by imitations and assimilations but also by the opposition it provokes, by the repugnance it excites, by the disputes it causes. A genius of Taine's calibre reacts not only on those who become his disciples but on all those who struggle in the grip of his imperious mind, who revolt, who find reasons for dissociating themselves from him.[1] For many writers of deep and lasting action— Molière, Fénelon, Rousseau, Voltaire, Renan—the paragraphs in Lanson's *Manuel* entitled "Polémiques," "Réfutations," etc. offer excellent material for any study of influence.

7. *Study of the public; intellectual environment; historical conditions; contradictory or more powerful influences.* Finally, a word remains to be said as to three branches of study that cannot accurately be termed means or methods of tracing or estimating an influence but are indispensable types of auxiliary research.

The first is the psychological study of the reading-publics and of the intellectual atmosphere with which a work comes in contact. To what social groups do the readers belong? How cultivated are they? What are their needs and aspirations? their favorite books? the general orientation of their opinions and tastes?[2]

ger"), 5363 ("Boileau et Lessing"), 5511 ("La Fontaine en Allemagne et en Angleterre"), 11,152–11,168 ("Rousseau à l'étranger"), 17,570–17,573 ("Victor Hugo à l'étranger"), etc.

[1] See a good example in Levi-Malvano, *Montesquieu e Machiavelli* (Bibliothèque de l'Institut français de Florence) (Paris, 1912). The influence of Machiavelli on Montesquieu is shown less by what Montesquieu has taken from him than by what he has rejected. Many of his affirmations are only negations of Machiavelli.

[2] What picture does a foreign influence give of its own country? See G. Chinard, *L'Exotisme américain dans la littérature française au XVIe siècle* (1911), and *L'Amérique et le rêve exotique dans la littérature française* (1913); A. Bisi, *L'Italie et le romantisme français* (Milan, 1914).

The next is the investigation of historical events and conditions—political, economic, or religious—that modify environment and public, preparing, checking, hastening, rehabilitating, the influence of a literary work.

The last is the examination of other literary influences that are at large at the same moment,—influences that sometimes strengthen, sometimes neutralize, sometimes overbalance, the one that we are studying. The influence of Rousseau blocks that of Voltaire in certain *genres*, whereas it aids that of Sénancour or Mme de Staël. There are phenomena of rivalry and phenomena of mutual assistance.

IV. Possible Errors and Necessary Precautions

Certain students are obsessed by an influence, as others are by a source. Instead of discovering it where it is really to be found, they see it on all sides just where they wish to see it. They conclude some contribution on a hitherto overlooked author by the triumphant assertion that he is responsible for nearly everything written or thought after his day. Such works obstruct our view of the interesting but less numerous instances where the influence is genuine and fruitful.

If we believe certain scholars, it is Lamennais who 'made' Hugo and Lamartine. Rousseau as well has been held responsible for a multitude of things—literary doctrines and political crimes, sentimental revolutions and new designs in gardens—for which his responsibility is, to say the least, shared with others. E. Martinenche has written a good book entitled *La Comédie espagnole en France de Hardy à Racine*,[1] which, however, is impaired by his "systematic effort to discover Spain in every direction" (even in *Horace, Cinna*, and

[1] Paris, 1901.

Polyeucte), and by his failure to "distinguish in Corneille's plays between what has been borrowed, adapted, suggested, and what is the normal and necessary development of Corneille's original conceptions".[1] Even the excellent work, by Chérel, entitled *Fénelon au XVIIIᵉ siècle*, which in many ways is a model for all studies of influence, does not entirely escape this danger. No writer who comes after Fénelon can express a literary, religious, or political idea that is not claimed by Chérel as Fénelon's if he can find the slightest excuse. He minimizes the fact that many of these ideas belong no more to Fénelon than to ten or a hundred others; that they form a part of that common and anonymous store on which every writer is obliged to draw.

I find some judicious remarks, widely applicable, in an article entitled "Montaigne et les poètes dramatiques anglais du temps de Shakespeare,"[2] in which Villey endeavors to discover and to measure the influence of the English translation of Florio.[3] That Shakespeare was familiar with parts of Montaigne there can be no doubt: it has been recognized since the eighteenth century that a passage of *The Tempest* is assuredly taken from the *Essais*. Since it is hardly conceivable that Montaigne's influence is so limited, hunting for Montaigne in Shakespeare has become a sort of game: a fantastic number of parallels have been amassed, and, from Stedefeld (1871) to J. M. Robertson (1909), theories of increasing audacity have been based on supposed resemblances. These theories are of value for the study of Montaigne's influence, says Villey, "if the resemblances are well

---

[1] Lanson, *Revue d'histoire littéraire*, 1901, pp. 332–333.

[2] *Revue d'histoire littéraire*, 1917, pp. 357–393. See also his excellent "Montaigne et François Bacon," *Revue de la renaissance*, 1911, pp. 121–158 and 185–203, particularly his prudent conclusions; and his article "Montaigne en Angleterre," *Revue des Deux Mondes*, September 1, 1913.

[3] 1603.

founded. But, for the most part, they reveal only *coincidences of thought*. . . . I have scrupulously examined all the similarities indicated . . . and I find few worthy of consideration. The retort will surely be made that their number is such as to carry weight. Beware lest that impression lead us astray! *One hundred zeros added together make only zero*. The grain of probability contained in each of these resemblances is so infinitesimal that the sum of all the grains does not make even the beginning of a demonstration." Cannot this remark be applied to all studies of the kind? Sometimes, he says farther on, it is a question "of ideas that may have reached Shakespeare through quite another channel than Montaigne, in particular from the ancients" or "from the common domain of all time"; or, again, it may be a question "of opinions that seem unnatural to us today but that were then banal". He advises us "to avoid the strange blindness induced in a scholar by the desire to prove a preconceived theory".[1]

Thus a writer's rôle as interpreter should not be confused with his rôle as instigator. In a multitude of cases an author translates the ideas, feelings, and tendencies of an entire public or environment. Those who succeed him may doubtless feel his influence, but they feel at the same time the influence of many others who are themselves the interpreters and heirs of this same place and this same public. How the rôle of Rousseau in French Pre-Romanticism has been enhanced, or that of Voltaire in the revolt against the Christian spirit! André Chénier voices the reviving taste of a whole public for Greek antiquity,—he does not create this taste.

[1] Loc. cit. pp. 383-385. Compare the question of Descartes's influence on French Classicism. See Krantz's exaggeration of his thesis in his *Essai sur l'esthétique de Descartes* (Paris, 1882), and Lanson's methodical discussion, "L'Influence de la philosophie cartésienne sur la littérature française," *Revue de métaphysique et de morale*, 1896, pp. 517-550.

In our desire to emphasize the influence of an author, we must not call him a starting-point when he is in reality an evidence of a more general movement. We should define his rôle rather as a 'point of condensation' and a 'centre of radiation.'

On the other hand, if it is our special concern to distinguish what is due to the work itself from what is due to the environment, we should make the knowledge of the environment a part of our preliminary studies. Currents of opinion or of thought, literary fashions and doctrines, the eddies and cross-currents of vague aspirations or clearly articulate needs, parallel or conflicting influences, general social evolution and historical events of wide renown,—all these should be definitely and constantly present in our minds. It is before this background that we must watch our principal characters live and act. Failing to take this precaution, we run the risk of seeing only one soldier where there is an army; of thinking him responsible for the victory, when he is but one in a thousand; and of placing on his head a crown that history, less partial and better informed, will sooner or later snatch from him.

CHAPTER XI

THE HISTORY OF LITERATURE IN CONNECTION WITH THE HISTORY OF IDEAS AND OF MANNERS[1]

It is not the purpose of the present chapter to discuss the best methods for a historical research of the transformation of ideas and the evolution of manners. Not, indeed, that the subject is uninteresting, or that among the publications of the last fifteen years there are no worthy models, but that we should be carried quite beyond the limits of this book. It seems, however, scarcely possible to ignore the question when we reflect how repeatedly the history of literature—in other words, of books—touches the history of manners and of ideas—of life. The student who undertakes any such investigation may feel not only that he is overstepping the boundaries of literature proper: perhaps he sees as well the dangers of the new country opening before him; his steps falter; he may even decide to retrace them without venturing into the perilous regions ahead. This prudence, however, is likely to cost him the best part of his work: the book— scanty, curtailed, incomplete—will not cover the subject. It may give an impression of conscientious, painstaking research; it will not give the more important and more praise-

[1] See Lanson, "L'Histoire littéraire et la sociologie," *Revue de métaphysique et de morale*, July, 1904; D. Mornet, *Le Sentiment de la nature en France de J.-J. Rousseau à Bernardin de Saint-Pierre* (1907), especially the Introduction and the Conclusion. I want to acknowledge here all I owe, in connection with the present chapter, to these two contributions, and perhaps still more to the personal teaching I received from Lanson and Mornet and to the precious conversations I held with them.

worthy impression of having brought to life in its entirety a moment, an episode, in the true history of human thought.

In what spirit should we approach problems of this type, since approach them we must? What attitude should we adopt toward them?

To Mme de Staël is generally attributed a formula that has met with much favor: "Literature", she is supposed to have said, "is the expression of society." This seems clear and obvious; and, relying more or less implicitly on this principle, many attempts have been made to study literary productions as mirrors of the society in which they were created, or, inversely, to study society as the source of literary productions. How has it happened that many of the earlier studies and interpretations rapidly became antiquated and are almost valueless today? Was it not because, in spite of the diligence applied to the work, it was basically unsound? As a matter of fact, those who within the last few years have shouldered the task afresh are often obliged both to accumulate documents and to build up a method. Nothing, indeed, is more necessary than to evolve processes of less dubious historical value, for the questions of literary history are rare that do not in some particular cease to be solely literary, that do not run more or less deeply into the history of ideas and the history of manners. Two important works—*Le Roman social en Angleterre*, by L. Cazamian, and *Le Sentiment de la nature en France de J.-J. Rousseau à Bernardin de Saint-Pierre*, by Mornet—furnish valuable suggestions of method together with an abundance of new material in the way of scholarly research. The latter is especially interesting to us, for it was through the very nature of the conditions existing during the period covered by the book that its author, whose first intention was to study Rousseau's feeling for nature from a purely literary point of view, was led to inquire into the ideas and manners that formed Rousseau's environment. He realized that nothing in Rousseau could be explained without the knowledge that round him on every hand had sprung up a curiosity about nature,—a taste for country life, for mountain scenery, for landscape gardening,—under conditions that placed Rousseau now ahead of his time, now behind it. We need only glance through the book to see at what cost of minute and scientific research, with what caution and wisdom, Mornet succeeds in determining the delicate reactions between literature and society, between manners and books.

If we consider the end of the seventeenth century and the beginning of the eighteenth, we find another problem, presenting itself in different terms, no doubt, but confronting us with similar difficulties. That problem, which I myself have attempted to treat and which I hope to be allowed to use here as an example, is the place held by the question of luxury in the philosophical literature of the eighteenth century,—an almost indispensable study for understanding Bossuet no less than La Bruyère, Voltaire no less than Rousseau. Writers of every type are observed to touch upon luxury: preachers, to combat it; satirists, to jeer at its excesses; moralists, to denounce its consequences; philosophers and economists, to study its processes and functions; and even novelists, to record or criticize the moral or social reaction to its changing manifestations. Thus the eighteenth century found ready at hand a certain number of important ideas over which to wage literary and philosophic war. Now these ideas doubtless did not spring fully armed from the brain of a few men of genius: they were laboriously forged and ground out during that obscure but active period of transition when, widely dispersed though they were, new theories were struggling to the light, new tendencies taking shape, opposing forces gaining strength. Notions of property, equality, commerce, luxury, civilization, and progress, of Nature and Revelation, were passing through an indispensable preparatory stage. A large part of the great philosophical works of eighteenth-century literature will remain unintelligible or obscure until we study the transformation undergone by each of these notions in passing from the moral consciousness of the seventeenth century—Christian, monarchical, classical, and speculative—to the moral consciousness of the eighteenth,—'libertin,' liberal, controversial, economic, and practical.

The results of this research I shall not yet set forth; I want merely to explain by means of examples (purposely few in number, to allow of detailed discussion) some of the difficulties we have to contend with; to point out useful practices; to suggest necessary precautions in investigating or in interpreting facts and documents; lastly, to determine the nature and import of the conclusions to which such studies may lead.

1. To convince ourselves that in treating questions that involve the history of ideas or of manners our methods should be enlarged and adapted, we have only to ask what would happen if we kept strictly to the point of view of literary history. The arbitrary, incomplete, false conclusions thus reached would soon prove that we were on the wrong road.

Doubtless, by limiting ourselves in this way, we could escape much labor. By relying exclusively on texts of literary reputation and value, without looking beyond them, it is easy to group quotations, to form definitions, to trace a current, and, easiest of all, to collect elements of polished antitheses, whose least fault is their complete inaccuracy. Let me make my meaning clear by taking as an example this same question of luxury. Let us confine ourselves to literary works, especially to those that literary history has classed as masterpieces. What do we see?

On the one hand, in the neighborhood of 1685 we find a general condemnation of luxury: viewed by the moralists as the blight of nations; blamed for many evils by La Bruyère, in his *Caractères* (1688); the subject of a merciless *Essai* by Nicole. Fénelon, in his *Télémaque*, banishes it from Salente and lauds the ancient ideal of frugality. The great preachers pursue its every manifestation: Massillon in the *Sermon sur l'aumône*, like Bourdaloue in the *Sermon sur les divertissements du monde*, asserts that the excesses of luxury have brought down the anger of God upon the close of the great reign.

On the other hand, fifty years later, about 1736, we see a general apology for luxury. Preachers still declaim, but to empty benches: philosophers and economists hold sway. *Le Mondain* of Voltaire is a clamorous declaration of war on the austere moralists, an airy and rather cynical justification of the superfluous, of comfort and sensuality; it is the gospel of eighteenth-century Epicureanism. Condemnation and vindication, respectively, are the watchwords of the opposing forces. Speaking strictly from the point of view of literary history, we can find little fault with this division. In fact, under one head or the other we might easily range the leading literary works without perverting their sense or coaxing a meaning from them that they do not contain.

Now, in reality, there is no such sharp division. If we are content to accept the opposition, we are far from tracing the curve of thought extending through these fifty years. Unless we accomplish this, we cannot give to literary works their full significance.

What we should do is to study the literary movement and the movement of ideas as inseparably linked and as reacting upon each other; when examining currents and tendencies —their direction, their points of contact, their origin, and their transformation—we should notice how far they are reflected in literature.

Here, however, the real trouble begins: the correlation once clearly established, how shall we isolate, how shall we select, the facts with which to work? Yet it is not so much a question of choice as of necessary guarantees and precautions of method.

2. To merge purely literary facts with facts of another nature, to study literary works not as isolated productions but in their relation to the social, political, or economic world to which they belong, is to become entangled in a mass of complications and difficulties.

a. The first and by no means the least difficulty consists in discovering in the texts not the exceptional nor the anecdotal matter but the usual, the normal. It is almost incredible to what extent the neglect of this practice has warped and still warps the history of ideas. H. Baudrillart's four-volume *Histoire du luxe* is the result of very creditable research: how is it that for our purposes it does not furnish half a dozen interesting facts? Because for no period has Baudrillart either asked or found what was, for the average individual, the average consumption of luxuries and the average idea of luxury,—information essential to any true interpretation and valuation of contemporary literary or philosophical texts. His book is, in the main, simply an amusing collection of anecdotes about the peculiarities of fashion, the exaggerated table refinement, the curious exactions of social etiquette, or the perplexing mysteries of feminine attire. The same objection is to be made to the works of the Goncourt brothers on the society and the women of the eighteenth century. Over and over again they quote and utilize texts that we also have to consult; but what do they seek in them? Not the average soul of the period but the extreme cases, the scandalous and eccentric features. The king's mistresses, the renowned courtesans, and the *filles d'opéra* do not constitute the eighteenth-century woman.

We find an instance of this striking contradiction in the case of Molière's successors in comedy, Le Sage, Regnard, Dancourt. They are supposed to have portrayed faithfully the French bourgeoisie of the period; the picture has been often reproduced—of the tradesman with his newly made wealth, the insolent and blustering upstart. It is a time when fortunes are made in the twinkling of an eye by the magic of credit. Speculation is rife; social distinctions totter and fall. All this is true, no doubt, but only partly and locally true. It is, in fact, the exceptional and the abnormal; other investigations, more extensive and more painstaking, give us insight into quite a different reality. Glance over those account books ('livres de raison'), those family registers in which, day after day, the bourgeois of the provinces or even of Paris set down their domestic accounts and the faithful record of their obscure existences. More than two hundred such books have been published, typifying the life of several localities, of many degrees of fortune, of various professions. Add to these the private correspondence, printed or in manuscript,[1] and we shall see a bourgeois society emerge very different from the first,—one composed not of a few irrational and unprincipled individuals but of a mass of unknown, good, industrious people. This is the bourgeoisie that works, thinks, and acts, that takes advantage of

---

[1] Besides the large number of references given in the *Catalogue des manuscrits des bibliothèques des départements* (Paris, 1849–1906), many private archives are accessible.

the progress of commerce and industry to build up, little by little, a comfortable and substantial competency. It is just this normal, average bourgeoisie whose existence we should recognize and whose mentality we should analyze, if we would understand the diffusion, the success, and the influence, at this time, of works in which a spirit of reform and a solicitude for national issues are manifest. To this class belonged the readers for whom La Bruyère, Fénelon, Vauban, and Boisguillebert wrote: these readers we need to know.

As is readily seen, if a literary work is considered by itself, or if it is considered a priori as a faithful and adequate exponent of the social stratum to which it corresponds, errors are bound to result. At this stage in our work, therefore, it behooves us to take additional precautions.[1]

b. The first precaution relates to literary works considered by themselves. As I have said elsewhere, we should not let ourselves be hypnotized by the masterpieces; for masterpieces are but rarely exact in their representation of contemporary public opinion and of the progress of ideas. "It is a mistake", said Bersot, "to believe . . . that the book that makes the most stir is the most characteristic of its epoch." Bossuet is ahead of his time: the Père Gerdil or the Père Provinquières, of faint renown, reflect it more accurately.

Secondly, it is specially important here to give to chronology the scrupulous attention that I have already insisted on. Famous men and famous works are often walled in by certain traditions, certain classifications, which it is hard to overthrow. How many people,—even cultivated people,—in speaking of eighteenth-century painters, name Watteau in the same breath with Fragonard, without realizing that

---

[1] This chapter finds its natural complement in Chapter X, "Questions of Success and of Influence."

Fragonard was born eleven years after the death of Watteau and that he was a contemporary of Napoleon I, Watteau of Louis XIV? Or let us turn to some of the authors who are involved in our study of ideas on luxury: Bossuet, Fénelon, La Bruyère, Fontenelle, Bayle. Each has his traditional niche in the history of the literature of his epoch; manuals and other scholarly works, I am well aware, are responsible for a large part of this. In these works Bossuet, Fénelon, and La Bruyère belong without question to the seventeenth century; there they are, ranged alongside the 'grands classiques,' as glorious representatives of French literature under Louis XIV. Fontenelle and Bayle, on the contrary, are always given a place apart. Once for all they have been baptized 'precursors' of the eighteenth century, which entitles them to a special chapter. They are thought to be closer to Montesquieu or Voltaire than to Fénelon or Bossuet. The fact is, however, that the *Dialogues des morts* of Fontenelle (1683) is anterior to *Les Caractères* and to *Télémaque* and that scarcely eighteen months elapsed between the *Pensées diverses sur la comète* of Bayle (1682) and the *Discours sur l'histoire universelle* of Bossuet (1681).

Lastly, for certain categories of writers we must disregard the individual and consider the group, in order to reach the average opinion. This method has to be applied, for instance, to preachers and jurists. Here personal doctrines matter little, unless in dealing with the great minds: we must, so to speak, take 'cross sections' at various dates and, by accumulating the evidence and verifying the variations, gain a knowledge of the general direction and intensity of the movement.[1] In regard to the preachers, a close examination

---

[1] This process has been clearly explained by Mornet in the Introduction to the book already cited, and analyzed by Lanson in a review of the same book, in *Revue d'histoire littéraire*, 1908, pp. 168–170.

of some three hundred sermons, from 1670 to 1730, shows that the question of luxury, originally discussed from the pulpit as a moral issue, becomes finally a social question: luxury, once the corrupter that interfered with the Christian duty of almsgiving, is denounced rather for disturbing the social hierarchy, upsetting existing conditions, establishing a sort of equality between social elements that it was in God's scheme of things to keep distinct. This point does not stand out, or stands out only dimly, if, instead of comparing groups of preachers, we limit ourselves to the best and most striking sermons of the few gifted and famous men.

The foregoing advice aims solely at associating literature and life. It should be supplemented by considering the following questions:

(1) In what measure does the work owe its creation and original form to the environment? First, let us remark that even if the book presents the author's thought to the public, it often returns—to quote La Bruyère's words—what the public has lent. The form that the writer gives to his work, the spirit that animates it, the way he develops his ideas, depend primarily on his own originality and creative force; but is it not true also that they depend to a certain extent on the readers for whom the work is destined? This relation should never be lost sight of. If, as Lanson says, "the mind of the author contains in advance the mind of his readers",[1] we must ask how far the author, in choosing his means of expression, in arranging his thoughts, in insisting on certain ideas, has obeyed—perhaps unconsciously—the imperious demand that reached him from his future public. Every study of the trend of ideas in the first third of the eighteenth century, for example, draws extensively on the *Lettres persanes* of Montesquieu. Now we can neither weigh the real

[1] *Revue de métaphysique et de morale*, p. 626.

value of his testimony nor measure the book's novelty or influence without first ascertaining to what extent it was 'ordered' by the public. On a close inspection we see that neither the form (an epistolary novel), nor the Eastern element, nor the conception of a social or political satire, nor even the utopian pages on the Troglodytes, are in any exact sense new. We see that they fit into an already existing series; that in this respect Montesquieu has created nothing, —he has satisfied a demand. He is therefore neither an innovator nor a precursor: he is, rather, the enlightened, intelligent, well-informed spokesman of a social group that has prepared in advance a form for his thought and polemic.

Does this imply that literary works are the faithful images of the average opinions and ideas of the society that gives them birth? Should we make this relation a postulate of our method of research? By no means.

Without speaking here of works that apparently have no direct relation to their environment,—products of isolated writers, resulting from prolonged meditations in soundproof "towers of ivory",—we must remember the books that express not what actually already exists in the social environment but what is yet to be realized—the aspirations and hopes of that environment. Again it is Lanson who finds a neat phrase: "In such cases", he says, "literature is not the *image* of society, but its *complement*."[1] Take as an instance the first *Discours* of Rousseau, "Sur les sciences et les arts": is it purely declamatory, expressing only Rousseau's personal sentiments and points of view, connected in no way with the social sphere in which it appeared? Nothing of the kind. Doubtless the work represents neither the society nor the customs of the time: it is in Voltaire and in the *Encyclopédie* that the thirst for civilization, for progress and luxury,

[1] Loc. cit. p. 635.

characteristic of this society, finds its true expression. The "Mondain" of Voltaire is a type that could be seen anywhere in the fashionable life of Paris and the provinces. Yet certain people felt a yearning that neither Voltaire nor the *Encyclopédie* could satisfy; they were filled with anxiety and scruples of conscience, with discontent and revolt; neither the social life nor the literature of the day could reassure or calm them. These mingled aspirations (contrary, we should note, to the general trend of the period), these regrets or dreams, which the preachers of fifty years before might have interpreted, find expression in the bitter, burning pages of the *Discours* of Rousseau. Here again, the environment is responsible for the literary work, but only in a particular, restricted, and almost negative sense.

(2) In what measure does the environment influence the subsequent life of the work? As we penetrate far into the study of the relations between literature and society we should repeatedly ask this question. It is of no avail to collate the various readings, to observe the development of a writer's ideas, and to state the results with scientific precision. We should seek the reason for this evolution,—the causes, often exterior, of this transformation. Many times it is not so much the writer himself who changes as the political, economic, and social conditions round him. Literature is only the echo of these conditions. The La Bruyère of 1695 is no longer the La Bruyère of 1688: a richer maturity, a keener observation, a sort of ambition that success has fostered from edition to edition, no doubt explain many of the alterations and additions in *Les Caractères*; but does not the difference between society and social conditions in 1688 and in 1695 count for much? A short passage from the *Maximes* of La Rochefoucauld illustrates this point with striking exactness. In 1664, in the first edition, we find:

"La politesse des États est le commencement de leur décadence, parce qu'elle applique tous les particuliers à leur
intérêt propre et les détourne du bien public." In 1665 the
phrase becomes: "*Le luxe et la trop grande politesse* dans
les États sont *le présage assuré* de leur décadence, parce que
tous les particuliers s'attachant à leurs intérêts propres, ils se
détournent du bien public." After 1666 it is suppressed.
What does this signify? Can we not trace here the reactions
of La Rochefoucauld's observant and thoughtful nature to
the pressure of events and experience? The first form of the
maxim represents traditional and current opinion: pomp and
excessive refinement corrupt nations, debilitate energy, and
encourage egoism. A few months later, Colbertism stimu-
lates a sudden and unexpected rise of industry. A large number of the most important manufactories are founded in 1664
and 1665. The effect is quickly felt in private consumption
and public expenditure, especially in Paris and in the aristo-
cratic circles that La Rochefoucauld frequents. Thus his
anxiety takes definite form; he expresses it more forcibly
and completely: "*Le luxe* et *la trop grande politesse* . . . *le
présage assuré* de la décadence." Then Colbertism carries
the day; its triumph seems definite and indisputable; the
king derives new glory from it; the nation, power and respect; and the moralist strikes out the reflection that contains a criticism of Colbert and his success.

I might make the same experiment on less celebrated
works, such as the *Essais de morale*, of Nicole, and the *Consi-
dérations sur les mœurs*, of Duclos. Or let me, rather, point
out the overwhelming effect of the same social and economic
changes upon the great Arnauld. I choose two letters by
him, one written in 1668, the other in 1685, in which he
replies to overscrupulous priests who ask how much severity
they should apply to feminine adornment, laces, and luxuri-

ous brocades. In 1668 he speaks in pure Jansenist vein: no tolerance of superfluous and diabolical ornaments,—those instruments of corruption and agents of immodesty. In 1685 the tone has changed together with the doctrine. Take care! advises Arnauld; be cautious! Be not, of course, indulgent toward Christians who forget the duty of almsgiving,—especially toward penitents inclined to a too liberal "nudité de gorge". But also, before condemning harshly, —Arnauld continues,—give heed to these points: first, that, as the price of luxuries has greatly decreased in the last ten years, more brocades and laces today do not necessarily mean more extravagance; next, that the manufacture of such commodities furnishes a living for a multitude of laboring men and women whom your condemnation would deprive of wages and bread. A curious evolution, indeed, to be explained only by the vast economic revolution that separates the two texts.[1]

(3) These instances are enough to show how we obtain through literary texts a 'snapshot' of the morals and opinions of a period profoundly stirred by the pressure of new economic and social conditions. If such is the general effect of the public on the book, we should also ask ourselves what is the effect of the book on the public. In the chapter entitled "Questions of Success and of Influence" I have analyzed more especially literary influences; now it is time to consider influence on life, manners, and moral ideas.

We already know with what extreme prudence it is necessary to speak of the influence of a book. The starting-point for such a study, as we have seen, is not the book itself but the opinion formed of it by the reading-public. To the examples given, it is possible to add one or two that are of special importance for the history of moral doctrines.

[1] For a more detailed discussion of these points see my *Apologie du luxe au XVIIIe siècle*. Paris, 1909.

Observe, for instance, how the 'libertins' of the seventeenth century utilized and transformed the Epicureanism of Gassendi. As a matter of fact, we find practically nothing of Gassendi's *Syntagma philosophiae Epicuri* in either Saint-Évremond, Ninon de Lenclos, or Mme Deshoulières. Yet they quote Gassendi, rest on his authority, are saturated with him. In 1678 his favorite disciple, the "joli philosophe" Bernier, published two widely circulated editions of an *Abrégé de la philosophie de Gassendi*, which, under the shelter of Gassendi's name, contains a system considerably different from his. Therefore, when we speak of the influence of 'Gassendism,' we should start not from Gassendi himself but from the sum total of the ideas that his disciples or indirect heirs have established in his name.

Mandeville's *Fable of the Bees,* a work of much importance for the history of ideas in the eighteenth century, has been similarly distorted. The book, published in England in 1706, was not translated into French until 1740. Before being translated, however, it was used and even occasionally imitated, though less well known in its original text than through the abstracts and reviews given in the periodicals. Now all of these—*Journal des savants, Mercure de France, Mémoires de Trévoux, Bibliothèque britannique*— were of one mind in stressing Mandeville's ideas on luxury and its function in social life. As a result, a chapter that is really supplementary to the original work, and that gives of the author's general ideas only a fragmentary and incomplete impression, appeared to the French public the most important and original part. If, then, we say that Mandeville has influenced the evolution of moral ideas in the eighteenth century in France, we must qualify our statement by admitting that it is not precisely Mandeville's own thought that has acted, but what the public has rightly or wrongly made of it.

Now if we want to push farther, we must ask ourselves whether the action of a literary work on its readers can really produce changes in the social or moral life of an epoch or an environment. The question is a very different one from that of a purely literary influence: here an actual, practical influence is to be determined; in other words, the changes, disturbances, or progress that it provokes in the lives of men or of institutions.

Influences of this type can, I think, be classified under three headings: a literary work may be an agent of liberation, an agent of preparation, or an agent of organization.

It may be an agent of liberation in the sense that it creates a general state of mind or of conscience so fundamentally at variance with certain political, economic, social, and moral conditions that these must either be modified or abolished. During the last years of the reign of Louis XIV and during the Regency occurs a joyous expansion of epicurism. When we see noble and bourgeois shaking off the gloomy yoke of moral austerity and rigidity; when we see people devoting themselves in all tranquillity of conscience to the enjoyment of worldly goods and to each day's increased comfort, without excess, debauchery, or even coarseness, but with firm determination to miss none of the ephemeral pleasures of a too short existence,—when we see this transformation in the manner of living, we should seek the cause not only in a material change of conditions but also in the deep influence of the freethinkers,—of Saint-Évremond, Gassendi, or Bernier, who have made all other modes and conceptions of life intolerable to their readers.

Again, a singularly interesting confirmation of such influence might be found on the eve of the French Revolution. Writers and philosophers who during the eighteenth century publicly aired their views helped to make the people intolerant of certain abuses, certain absurdities, of the Old Régime. Readers fed on Montesquieu, Voltaire, and Rousseau could not live happily within the narrow limits of a political organization imposed by monarchical absolutism, by a judiciary system founded on the selling of positions and the bribing of judges, and by a disastrous inequality of conditions and classes. The structure was bound to crumble, not only because it was beginning to crack but because this enlightened public who must live under it would accept it no longer. When the representatives of the people transferred the bodies of Voltaire and of Rousseau to the Panthéon, they were not merely obeying a fanatical impulse or a desire to spite the late régime: their action was symbolic and significant.

Is there not a certain similarity in all this to the rôle played by *Uncle Tom's Cabin* in connection with the struggle against slavery?

A literary work may be also an agent of preparation. This is too obvious to dwell upon. Social, legislative, and political changes imply a long and thorough preparation in which literary works take an active part. The theatre and the novel 'prepared' the French laws on divorce, on the legal status of women, on education. When between 1900 and 1914, after a decided falling away of patriotism in France, a splendid revival took place, the writers who gave expression to the feeling were not only the echoes of their public: they were its guides and instructors, oftentimes checked by irony and opposition. They were preparing; and the enthusiasm of 1914 has proved that the voices of authors heard through their books are not powerless to stir a nation's soul to its depths.

Lastly, a literary work may be an agent of organization. It is a means of communication between minds; it helps to form opinion, either in the public at large or in a group. Like a tiny quantity of some chemical substance thrown into a solution already saturated with the same substance, it causes a sudden crystallization that alters completely the existing conditions. Here two cases may arise:

(*a*) A book may brusquely penetrate an environment where many minds are unconsciously preoccupied with identical needs. To this tie, real but not sensed, it gives concrete form. It unites the members of a group and helps them to know and to understand one another. In 1734 the economist J. B. Melon's *Essai politique sur le commerce*, which takes up once more the question of luxury, fell in the midst of a public whose ideas on the subject, in the preceding twenty years, had undergone a profound change. Gradually yet progressively the question had shifted from a moral to an economic basis. Of this everyone was vaguely conscious, but no one had said it in so many words. Melon did say it, distinctly, in a few vivid, striking pages which interpret admirably the unexpressed or ill-expressed opinions, moral, economic, and social, of the upper classes of the bourgeoisie. This, then, is one instance of a book's giving to the opinion of a social group the homogeneity that it had but imperfectly achieved and the formula that it totally lacked. It was an agent of unification.

(*b*) A book may also serve to draw together a few isolated individuals who, lost in the throng, are opposed to the generally accepted views both in their habit of mind and in their personal beliefs. It states this opposition precisely and is a rallying-point for these scattered skirmishers. A small, independent faction is formed, a veritable party with a platform; the party, however, does not make the platform,— the platform makes the party. Such a platform is the first *Discours* of Rousseau,—a paradoxical and blatant work, flung in the face of a public that held the sanctioning of luxury an almost incontestable truth. Rousseau, among a mass of adversaries, discovered a handful of followers opposed to the economic rehabilitation of luxury. From 1750 they are a force to reckon with. This group, in a measure restoring the question to the moral footing that had been disregarded for nearly half a century, appeared as a sort of new cell in the total social organism at that date. The discourse acted as an agent of dissociation.

Such are the various contacts that a work may have with the society that gives it birth, and such are their principal actions and reactions. In attempting to discover and to define these, we must not forget to ask another question:

How wide has been the diffusion of the work? We have seen already[1] that by means of bibliography, the history of printing, a study of the press, memoirs, and correspondences, as well as by considering the use to which the work is put as the source of subsequent authors, we may answer this question with a satisfactory degree of certainty.

Without these precautions we shall surely form false estimates of the extent of the action of a book on society. Originality or novelty is not a guarantee of popularity or influence, nor is it often a reason for either. Thus we should at the outset make sure that the book has ever had popularity or influence. If we find no signs of these, either at the time of publication or afterwards, we must give up trying to fit the book into a preconceived rôle. For instance, in the very obscure *Cours abrégé de philosophie*, published in Switzerland in 1697 by the equally obscure French refugee Le Sage de la Colombière, is set forth practically the entire mercantilistic theory of commerce and luxury that was later to meet with great success in the writings of Melon and Voltaire. This fact is strange; it is amusing—but that is all

[1]See chapter entitled "Questions of Success and of Influence," p. 225.

there is to it. Nowhere in France, in the works of famous or of insignificant writers, in reviews or in newspapers, in libraries, or in volumes of collected essays, is the slightest trace to be found of any knowledge of Le Sage de la Colombière. His thought was original and striking, without doubt. That it has lain dormant, taking no part in the history of ideas, there is even less doubt. The yeast may lie close to the dough indefinitely and remain inactive: they must be mixed before the bread will rise.

After these varied investigations have put us in possession of the facts, we must turn them to account—group them, organize them, and interpret them.

Le Sentiment de la nature en France de J.-J. Rousseau à Bernardin de Saint-Pierre, by Mornet, is full of interesting suggestions as to what method to pursue at this point.[1]

First, it is well, as Mornet expresses it, to form "homogeneous groups" of facts having the same character, the same origin, and a similar bearing, in order to eliminate as far as possible individual differences. Too often "entertaining documents have been collected to the neglect of chronology and truth. Here we have gathered them in together with everything that surrounds them—obscure examples, works forgotten almost as soon as written, humble records of mediocre people, that give the surest proof of the depth an influence may attain." Thus Mornet groups in series every fact he can gather relating to his special subject: evidences of the growing taste for travel, the new interest in ocean or mountains, the transformation in architecture and landscape gardening, or the effect of these modifications on literary inspiration and form. Similarly, whoever wants to study a problem such as that of ideas on the nature of money, commerce, or luxury which prevailed between 1660 and 1750

[1] See pages 9 ff.

must take into account not only the doctrines and opinions expressed in the masterpieces of Bossuet, Montesquieu, or Rousseau but also the average doctrine and opinion of preachers and moralists, of magistrates and of the bourgeoisie. By dropping all writings—individual caprice, pure paradox, or trivial anecdote—into one melting-pot, we may hope to extract the general cast of mind or moral consciousness of a given period.

This first suggestion is supplemented by another: We should try to determine the flow of converging facts; only by this means can we measure the information gained through particular investigations. "The transformations in manners", says Mornet, "are not simple in their courses. Opinion seems to progress as a rising tide, whose waves alternately advance and recede. From the innumerable mass of volumes spread out before the historian of the eighteenth century, it is easy for him to choose quotations that prove anything he pleases. The experiment has been made. The true meaning of a movement does not become clear until, instead of contrasting a few facts with nothing, we contrast a group that expands with one that contracts."[1] It will be well to notice, in his book as a whole and especially in the concluding chapter, how skillfully he applies this method.

Once more let me repeat that its application to the problem of ideas on luxury simplifies a mass of facts that are often obscure and always complex. I dwell on this point as an illustration of the service rendered to scholars and students by those who know how to organize and formulate useful methods. When, in the course of my work, Mornet's book was published, I felt as if I were emerging from a forest full of misleading tangled trails into a garden squared off by orderly paths with signposts at their intersections.

[1] Loc. cit. p. 9.

Therefore, with Mornet's directions to guide us, let us review the question of luxury as a whole and see what results we reach. Toward 1670 what do we find? Facts that prove a general opposition to luxury preponderate: preachers, moralists, philosophers, historians, and magistrates are almost unanimous; sumptuary laws multiply; the government is in sympathy with prevailing sentiment. Here we have the dominant group. Not the only group, however, for round it are forming opposing tendencies. First, economic facts, whose moral and social bearings are only partly disclosed, though already in embryo, and perceptible either in a few daring thinkers or in sporadic occurrences of daily life—a restricted group, not yet to be compared to the preceding one. Secondly, as an undercurrent, still obscure and intangible, the 'libertin' Epicureanism of Saint-Évremond, of Ninon de Lenclos, of Bernier, and of a few others, which spreads farther and farther, takes on a thousand shapes, penetrates into theoretical morality, and echoes in everyday life. This last influence has at that date no direct connection with the question of luxury, but prepares a more indulgent attitude toward it: the epicureans who seek to extract from life all the pleasures and comforts it affords are quite ready to join hands with the defenders of luxury as a source of pleasure and purveyor of material comfort.

Thirty years later let us take another cross section and examine the condition of the various groups. The first, preponderant in 1670, has dwindled and disintegrated: Christian preaching either persists in traditional oratory, to which no one listens, or allows itself to be pervaded by a spirit of indulgence toward luxury; the moralists, for their part, go over to the enemy. The second group—economic facts— has taken a leading place; we feel the effects of the great industrial and commercial transformations at the close of the reign of Louis XIV; new conditions hold sway over public opinion and modify it profoundly. This group is still swelling. Lastly, the third group—'libertin' and epicurean ideas —makes a new move: it joins forces with the preceding one. Henceforth the connection is clear between the economic aspect of the question of luxury and its moral significance: the progress of luxury in everyday life leads to its justification in moral and philosophical theories.

Finally, another thirty years later, we see a very different relationship. The first group is seemingly submerged and, for the time being, practically reduced to silence. We must not, however, cease to heed its murmurings: toward 1750, with the coming of Rousseau, it will forcibly raise its voice again. The other groups, on the contrary, enlarge and extend their influence with extraordinary rapidity. Henceforth the question of luxury is placed on an economic basis, and, as such, luxury finds, among those who most faithfully reflect the general opinion of their time, only enthusiastic apologists. It is the period of *Le Mondain* of Voltaire: literary thought is imbued with economic preoccupation; we find a complete reversal since 1670 in the importance of the various groups of facts that we have been considering.

It would be perverting the sense and the spirit of the method just sketched to conclude that it deals with groups of facts, of writers, or of ideas, to the exclusion of individual elements. Far from this, it enables us to define, to limit, with great precision the rôle of the individual. Though I have insisted upon the interest and importance of organizing facts into coherent and homogeneous groups, you must not forget that this is merely one process among many and that elsewhere I have tried to explain the action of an individual or of a book and to facilitate its analysis. It is, indeed, by digging in both these directions that the student will find the richest treasure. He should discriminate between group psychology and individual action. He should contrast the times when writers echo one another, in a tireless round, with the moment when a fresh, vigorous thought, original or rejuvenated, sounds a new note in the monotonous concert. He should mention how and when this element, the product and image of some individual, becomes the point of departure for a new series—the generative cell of a new group; he should trace this group until in its turn it is broken up or transformed by a personality or an event that marks its end, as some other personality or event has marked its beginning. In short, he should point out in the analysis and the history of these complex relations the respective places of the two elements called by Tarde "imitation" and "invention". "Social transformations", as he tells us, "are explained by *imitated individual initiative.*"[1] This phrase, taken in its true meaning, contains a programme for our studies. In the history of "social transformations" what is the book if not an "individual initiative"? Let us therefore ask (1) whether the book possesses the quality that may accurately be called "initiative"; (2) whether this initiative has been "imitated", —that is, whether the success or the influence of the book has created a group; (3) whether the group has been sufficiently powerful to transform in any degree the existing social conditions.[2] I believe that, thus approached, our pro-

[1] G. Tarde, "L'Invention considérée comme moteur de l'évolution sociale," *Revue internationale de sociologie*, 1902.

[2] In the article already cited Tarde gives a good illustration of the rôle played in the transformation of social conditions by the individual,—by 'invention,'—which for us means the writer or the book. He explains that the consequences of an influence may appear to the superficial observer disproportionate to the actual value or force of that influence, owing to the fact that an individual influence often merely "destroys the equilibrium": "When the touch of a bird's wing starts an avalanche, it is indeed a very tiny force compared

gramme is justly divided between the individual and the mass, the genius[1] and the group.

No chapter in this book has inspired me with so keen a desire to conclude by giving a few judicious, clear rules; no chapter has made me feel so surely the impossibility or at least the imprudence of such a step. I shall limit myself to summarizing by certain suggestions and warnings my attempt to define the attitude of mind in which to begin and to carry on the study of literature and life in their mutual relations.

Remember that few problems of literary history are confined to the domain of literature proper, without overstepping its bounds on one side or another or bringing us into direct contact with the general history of ideas or of civilization. Do not try, then, to save trouble by arbitrarily restricting your study to the literary aspect of the question; on the contrary, face the difficulty squarely, with the understanding that here lies the principal interest, the true value, of your subject.

Never be content, in comparing a literary work with the manners or the ideas of an epoch, to collect anecdotes or isolated facts, no matter how interesting and pointed. Seek the general, the average, the normal—the ensemble of the social, moral, worldly life of the place or period studied.

with that of gravitation and molecular cohesion—constant forces whose unstable equilibrium has been jarred by this slight, accidental shock. The shock is none the less the explanation of the avalanche. . . . It is the same in the world of human beings. The variable element, accident, germ, is represented here by individual initiative, invention. The stable element is made up of climate, soil, race, as well as of traditions, customs, inculcated ideas, acquired habits."

[1] When I say 'genius,' I do not mean to imply that only the very great minds or the very great writers represent the 'individual' element that originates social transformations. I mean simply the personality that invents something new or that rediscovers something old. Tarde himself says, "The leaders of the world are not its great men but the great thoughts that not infrequently take up their abode in small men ".

In particular, apply this principle to the books themselves. Give to the masterpieces, or to the works that show inventiveness, the place they deserve as elements of transformation; but do not forget that they reflect less exactly the average opinion or the general environment than does the mass of imitative works that succeeds them.

In studying mutual transformations and reactions a minute precision in chronology is the sole means of tracing exact 'curves' and of placing each modifying agent in his true historical position.

Again, as these transformations and these modifications are the result of the reciprocal influence of book and public, take care to define with extreme exactness the nature, depth, and duration of this influence. Do not merely affirm and guess, but exhaust every means of investigation.

Finally, once in possession of the facts, group them: associate those of coherent, homogeneous character. Examine the groups: at a given date study their mutual relations, their comparative sizes, the general trend of their courses. Do they sink deep or spread out upon the surface? At other dates make the same study, the same measurements. Then compare results. You will find that the curves along which these transformations are moving, the points of intersection of literature and of life, are tracing themselves before your eyes. If, on the summits of these curves,—that is, at the points that mark a change of direction,—you succeed in placing the individual or the book that has caused the change, I believe that you will have done all you can to draw a true picture of a moment in the history of thought and the history of manners. Doubtless you will not always solve every problem; but you will, at least, have clearly stated its terms, and when you have failed to find the answer, you will know how and why.

CHAPTER XII

PREPARATION AND REDACTION OF A THESIS

In my opening pages I explained that the aim of this book was to help advanced students of French literature to engage successfully in research work. Up to this point we have been occupied more particularly with the methods of discovering, criticizing, and preparing, the material: we must now turn to constructing and organizing. We want to build, with the stones that we have hewn, a consistent and harmonious edifice; to do this we must consider each step of the work in turn. I am far from intending to summarize in a few pages the arts of rhetoric and of composition; I should like merely to ask the inexperienced scholar to reflect on certain foreseeable difficulties and certain usual mistakes.

I. Choice of a Subject

The choice of a subject is undoubtedly the capital point; it is also the point that is commonly treated in the most casual and shortsighted manner. It would be superfluous to say that to write a good thesis requires a good subject, did not the all-too-general practice prove that this advice is frequently needed. What is likely to take place? The student hunts up some professor and straightway asks, "Will you give me a subject for a thesis?" After a more or less hurried discussion the student departs with his subject in his notebook—a subject naturally in far greater accord with the preoccupations and tastes of the adviser than with the ability and preference of the prospective writer. To begin in this way is neither logical nor reasonable. Never forget that a subject should be not a point to start from, but a decision to reach: I mean that when you have made up your mind to attempt a piece of research work or a thesis, you should next decide upon a field of special interest—an author, a century, a question—vast and vague. You should then read, explore, reflect; little by little circumscribe the field, contract the horizon, until such time as you shall have clearly defined the subject that deserves your interest and labor. You will then be no stranger to it: you will be on familiar ground, with a wide background to supply solidity and vigor to your research.

Remember that any thoroughly good subject conforms as far as possible to the following requirements:

1. It should not be too large: an unlimited subject is a great handicap. Shun those fine, broad topics that entail a knowledge of the literature and the history of several countries. They are too heavy for your unaccustomed shoulders.

2. It should possess genuine interest; that is, it should be so linked with the general history of literature or of civilization as to be not a sterile exhumation of dry details but a real contribution to the fund of literary or historical knowledge.

3. It should be new. Before proceeding, you should make sure that the bloom has not been rubbed off. Be on the lookout for articles hidden away in reviews, or you may be disillusioned by finding that your subject has already been thoroughly investigated.

4. Do not struggle against physical impossibilities. Before becoming deeply involved inquire where and how you can find the materials essential to you. Measure the amount of work that you can accomplish here in America and the amount that you can do only in France. Take into con-

sideration the resources of the libraries to which you have
access; the complete or incomplete collections at your disposal,—in short, do not rush ahead until you know exactly where you intend to go, why and how you expect to
arrive there.

5. Lastly, be loyal toward your work, which means that
you should be the master and not the slave of your subject.
It is while working that you will determine its exact scope
and limits. You may well find that a subject, tempting at
first, does not exist in the form you supposed. Do not hesitate an instant: give it up. Stretch it if it is too narrow;
shrink it if it is too broad. Preparing a thesis is not like
answering definite questions on the day of an examination:
for your thesis you yourself ask the questions; you yourself
are responsible for the value and intelligence of the questions no less than of the answers.

II. Approach and Preparation

As you advance in your work, as you clear the ground in
all directions, various problems will spring up before you.
You will then have occasion to apply the advice and suggestions given in the preceding chapters; whether dealing with
biography or bibliography, sources or influence, chronology
or authenticity, you will continually have to follow the same
processes: investigation and criticism of materials, elimination, organization, redaction. To what has already been said,
it is necessary to add only some general remarks.

1. Establish your bibliography with minute care, with
no preconceived ideas as to the utility or futility of any
reference. Your cards should be clear and full, as has been
explained at the end of the chapter entitled "Implements and
Tools." They should be arranged alphabetically and by sub-

ject in such a way that you can instantly put your hand on any reference either to a given author or to a specific part of your work.

2. Follow a rigid discipline in your reading; that is, organize it logically, according to a definite scheme. First, read the texts by your author, or the original texts relating to your subject. Read them thoroughly: do not be content with a superficial and uncertain acquaintance; make them part of yourself. Read and reread them until you can at once locate any allusion, word, comparison, or shade of thought. You will not work to full advantage on a text until the day when you know it practically by heart. Next, choose all the reading which, though it may have no direct bearing on your subject or no immediate usefulness, yet gives you the historical, literary, or philosophical atmosphere requisite to its proper treatment. You must be master of this background, under pain of producing only shallow work without import or interest. Finally, run through all the works, all the references, compiled in your bibliography. Very soon experience will enable you to distinguish what is essential from what is superfluous or worthless. Never feel obliged to discuss seriously the conclusions of any works not in themselves serious. A brief note at the bottom of a page, or even in your bibliography, will generally do them full justice. On the other hand, examine with the utmost conscientiousness everything that supplies you with any important information or point of view. Never let anything turn up without immediately making a note of it.

3. You must, however, understand how to take notes and, later, how to use them. Make them abundant, complete, exact.

Make them *abundant*. If, your research ended, many still remain unused, so much the worse. Yet this is better than to regret not having taken them when you had the chance. Besides, if they have served no purpose on this occasion, they may perhaps do so on another; in the meantime you have learned something in the taking.

Make them *complete*: do not, in order to gain a minute or two, summarize instead of transcribing a passage, if it is worth preserving at all.

Make them *exact*, so as to be able, when the time comes, to incorporate them in your work as quotations or references without consulting again the books from which you copied them. Some writers have a habit of inclosing their notes in quotation marks whenever the text is exactly reproduced. These signs show that the extract may be inserted as it is; their absence, that the note is merely a résumé or an approximation of the text. I consider this a good practice.

Always write your notes on loose leaves,—never in bound notebooks. Always use the same size, not so small that the note will be cramped or will run over several pages, nor so big as to be clumsy. Never write on more than one side of the paper, and put only one note on a page. Otherwise, in sorting your notes you will have to copy many of them.

While working on a writer, you will be handling at least three classes of notes: quotations taken from his books; extracts from books or documents contemporary with him; notes on modern works of erudition, criticism, or reference. As a help in classifying your material, why not choose different-colored paper for each kind of note?

Whenever possible, immediately upon taking a note give it some title, even if nothing more than a heading that defines, summarizes, and emphasizes its interest and significance. This precaution will compel you to reflect, to weigh the interest and the value of the text that you have copied, to extract from it some useful suggestions; without it the same text, reread several weeks or months later, might convey to you no idea whatever.

Finally, do not accumulate notes by the hundred and then by the thousand, only to let them lie in your boxes until the day when, deciding that your search for material is completed, you turn to its redaction. This is a deplorable method. On the contrary, reread your notes continually, the oftener the better; reread them, varying the order; reread them each time that you add another extract. This constant contact with your swelling mass of notes will be an incentive to reflections, doubts, associations of ideas, discoveries of relations and connections, that at the outset you had not even suspected. Each time that an idea strikes you in this way, jot it down, without waiting a second, without waiting even to read the following note. Nothing is so fleeting as these associations or thoughts: if you do not close your hand on them when they first occur to you, they will escape and may never come back. Experience proves the utility of this practice: after some months you will be astonished to see the amount not only of external material but of personal work thus collected, and to discover how helpful are the results of this method when it is time to construct and organize.

III. WORK OF ORGANIZATION: DETERMINATION OF PROBLEMS

Let us suppose that you are now in possession of all your documents. You have read and reread your notes; you have added your personal thoughts and reactions to the information collected from your reading. Do not believe that from this time forward you should rush headlong, write at top speed, race from page to page. You will save time and inevitably improve the quality of your work if you allow all this material to ripen and mature in your mind for a fairly long period. Force yourself to talk about the results of your researches and of your deliberation; there is no better way of learning to express definitely the ideas still seething nebulously in your subconscious mind. If some interesting point is brought to light in this way, verify it and make a memorandum of it after the conversation is over. Then, when you have completely mastered your subject, begin to arrange and to write.

At this stage be governed by a new consideration: pick out every problem contained in your subject and try to give to every point the form of a problem. Do not be content merely to arrange your notes in a logical or a chronological order or to divide your material into chapters and paragraphs. Keep repeating to yourself that in every question, general or particular, there is always some obscurity to clear up, some uncertainty to dispel. Try to find the definite or approximate solution or, if no solution is possible, give the reason. By this method you will create centres of interest and supply a principle of organization.

Again, in the heterogeneous mass that you have gathered, some is new and some is old. Be loyal toward yourself and toward your readers in differentiating clearly between the two and in making the new predominant, the old subordinate. The reader of any work of this type is already well informed on the subject and expects from you only what you are able to offer as a personal and original contribution; anything else, no matter how cleverly disguised, how cunningly unlabeled, is mere rhetorical amplification.

The plan of the work admits of no general advice: each subject has a plan of its own, and yours will be good if it allows you to bring out every discovery pertinent to the question; if it does not interfere with the logical or the chronological order; if it does not necessitate dispersing through several chapters a question that should be dealt with as a whole; and, finally, if it does not entail unacceptable repetitions. This last fault occurs repeatedly in monographs in which both the life and the works of an author are considered. Should they be treated separately? Should the criticism of his works be incorporated into the history of his life? There are as many answers as there are subjects; one thing, however, is certain: if, in discussing the works, you are forced to repeat what you have already said in the biographical chapters, your plan is poor, and you must seek one that does not separate what in reality is inseparable.

Here again the scrutiny of well-constructed works will furnish many suggestions. Choose some good theses, some monographs; pen in hand, attempt to discover how they have been built up; set yourself the task of reconstructing the stages of composition through which the author has passed. This is the best possible discipline.

I have always considered V. Giraud's *Pascal*[1] very helpful in this respect. It is composed of inedited notes—the outline and the subject matter of an excellent course given at the University of Fribourg. In it you may observe a work in the stage intermediary between the search for documents and the definite redaction of the book, with the skeleton, the joints, the processes of arranging facts and ideas, frankly visible.[2] More helpful still, because of the scope of its research and the variety of the points discussed, are Lanson's

[1] 8vo. 1898.

[2] From the first lecture of Giraud's book I detach this page, which offers a widely applicable programme:

"Certain principles of criticism should be kept constantly in mind while writing a literary monograph:

"1. *Every individual is a member of a group*; therefore it is necessary to determine exactly the influence exerted over him by this group.

notes and outlines for his course at Columbia University, *Esquisse d'une histoire de la tragédie française.*[1]

Let me add two remarks:

1. Beware of exaggerating the importance of the hero whom you have chosen. Many secondary writers not only deserve but demand investigation. Nevertheless, the false idea that such investigations should inevitably take the form of a rehabilitation accompanied with imprecations on an unjust and blind posterity detracts from the value of many theses and essays. Throwing light on an author does not mean surrounding him with a halo. Give him, not a better place than he had, but his true place in his own time and environment.

2. In order to succeed in this, never lose sight of time and environment. For all good portraits the background has an importance that the genuine artist never slights. He realizes that the figure will acquire its just value only if the setting is correct and appropriate. In your turn, if you neglect the background of your canvas, if you isolate your author instead of painting author and environment together, you cannot properly bring out his significance.

IV. FORM AND EXPRESSION

Lastly, use the same artistic care in the final redaction of your work. Even though you may have planned your outline

---

"2. *Every individual affects the group he belongs to*; therefore it is necessary to study the influence exercised by him upon his contemporaries and successors.

"3. *Every individual develops with the passage of time*; therefore it is necessary to conform to chronology and to follow, step by step, the successive phases of his development.

"4. *Every individual is infinitely more valuable through his work than through his personality*; therefore it is necessary to subordinate the study of the man to the study of his work." (P. 11.)

[1] Columbia University Press, New York, 1920.

correctly, it is not enough to empty your box of notes into a well-proportioned frame. You should give to your ideas the most artistic and the most agreeable form discoverable. I do not mean that you should employ some affected coquetry of style, or trim up facts, dates, and discussions with meaningless frills and niceties. There is, however, no reason why a scholarly piece of research work should be dull, heavy, unreadable. Why not remember Michelet's sound advice? "Criticism and History", he said, "being works of art as well as of science, should be presented free from the contrivances and scaffoldings used in their construction." This means: Do not attempt to impress your reader by the enumeration of superfluous bibliographical references or by unassimilated, inconsequent footnotes. Produce all your proofs, all your facts, all your dates, on condition that they signify something. Always tend to lighten and eliminate, never to pad and amplify. Above all, be terse, and remember that this can be attained only through patient toil: Pascal wrote, at the end of the sixteenth *Provinciale*, "I have made this letter so long because I have not had time to make it shorter".

Furthermore, you must keep in mind a last, but important, requirement. Your work should be a harmonious whole, and its general tone suitable to the subject. A style that is perfectly appropriate if you are dealing with Voltaire would be out of place if you are writing about Bossuet. If I read a thesis on Villon, I should be willing to accept a somewhat less formal attitude on the part of the writer than would be tolerable in a book on Vigny. Sainte-Beuve, who was not only a scholar but also an artist, understood how to modulate his voice differently when speaking of Rabelais than when speaking of Chateaubriand.

In short, raise your ideal above the simple gathering of facts and of names, no matter how accurate and trustworthy the data; constantly ask yourself whether you may not be able, without detracting from the value of your work, to lend it a more persuasive force and a more pleasing exterior. In this manner you will escape calling down about your ears the cruel condemnation with which Voltaire crushed the honest and unfortunate Abbé Trublet:

> Il compilait, compilait, compilait . . .
> Et nous lassait sans jamais se lasser.

CONCLUSION

The foregoing chapters certainly do not exhaust all the problems with which the student may satisfy his curiosity: they present examples merely of possible undertakings and explain by what methods to obtain results. Literary history, like all historical research, is a route strewn with obstacles, difficulties, and snares; to describe them to the inexperienced traveler, to warn him, to save him from aimless roving, from costly squandering of time and strength,—this is all that can or should be done for him. Guided in this way, he is more likely to acquire the valuable qualities so often mentioned in these pages: a regard for accuracy in detail, a habit of orderly and methodical investigation, and especially that scientific sense quick to distinguish between degrees of certainty, and scrupulous to affirm nothing that has not been clearly established and recognized as true.

Nevertheless, no matter how excellent these results may be, this book would completely fail in its intention were it not to encourage the student to look farther and higher. Although the author wants to help him in his effort to become a faithful servant of the science that discovers and studies facts, he would be singularly averse to seeing him become a "worshiper of facts", to quote an expression that has been used in reproach. Doubtless the most elementary scientific loyalty requires subjection to facts, but only so far as facts are a basis for deductions and conclusions: facts are not an end in themselves.

The very name "literary history" includes two sorts of intellectual activity: history on the one hand, literature on the other. As *history* it entails a combination of minute documentation, exact research, and scrupulousness of method. As *literature* it implies the faculty of reacting to a work of art with all possible delicacy, sensitiveness, and taste; it implies comprehension, appreciation, enjoyment.

The discipline that a student of literary history is invited to undergo should, then, on no pretext whatever divert or distract him from the impressionism that is not only legitimate but essential: it should lead him there by the straightest and surest paths, secure from wasting himself in vain and empty words.

The final aim of these researches is not to form narrow, circumscribed minds, absorbed in childish curiosity about learned details, or in the heaping up of interminable and undigested commentaries; it is not to lose sight of the forest while wearing oneself out, microscope in hand, studying a bit of leaf or a dried flower; still less is it to consume brain and life in commentating on commentators, and on the errors and stupidities with which they so often clutter the great works of literature. If certain clumsy enthusiasts have done this, they have been false to the ideal of literary history and have simply shown the inadequacy of their skill and literary sense. They have failed to understand that the true literary historian is he who places an irreproachable scientific loyalty and a tried method at the disposal of a keen sensibility, an exquisite perceptiveness, and a delicate taste.

"Philology", wrote Taine, "is a subterranean passage, dark, narrow, and bottomless, along which people crawl instead of walk; so distant from the air and the light that they forget the air and the light, and end by finding satisfactory and natural the smoky rays of the dismal lamp that they trail behind them. After staying there a few years they declare that the sky is a dream of the feeble-minded."[1]

Let the student take this admirable image as a sharp warning. Even if in this book the author has intended to hand him the little lamp to guide him through the labyrinths and obstacles of the blind tunnel, he would prefer never to see him enter there if by so doing he must lose sight of the splendor of the open sky and shut out from his lungs the fresh, life-giving breeze. Let him become a good workman in the mine of science; but, first and foremost, let him become or remain a man of taste, an artist, and—to use an old word of rich significance—a connoisseur.

Taine said also, "If we want to *understand* a work of art, we must *believe* in it". This saying, on close inspection, contains an entire programme for our young students of literature, a programme made up of two consistent parts: *faith* in a work of art, and a *method* of understanding and appreciating it.

Faith in a work of art is the conviction that art broadens and brightens our lives, and that, since the creation of beauty by the artist corresponds to the discovery of truth by the scholar, we should let ourselves be carried away by beauty just as whole-heartedly as we acquiesce in intellectual certainties. To have faith in a work of art, literary or plastic, is to keep the fresh, precious faculty of admiration from withering within us; it is to seek that peaceful communion with ourselves, that activity of intimate life, that is a condition of the budding and blossoming of taste. This is what our students, even those most attached to the scientific spirit, must never lose sight of: the infinite worth of the inner life; the conviction that in the midst of the driest researches they should, deep down in themselves, preserve a quiet retreat;

[1] *Les Philosophes classiques du dix-neuvième siècle* (1868 edition), p. 194.

the conviction also that they shall not come to grief if they respond in good faith to the things that 'grip' them, that time spent in rousing the beauty that sleeps in every page is not ill-spent, and that to admire is not necessarily to be deceived.

But to this faith must be added an understanding of the work of art: to stop short at this sincere and lively emotion would be to halt midway. There must be also—and here literary history is essential—a clear insight into the work and the myriad relations, both delicate and complex, that define and explain it. The student should know how to ask questions that will help him to discover its meaning and value. He should realize that a masterpiece remains sealed and dead to all who do not try to grasp it by a strict and wise method, and that real admiration is not an attitude of lazy relaxation but the reward of a hard, wholesome struggle between the admirable work and the admiring man. "What is this work?" he will ask himself, "and what artist has imagined and produced it? What inspiration stirred his mind or heart? To what lineage does it belong? Has it antecedents and sources? Under what conditions was it written and published? With what artistic ideal is it connected, and in what degree does it reach perfection? What is its technique? What society does it reflect? From what vast currents of ideas is it derived, and what has been its influence? In what do its lasting value, its attraction, its charm, its life-blood, consist?" Only by answering these questions will he judge sanely and with taste and produce a justifiable æsthetic reaction.

The author knows that this point of view will not fail on certain sides to raise violent objections. He knows that, for many people, it comes too close to that "rusty learning of the pedants" spoken of by Molière. He knows that others see no reason for the existence of any type of criticism not

founded on a preëstablished philosophical, religious, or æsthetic doctrine. Lastly, he knows that this idea of turning
taste into a sort of historical method is revolting to certain
minds,—minds that may be excellent but that are less inclined to enter upon patient, rigorous, scholarly work than
to protest with expressions of injured sensibility against the
day predicted by Joubert when "lusty laborers will make it
their business to judge the flowers of literature".

We should, however, take no part in these revolts or ap-
prehensions but should be confident that just such discipline,
scientific in its aim, historical in its methods, æsthetic in its
inspiration, far from "treating matters of feeling geometri-
cally", will preserve in the many "esprits géométriques" of
our day the necessary proportion of "esprit de finesse". It
will give them a "clear vision" for those "delicate principles" in literature that do not attract the admiration or the
blame of the vulgar. It will decline to form those dull, empty
minds that Pascal says are "ni fins, ni géomètres".

The task is unassuming and slow, but it may prove tempting. It lends itself, for masters and disciples alike, to no brilliant dissertations or neat witticisms. But it is based on firm
ground and leads to sure, if limited, conclusions. When our
students branch out on their own account,—although they
will not with aggressive confidence settle questions in every
field of thought and art, sometimes correctly and sometimes
incorrectly,—they may at least hope for the upright conscience of the critic who judges only what he knows,—and
perhaps also for what Anatole France calls "a natural friendship for beauty".

INDEX

NOTE. The reference is to pages. Reference to a note is indicated by a figure followed by *n*.

Academic dissertations, 25–26
Académie française, 132
Ackermann, Mme, 233
Alline, H., 95 *n.*
Amiel, 233
Amyot, 94 *n.*, 96, 99, 101, 188
Anaxagoras, 107
Anonymous books, 24
Arbelet, P., 101 *n.*
Armaingaud, Dr., on authenticity of the *Contr'un*, 176–189
Arnauld, 175, 275
Arnould, L., 211 *n.*
Arrian, 97
Ascoli, G., 189 *n.*
Ashford, Daisy, 157 *n.*
Ashton, H., 252 *n.*, 257 *n.*
Asselineau, Ch., 69 *n.*
Attribution, problems of, 157–193
Aulard, A., 160 *n.*
Authenticity, problems of, 157–193

Babbitt, I., 12 *n.*
Bacon, F., 260 *n.*
Baldensperger, F., quoted, 16 *n.*, 29, 46 *n.*, 220 *n.*, 226 *n.*, 232 *n.*, 244, 249 *n.*; *Bibliographie critique de Goethe en France*, 81; on Vigny, 123; on *Héléna's* date, 142; *Goethe en France*, 247
Balzac, influence of, 231
Banville, Th. de, 213
Barber, M., 101
Barbier, A., 24

Barckhausen, H., on Montesquieu, 90 *n.*; on the *Contr'un*, 176 *n.*
Barine, A., 220 *n.*
Barre, A., 136
Barrère, J., 176 *n.*
Barrie, J. M., 157 *n.*
Bartram, W., 97
Baudelaire, editions of, 37 *n.*, 200 *n.*
Baudrillart, H., 268
Bayle, 107, 189 *n.*, 271
Beaugrand, C., 189 *n.*
Beaulieux, 21 *n.*
Beaunier, A., 200 *n.*
Becq de Fouquières, 107, 197
Bédier, J., on the *Entretien de Pascal avec M. de Saci*, 41–42; quoted, 47 *n.*, 97 *n.*; on text of *Les Tragiques*, 48–50; on Chateaubriand, 99 *n.*, 214; on the *Paradoxe sur le comédien*, 160 *n.*, 166–169
Bengesco, G., 70
Berger, B., 172
Bergerat, E., 127 *n.*
Berkeley, 248
Bernard, Cl., 69 *n.*, 133
Bernardin de Saint-Pierre, 264
Bernheim, E., 157 *n.*
Bernier, 277, 278, 284
Berret, P., on *La Légende des siècles*, 68, 97 *n.*, 98 *n.*, 103–104, 122, 126; on chronology of *Les Contemplations*, 149 *n.*
Bersot, 270
Betz, L. P., 29

Beuve, 254 n.

Bibliographical evidence, in problems of authenticity, 170

Bibliographical index cards, how to make out, 34–35

Bibliography, general bibliography, and bibliography of modern French literature, 13–36; national bibliographies, 20–24; establishing a critical bibliography, 70–81

Bibliothèque nationale, various catalogues, 27

Binet, Cl., 68

Biography, treatment of biographical material, 210–224

Birch-Hirschfeld, 169 n.

Biré, E., 220 n.

Bisi, A., 258 n.

Bissipat, G. de, 171

Blanchemain, editor of Ronsard, 53, 171

Blossom, F. A., 156 n.

Boileau, 207, 258 n.

Boisguillebert, 270

Boislisle, De, editor of Saint-Simon, 64

Bonnefon, P., 128; on the Contr'un, 176 n., 184–186

Bossuet, books on, 28 n.; text of, corrected, 46 n.; specimen of spelling, 58 n.; critical bibliography, 76; ideas of, on luxury, 265, 270, 271

Boston Public Library, 28

Boswell, 255 n.

Boulenger, J., editor of Rabelais, 169 n., 255 n.

Bourdaloue, 267

Bourmont, A. de, 40 n.

Bourrilly, 68

Bouvy, 257 n.

Braunschvig, M., 19 n.

Breuillac, M., 234 n.

British Museum, General Catalogue, 26–27

Brockhaus' Konversations-Lexikon, 34

Bruguière de Sorsum, 142

Brunel, L., 160 n., 161 n.

Brunet, G., 24

Brunetière, 11 n., 12 n., 19 n., 44, 127, 200 n.

Brunot, F., 30, 58 n.

Brunschvicg, L., 66

Buffenoir, H., 254 n.

Buhle, P., 126 n.

Burke, 239, 240

Byron, 123, 140, 141, 247 n.

Cæsar, Julius, 153

Cahen, A., editor of Télémaque, 68

Cailhava, 160

Calvin, text of the Institution chrétienne, 52

Canfield, D. F., 257 n.

Caro, A., 233

Caron, P., 14 n.

Carré, J. M., 247 n.

Cassagne, A., 127, 200 n.

Castel (le père), 105

Catalogues of libraries, 26–28

Caussy, F., 93

Cazamian, L., 264

Celani, H., 24 n.

Cesalpino, 107

Chamard, H., editor of Du Bellay, 66; on La Princesse de Clèves, 104 n.; on Quintil Horatian, 189 n.

Champion, P., 68, 255 n.

Charavay, A., 72 n.

Charles d'Orléans, 255 n.

Charlevoix, 99

Charlier, G., 246 n.

Charpentier, G. H., 251 n.

Chastellain, G., 171

Chateaubriand, sources, 97, 99; Chateaubriand and Vigny, 123; biography, 212, 214; influence, 237, 239, 256

Chatelain, H., 200 n.

Châtelet, Mme du, 110
Chénier, A., a line of, corrected, 44; editions, 51; punctuation in *Le Jeune Malade,* 61; influence on Romanticism, 86; sources of *La Jeune Tarentine,* 107–108; influence on Vigny, 140, 142; versification, 207; influence, 257, 261
Chénier, M. J. de, 246
Chérel, A., 245 *n.,* 251 *n.,* 254 *n.,* 260
Chinard, G., 99, 258 *n.*
Chronology (in literary history), 132–156
Cirot, 134
Clairon, Mlle, 160, 163
Claudin, A., 252 *n.*
Cleaning up, correcting a text, 42–47
Clédat, L., 58 *n.*
Clément, L., 200 *n.*
Cohen, G., 4
Colbert, 275
Cole, G. W., 73 *n.,* 76 *n.*
Colet, Louise, 69 *n.*
Commentary, in an edition: linguistic and grammatical, 62–63; literary, 63–64
Comparative literature, bibliography, 28–29
Comte, A., 248
Condillac, 257
Cons, L., 169 *n.*
Constant, B., edition of *Adolphe,* 68; bibliography, 78; biography, 220 *n.*
Cooper, F., 125, 255 *n.*
Corbière, T., 69 *n.*
Cordier, H., 78 *n.*
Coréal, Fr., 111
Corneille, P., bibliography, 28 *n.*; date of *Le Cid,* 132; date of *Polyeucte,* 136; P. Louys on Corneille and Molière, 189 *n.*; versification, 200 *n*; Corneille in England, 257 *n.*; Corneille and Spain, 260
Courteault, P., 220 *n.*
Courtney, W. P., 16

Critical apparatus, how to arrange, 56–58
Croiset, A., 46 *n.*
Currier, T. F., 28
Cyrano de Bergerac, 254, 256

Dalmeyda, G., 44 *n.*
D'Ancona, as editor of Montaigne's *Voyage,* 44
Dancourt, 269
Dannheisser, E., 138 *n.*
Daragon, 254 *n.*
Darmesteter, A., 30
Darwin, 133
D'Aubignac, Abbé, 137
D'Aubigné, A., text of *Les Tragiques,* 48–50, 68
Daubigny, 126
Dedieu, J., 89
Delille, 241
Dellon, 125
Descartes, 133; influence, 248, 257, 261 *n.*
Deschamps, E., 69 *n.*
Des Cognets, 59
Desfeuilles, 66
Des Granges, C. M., 134 *n.,* 255 *n.*
Deshoulières, Mme, 277
Desnoiresterres, 220 *n.,* 254 *n.*
Despois, 66
De Vinne, T. L., 73 *n.*
Dezeimeris, A., 176 *n.*
Dickens, 256
Diderot, 115; authenticity of the *Paradoxe sur le comédien,* 158–166, 277 *n.*
Didot, 34
Dietrich, F., 32
Dimoff, P., 51
Diogenes, 107
Dissertations, academic, 25–26
Dorbec, P., 125 *n.*
Dorchain, A., 197
Dorison, L., 44
Doumic, R., 160 *n.*

Dreyfus-Brisac, E., 87
Dreyss, C., 133
Drouet, Juliette, 147
Druon, 214
Du Bellay, 66, 86, 118–119
Du Camp, M., 127 n.
Duclos, 275
Dufourcq, 134
Dumas, A. (père), 69 n.
Dumesnil, 218
Dunn, W. H., 211 n.
Dupin, H., 145–148
Dupuy, E., quoted, 120, 123; on Vigny, 126; on Verlaine, 136; on Héléna's date, 138–140; on the Paradoxe sur le comédien, 158–166, 220 n.
Duras, Mme de, 124
Du Resnel, 249 n.

Edition, preparation of an, 37–69
Encyclopædias, 33
Encyclopédie, 238, 273
Enjambements, 207
Entretien de Pascal avec M. de Saci, text, 41–42
Erasmus, 91
Estève, E., 12 n., 45 n.; on Héléna's date, 139–142; on Byron in France, 247 n., 257 n.

Faguet, E., on the Paradoxe sur le comédien, 160 n., 162–166; on Rousseau, 220 n.; on Chénier, 222
Falconet, 227 n.
Faxon, F. W., 32
Fénelon, bibliography, 28 n.; edition of Télémaque, 68; influence, 245, 246, 251, 254, 258, 260, 267, 270, 271
Ferrière, A., 226 n.
Feydeau, E., 69 n.
Flaubert, sources, 104 n., 127; composition of Salammbô, 156 n.; biography, 218
Florio, 260

Fock, G., 26
Fontenelle, influence, 241, 271
Fortescue, G. K., 27
Foulet, 68
Fragonard, 270
France, A., 12 n., 303
French language, bibliography, 29
Fromentin, 69 n.; critical bibliography, 78 n.; sources, 124; influence, 239
Fuchs, A., 231, 255 n.
Funck-Brentano, F., 71 n., 76 n.
Fustel de Coulanges, 133

Gallas, K. R., 16 n.
Garcilaso de la Vega, 111
Gassendi, 277, 278
Gautier, Th., 69 n.; sources, 126, 127
Gayley, C. M., 12 n., 19 n.
Georgi, T., 21
Gerdil, 270
Gerig, J. L., 25
Germany, national bibliography, 23
Gilbert, N., 214
Girard, A., 135 n.
Girardin, F. de, 254 n.
Giraud, J., on Vigny, 123; on Flaubert, 127
Giraud, V., 11 n., 12 n.; Bibliographie of Taine, 74 n., 77; on biography, 224, 245 n., 250 n., 296
Girodet, 125
Glachant, 51 n., 59 n.
Glatigny, 69 n.
Gobineau, 233
Goethe, 81, 233, 247
Gohin, F., editor of Heroet, 66, 171; on Stendhal, 101 n.
Goncourt, E. and J. de, 268
Goncourt, J. de, 69 n.
Gongora, 242
Gosse, Ed., 239, 240
Gossez, M. A. N., 127 n.
Gournay, Mlle de, 150
Grammont, M., 196, 197, 201, 204 n., 207 n.

Grande Encyclopédie, 33
Grappe, G., 160 *n.*, 162
Great Britain, national bibliography, 23
Gringore, P., 213
Guicciardini, 153
Guiffrey, 171
Guizot, 69 *n.*, 101 *n.*
Guy, H., 171, 256 *n.*; on Gringore, 213–214

Haase, A., 30
Hamilton, A., 104 *n.*
Hardy, Alex., 88
Hartsoecker, 109
Hatzfeld, A., 30
Hauvette, A., 45
Havet, L., 43
Hazard, P., 29, 226 *n.*, 248 *n.*, 253 *n.*
Heine, H., 234
Hennequin, E., 12 *n.*, 255 *n.*
Henriot, P., 101 *n.*
Herder, 247 *n.*
Heredia, J. M. de, 51, 60 *n.*, 205
Heroet, 66, 171
Herrera, 112
Herrig, L., 33
Herriot, E., 19 *n.*
Hinrichs, 23
Hoffmann, W., 233, 234
Horluc, 30
Hugo, V., text corrected, 43 *n.*; edition of *La Légende des siècles* by Berret, 68; sources of *Les Trois Cents*, 95, of *Les Pauvres Gens*, 97–98, of *William Shakespeare*, 101, of *La Légende des siècles*, 103–104, of *Notre-Dame de Paris*, 104 *n.*, of *Ruy Blas*, 120–121; chronology of *Contemplations*, 145–148, 156 *n.*; versification, 200 *n.*, 201, 207; biography, 212; influence, 241, 253, 256, 258 *n.*, 259
Huguet, E., 30, 104 *n.*

Ideas, literary history in connection with history of, 263–288
Influence, questions of success and, 225–262
Italy, national bibliography, 23

Jal, 34
Jamyn, A., 172
Janin, J., 69 *n.*
Jannet, P., 171
Jasinski, 200 *n.*
Jellinek, A. L., 29, 32
Johnson, Dr., 212
Joinville, 95
Jordell, D., 31
Journal de la librairie, 22
Jubinal, 98, 122
Jusserand, J. J., 249 *n.*
Justus Lipsius, 91

Kahn, G., 201
Kant, 248, 253
Kastner, 43 *n.*, 198
Kauffmann, A., 121
Kaulek, J., 40 *n.*
Kayser, C. G., 23
Klopstock, 123
Klussmann, R., 26
Kont, 257 *n.*
Krantz, 261 *n.*
Kroeger, A. B., 16
Kurtz, B. P., 12 *n.*, 19 *n.*

La Boétie, authenticity of the *Contr'un*, 176–189
La Bruyère, 66, 244, 265–274
Lachèvre, F., 70, 251 *n.*
La Fayette, Mme de, specimen of spelling, 58 *n.*; sources of *La Princesse de Clèves*, 104 *n.*; influence, 252
Lafenestre, G., 125 *n.*
Laffay, 214
Lafont, C., 97 *n.*, 98
La Fontaine, 125, 212, 258 *n.*

Lamartine, 200; corrections of text, 45; edition, 53; versification, 200 n.; biography, 212; success and influence, 233, 236, 243, 244, 253, 257, 189 n.

Lamennais, 88, 259

Lancaster, H. C., 121 n., 138 n.

Landry, E., 194, 201

Langlois, C. V., Manuel de bibliographie historique, 13–14, 216

Langlois and Seignobos, Introduction aux études historiques, 47 n., 157 n., 189 n.

Lanson, G., teaching of, at the Sorbonne, Introduction, iii–iv; on methods in literary history, 2, 3 n.; Histoire de la littérature française, 11 n.; Manuel bibliographique, 16–19; on text of Lettres philosophiques, 45; editor of Lettres philosophiques, 47, 54; on Calvin, 52 n.; editor of the Méditations, 53; on editing, 64, 67 n.; on Lamennais, 88; on Voltaire's sources, 102 n., 106 n.; on methods of investigation of sources, 114–115, 130; on sources of Ruy Blas, 120–121; on sources of Fantasio, 122; chronological tables in Manuel, 134 n.; on chronology of the Méditations, 145 n.; on Diderot's Paradoxe, 160; on authenticity of Pascal's Factums, 173–175; on attribution of the Discours sur les passions de l'amour, 175 n.; on French versification, 198 n.; on biography, 211 n.; on Voltaire's biography, 220 n.; on problems of influence, 226 n., 228, 247 n., 248 n., 249, 251 n., 252 n., 253 n., 257 n., 258, 263 n.; on Voltaire's influence, 241; on Gongorism, 242; on Descartes's influence, 261 n.; on social influence of literature, 271, 272, 273; on French tragedy, 296

La Rochefoucauld, 274, 275

Larroumet, G., 160 n., 161

Lasteyrie, R. de, 216 n.

Laumonier, P., editor of Ronsard, 53, 68; on chronology of Ronsard's lyrics, 145, 156 n.; on attribution of some lyrics to Ronsard, 171, 172 n.

Lautrey L., editor of Montaigne's Voyage, 44

Lauvrière, 218

La Vicomterie, 126

Lavisse, E., 14 n.

Le Brun, 125

Leconte de Lisle, 104 n., 127

Lee, S., 211 n.

Lefèvre-Pontalis, 216 n.

Lefranc, A., editor of Rabelais, 52, 169 n.; editor of Calvin, 52

Le Goffic, Ch., 196

Leibnitz, 105

Le Maître, 73

Lemaître, J., 240

Lenclos, N. de, 277, 284

Lenglet-Dufresnoy, 243

Le Sage, A., bibliography, 28 n., 78 n., 269

Le Sage de la Colombière, 281

Le Soudier, H., 22

Lessing, 233, 258 n.

Letourneur, 249 n.

Levi-Malvano, 258 n.

Libraries, large catalogues of, 26–28

Library of Congress, 28

Littré, 30

Logau, F., 233

Lorenz, 21

Lote, G., 194, 201

Loth, 254 n.

Louys, 189 n.

Low, S., 23

Lyonnet, H., 189 n.

Macaulay, 123

Machiavelli, 258 n.

McKerrow, R. B., 51, 72

Madan, F., 73 *n.*
Maeterlinck, M., 233
Maigron, L., 241
Maire, A., 26, 78 *n.*
Mairet, J., 138 *n.*
Maistre, J. de, 248
Malherbe, 207, 231
Mandeville, B. de, 277
Mantegna, 126
Manuscripts, reading of, 39 *n.*
Manzoni, 233
Marchangy, 123
Maréchal, C., 88
Marinet, 30
Marot, Clément, 171, 256
Marot, Jean, 171
Marsan, J., 251 *n.*
Martinenche, E., 259
Martino, P., 45 *n.*, 78 *n.*
Martinon, P., 43 *n.*, 189 *n.*, 200 *n.*; on strophes, 208–209
Marty-Laveaux, editor: of Ronsard, 53, 171; of Corneille, 136; of Rabelais, 169 *n.*
Massillon, 268
Masson, P. M., editor of the *Profession de foi*, 47, 57–58, 67; on Vigny, 123, 139 *n.*, 142, 156 *n.*; on Mme de Tencin's biography, 221; on literary influences, 237; on Rousseau's influence, 248, 257 *n.*
Mathews, W., 211
Melon, J. B., 279, 281
Mérimée, 69 *n.*, 101 *n.*
Mesnard, 66
Meusnier de Querlon, 43
Michaud, 34
Michaut, G., 66, 78 *n.*, 220 *n.*
Michelet, 69 *n.*, 298
Mirbeau, O., 233
Mistral, 233
Molière, bibliography, 28; edition, 66; Molière and Corneille, 189 *n.*; biography, 213; influence, 254, 258
Monglond, A., 16 *n.*

Monnier, H., 69 *n.*
Montaigne, editions, 40 *n.*, 43, 67; sources, 90–92, 95, 96, 99, 101; quoted, 130; chronology of the *Essais*, 149–156; Montaigne and the *Contr'un*, 176–189; influence, 237; Montaigne and Shakespeare, 260
Montalembert, 69 *n.*
Montchrestien, A. de, 199
Montesquieu, 89, 258 *n.*; influence, 272, 279
Montluc, B. de, 220 *n.*
Moore, Th., 123
Moratori, 111
Morel, J., 102, 115, 116
Moreri, 103
Morley, J., 246
Mornet, D., on methods, 12 *n.*, 264, 265, 282–283; works or articles mentioned, 16 *n.*, 231 *n.*, 243 *n.*, 253 *n.*, 255 *n.*, 263 *n.*; on versification, 60 *n.*, 200 *n.*; on biography, 210 *n.*, 222; on Rousseau's influence, 236 *n.*, 252
Morris, G. D., 255 *n.*
Musset, A. de, 212; quoted, 87

Naigeon, 158–166
Nebout, P., 200 *n.*
Newton, 102, 110
New York, libraries, 28
Nichol, J., 134
Nicole, 267, 275
Nietzsche, 240
Notes, how to take, 292–294

Ohnet, G., 240
Omont, H., 21 *n.*
Orthography, reproduction of original, of a text, 58–59
Ossian, 247 *n.*, 257
Oulmont, C., 213, 214 *n.*

Pagliaini, A., 23
Pailhès, G., 124 *n.*

Pailleron, 211
Pascal, manuscript of *Pensées*, 39 *n.*; text of *Pensées*, 50; editions, 66–67; bibliography, 78 *n.*; attribution of the *Factums*, 172–175; influence, 237, 245; quoted, 298, 303
Pauthier, H. J., 12 *n.*
Peabody Institute, 28
Peddie, R. A., 20, 21 *n.*
Pemberton, 102
Periodical literature, 30–33
Periodicals, of interest for French literary history, 33
Petit de Julleville, L., 19 *n.*, 30
Petzholdt, J., 14
Pichot, 142
Picot, E., 21 *n.*
Pirot, 175
Plan, P. P., 189 *n.*
Plantet, E., 40 *n.*
Plattard, J., 68, 85
Pluche, Abbé, 110, 243
Poe, E. A., 234, 255 *n.*
Poizat, A., 189 *n.*
Pons, A. A., 254 *n.*
Poole's Index, 31
Pope, 212, 246 *n.*, 249 *n.*
Port-Royal, 132
Potez, H., 122, 214 *n.*
Pouqueville, 141
Poussin, 125
Prévost, Abbé, 244
Prévost-Paradol, 69 *n.*
Prou, M., 39 *n.*
Provinquières, 270
Prudhomme, Sully, 201
Pseudonymous books, 24
Punctuation in an edition, 60

Quérard, J. M., 21, 24
Quinet, E., 69 *n.*
Quintil Horatian, 189 *n.*

Rabbe, A., 121

Rabelais, text, 52; editions, 68; authenticity of Book V, 169 *n.*; influence, 256
Racine, bibliography, 28 *n.*; sources, 88; library, 128 *n.*; influence, 257 *n.*, 259
Rageot, G., 226 *n.*
Ramin, H., 73 *n.*
Ramsay, 246
Ratisbonne, L., 144
Reader's Guide, The, 31
Readings, various, how to collate, 40 *n.*
Rébelliau, A., 46 *n.*
Regnard, 28 *n.*, 269
Régnier, H. de, 231
Renan, 133, 225, 244, 258
Renard, G., 12 *n.*, 226 *n.*
Research work, 291–294
Rhyme, 206
Rhythm of French verse, 200–204
Richter, J. P., 123, 125
Rieux, A. de, 95
Rigal, E., on *Polyeucte*, 136; on the *Contemplations*, 156 *n.*
Rigault, H., 242 *n.*
Robertson, J. M., 260
Rochette, A., 200 *n.*, 201
Roland, Mme, 243
Roney, I., 144
Ronsard, text, 53; editions, 87; pieces attributed to, 171; influence, 231, 251, 256
Rostand, 199
Rotrou, 138 *n.*
Rousseau, J. B., 241
Rousseau, J. J., edition of the *Profession de Foi*, 47, 57–58, 67; spelling in works of, 59; punctuation in works of, 60 *n.*; *Les Confessions*, 64; *La Nouvelle Héloïse*, 86; sources, 115–116; influence, 235, 236, 237, 239, 248, 251, 254, 258, 259, 261; first *Discours*, 273, 281
Rudel, G., 254

Rudler, G., 220 n.; editor of *Adolphe*, 68; bibliography of B. Constant, 78; on *La Princesse de Clèves*, 104 n.

Sainte-Beuve, quoted, 11 n., 74 n.; bibliography, 78 n.; on Vigny's *Héléna*, 138; on biography, 210 n., 214, 217, 218, 219, 220; on influence, 231, 246
Saint-Évremond, 238, 277, 278, 284
Saint-Hyacinte, Th. de, 243
Saint-Simon, 64
Sand, G., 69 n., 254
Scherer, 233
Schopenhauer, 227, 238 n.
Senancour, 66, 259
Seneca, 92–93
Serrurier, C., 12 n.
Servois, 66, 251 n.
Shakespeare, in France, 249; Shakespeare and Montaigne, 260
Shelley, 141
Silvestre de Sacy, 95
Sources, investigation and interpretation, 82–131
Souriau, M., 200 n.
Souza, 201
Speroni, Sp., 119
Spinoza, influence, 247, 248
Staël, Mme de, source of Vigny's *Le Mont des Oliviers*, 123; influence, 239, 240, 259, 263 n.
Stapfer, P., 226 n., 233 n., 244 n.
Stedefeld, 260
Stein, H., 15
Stein, L., 211 n.
Stendhal, 101 n., 214
Stevenson, F. S., 211 n.
Stiefel, A. L., 138 n.
Strowski, F., 67, 176 n.
Stryienski, C., 101 n.
Success and influence, questions of, 225–262
Swift, 256

Taine, quoted, 11 n., 300; Giraud's *Taine, bibliographie critique*, 77; on biography, 266
Tarde, G., 226 n., 286
Temple, W., 242
Tencin, Mme de, 221
Text, how to establish a correct, 39–42
Texte, J., 240
Thayer, W. R., 211 n., 220 n.
Thémiseul de Saint-Hyacinte, 243
Thesis, preparation and redaction of a, 289–299
Thieme, H. P., *Guide bibliographique*, 22; on versification, 195
Thiers, 69 n.
Thieulin, 196
Thiry, 134
Thomas, A., 30
Thomas, W., 239 n.
Thurot, J., 44
Tilley, A., 169 n.
Tillier, Cl., 233
Tobler, 198
Toldo, P., 256 n.
Toulouse, Dr., 218
Tourneux, M., 160 n., 161, 163
Tournoux, G. A., 78
Tronchon, 247 n.
Trublet, Abbé, 299
Turgenev, 256

United States, national bibliography, 24
Urbain, C., 12 n., 76

Vaganay, H., 80 n.
Vairasse, D., 106
Vallée, L., 15 n.
Vandeul, Mme de, 162, 163
Van Tieghem, P., 247 n., 254 n., 257 n.
Vauban, 270
Verlaine, bibliography, 78; date of *Art poétique*, 136; versification, 201
Verlaque, 77 n.
Verrier, P., 194

Versification, methods in questions of, 194–209

Vianey, 104

Vicaire, G., 22

Vigny, A. de, corrections of text of *L'Esprit pur*, 44; corrections of text of the *Journal d'un poète*, 45; sources, 123, 125; date of *Héléna*, 138–143; chronology of the *Journal*, 143–144; biography, 214 *n.*, 218, 220 *n.*; influence, 230, 251, 257

Villey, P., on Montaigne's sources, 90 *n.*, 91 *n.*, 92 *n.*, 94 *n.*, 95 *n.*, 97 *n.*, 101 *n.*; on Du Bellay's sources, 118–119; on chronology of the *Essais*, 149–156; on Marot, 171 *n.*; on the *Contr'un*, 176 *n.*, 186–189; on Montaigne and Shakespeare, 260

Villon, 254

Vollmöller, L., 25

Voltaire, text of *Lettres philosophiques*, 45, 54; text of *Candide*, 47, 52, 55; spelling, 59; correspondence, 68, 85; sources of the *Essai sur les mœurs*, 93; sources of *Candide*, 94, 104–106, 109–112, 116–117; sources of *Lettre philosophique XIII*, 106–107; biography, 220 *n.*; influence, 236, 241, 244, 251, 254, 256, 258, 261; Voltaire and Shakespeare, 246; ideas of, on luxury, 267, 273, 279, 281, 284

Waddington, Q., 21 *n.*

Wailly, L. de, 121

Waterhouse, G., 25

Watteau, 270

Whibley, 257 *n.*

Whitney, J. L., 28

Wolf, Ch., 105

Wright, C. H. C., 19 *n.*

Young, Ed., 239

Zangroniz, De, 96 *n.*, 99 *n.*

Zola, E., 218